First
Thesaurus

First
Thesaurus

Bounty
Books

Author: John Grisewood
Designer: Angela Ashton
Editor: Sue Churchill
Project Management: Sarah Eason
Editorial Assistance: Liz Dalby and Helen Parker
Artwork Commissioning: Susanne Grant and Lynne French
Production: Jenni Cozens and Ian Paulyn
Art Director: Clare Sleven
Editorial Director: Paula Borton
Director: Jim Miles

First published in Great Britain in 1999
by Chancellor Press (Bounty Books)

This edition published in 2007 by Bounty Books,
a division of Octopus Publishing Group Ltd
2–4 Heron Quays, London E14 4JP

Copyright © Octopus Publishing Group Ltd 1999

Produced by Miles Kelly Publishing Ltd, Bardfield Centre,
Great Bardfield, Essex, England CM7 4SL

ISBN-13: 978-0-753715-23-9
ISBN-10: 0-753715-23-6

A CIP catalogue record for this book is available
from the British Library

Printed and bound in China

CONTENTS

INTRODUCTION 6

STORY OF ENGLISH 7

THE SPREAD OF ENGLISH 12

HOW TO USE THIS BOOK 14

THESAURUS 15

ACKNOWLEDGEMENTS 128

INTRODUCTION

writer

A **thesaurus is a collection** of lists of words with similar meanings. It is a kind of word finder that should help you find the exact word you are looking for by giving other words that have similar meanings to the one you are thinking of. So listed under 'funny' you will find: amusing, comic, humorous, ridiculous, witty, laughable, droll; and also strange, weird, peculiar, odd, curious.

There are also lists of words associated in meaning with a particular word (the headword). They cannot replace that word but nevertheless belong to the same group.

So, under 'mathematics' are listed the following associated words:

- add up
- subtract
- take away
- divide
- multiply
- count
- measure
- calculate
- work out

This is not a comprehensive thesaurus. We have mainly chosen words that younger readers will be familiar with, particularly such overworked words as get, good and nice. So, for example, you could say: 'I had a nice time at the party. The people were nice. The food was nice and we played lots of nice games.'

But instead, you might say:
'I had a wonderful time at the party and I met several interesting people. The food was delicious and we played some amusing games.' Do you think that's nicer?!

It's not quite true to say that a synonym is a word with exactly the same meaning as another word. More often synonyms are words with perhaps very similar meanings but which may be used in slightly different senses.

We talk about a tall man, tall trees and a tall building but we say a high mountain (and also a high building), but never a high man (or woman) or high trees.

You may get on your 'high horse' but the horse you ride is a tall horse. You might also think that fast and quick are interchangeable, but some people drive fast cars and so make quick journeys.

It is important to look up in a dictionary any word you do not understand or are not sure about. A thesaurus does not give definitions.

The word 'thesaurus' comes from the Greek word for 'treasury' and, indeed, this is what it is – a treasury of words. By helping you to find the exact word you are looking for, we hope that we will help you to write in a more interesting and vivid way.

*Enjoy our
rich language!*

THE STORY OF ENGLISH

During the 100 or so years after the Roman armies left Britain in 408 AD to defend Rome against invaders, tribes from northern Germany and Scandinavia (the Anglo-Saxons) conquered Britain and drove the native Celtic British people into Wales and Cornwall. There they continued to speak their own language. (Welsh survives but the Cornish language died out in the 18th century).

We now call the language of the invaders Anglo-Saxon or Old English. Here is a clear example of Old English, from the Anglo-Saxon Chronicle of the 800s:

Breten iegland is eahta hund mila lang, and twa hund mila brad; and here sind...

Britain island is eight hundred miles long and two hundred miles broad; and here are...

...on thaem ieglande fif getheodu: Englisc, Brettisc, Scyttisc, Pihtisc and Boc-laeden.

...on this island five languages: English, British, Scottish, Pictish and Book Latin.

This language is the basis of modern English and provides us with most of our very basic vocabulary and grammar, parts of the body, relationships, names of animals, geographic features and so on. The Vikings from Scandinavia, who later plundered and settled in parts of the country, introduced new words. Many of our words beginning with sk– (such as sky, skill and skirt) are Viking words. And they gave names to the places where they settled: the 'dale' in

Grimsdale means 'valley', the 'by' in Rugby means 'village' and 'wick' in Blowick means 'bay' or 'inlet'. And their pronouns: 'they, them, their' etc. replaced Anglo-Saxon ones.

The enrichment of English with the introduction of new words from different languages has led to some duplication of words which allows for subtle and delicately different shades of meaning. We can have an English wedding or a French marriage, we can be brotherly or fraternal and we can forgive or pardon folk or people. This huge range of choice can be seen in this thesaurus with its variety of synonyms.

When English, once regarded as a 'rough, uncouth tongue', returned as the language of the ruling classes in the 14th century it had changed greatly and had absorbed thousands of French words. Norman French provided English with new ways of expressing more abstract ideas and emotions such as charity and passion; or words to do with administration and justice such as jury, felony, govern, prince, duke. And Norman cooks served pork, mutton and beef rather than English pig, sheep and cow.

ski

sky

Viking

7

OLD ENGLISH

On the following pages you can find out where words that we use today came from originally, and how the English language has changed over time. You can see the beginnings of the language in the examples from Old English shown on this page. There is a section which shows some of the main differences between American English and British English, including lists of things which are called by completely different names, as well as points about the major spelling differences between the two branches of the language. Also included are lists of words which have been taken into the English language from other languages, and a collection of common idioms. Finally, a map demonstrates how widely used the English Language is, as an official language or as a second language, in many countries around the world.

A simple Old English vocabulary:

English	Old English
cold	cald
cow	cu
day	daege
green	grene
hill	hill
king	cynning
land	land
man	mann
milk	milc
moon	mona
mouse	mus
night	niht
street	straet
sun	sunne

OLD WORDS WITH NEW MEANINGS:

Acre: this was once a field but now means a measure of land.
Fond once meant foolish but now means loving.
A **knave** was once a servant but is now a rascal.
Nice once meant fussy and hard to please.
Silly once meant blessed but now means stupid.
A **villain** was once a peasant but has now become a rogue.

moon

man

land

8

AMERICAN ENGLISH

American English is different from British English. Some words have different spellings, and some words that are used to describe the same thing are completely different. Today these differences do not seem so noticeable, as British and American people are both exposed to each other's cultures through films, television and books, and so tend to be able to understand each other. This was not always the case. Even up until the Second World War, the situation was quite different. For example, a book published in America might have needed a glossary to explain certain words in the British edition.

HERE WE SHOW SOME OF THE COMMONEST DIFFERENCES BETWEEN THE TWO VARIATIONS OF THE ENGLISH LANGUAGE.

Some common differences between British and American spelling:
British **re** (centre, fibre, theatre) usually becomes **er** (center, fiber, theater.)
British **our** (colour, harbour, honour) becomes **or**, (color, harbor, honor.)

WHERE THE BRITISH HAVE LL THE AMERICANS HAVE L TO INFLECT WORDS LIKE TRAVEL (TRAVELLING, TRAVELLED – BRITISH), TRAVEL (TRAVELING, TRAVELED – AMERICAN).

Here are some common examples of differences between British and American English spellings: (American spelling appears first.)

aluminum/aluminium	theater/theatre
defense/defence	molt/moult
gray/grey	mold/mould
check/cheque	labor/labour
plow/plough	fiber/fibre
skillful/skilful	woolen/woollen
color/colour	

American English also has over 4000 entirely separate words. Here are just a few: (American words appear first)

ladybug/ladybird

ball park/playing field
bill/banknote
candy/sweets
checkers/draughts
cookie/biscuit
drapes/curtains
fall/autumn
first floor/ground floor
gas/petrol
homely/ugly
hood/car bonnet
trunk/car boot
jelly/jam

drapes/curtains

ladybug/ladybird
antsy/fidgety
drapes/curtains
cotton candy/candyfloss
crosswalk/pedestrian crossing
downspout/drainpipe
duplex/semi-detached house
ground round/best mince
lightning bug/glow-worm
pacifier/baby's dummy
diaper/baby's nappy
realtor/estate agent
station wagon/estate car

teeter-totter/see-saw
yard/garden
zucchini/courgette
eggplant/aubergine
sidewalk/pavement
gasoline/petrol
pants/trousers
airplane/aeroplane
trash/rubbish
mad/angry
movie/film
chips/crisps
french fries/chips

teeter-totter/see-saw

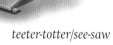

trunk/car boot

hood/car bonnet

BORROWED WORDS

Some words from other languages have become part of the English language. Here are some examples.

Arabic

cotton, algebra, sofa, sugar, chemistry, cipher, genie, yashmak, wadi, mohair

Greek

alphabet, geology, philosophy, chemist, character, oxygen, angel, coriander, symphony, rhinoceros, crocus, pylon, chaos

pylon

Latin

dental, focus, exit, circus, rostrum, ibex, pavement, juniper, damson

circus

Dutch

boom, skipper, landscape, yacht, gas, coffee, tea, cork

Turkish

divan, kiosk, yoghurt

Spanish

patio, zero

yacht

divan

Hindi and Urdu

bandana, bangle, dinghy, loot, shampoo, cowry, thug, sari, dungarees, guru, kedgeree, mynah

Polynesian

tattoo

loot

Italian

piano, pizza, ballot, bandit, opera, crescendo, pantaloon, porcelain, confetti

piano

Native American

canoe, moose, tomahawk

Afrikaans

springbok, aardvark, apartheid, kraal, veld

springbok

French

gateau, chamois, grill, beef, picnic, flute, giblets, fort, fortress, fairy

Icelandic

fairy, saga, geyser

Inuit

kayak, anorak, igloo

flute

Norwegian

lemming

Persian

shah, bazaar, paradise, shawl, cushy

Portugese

palaver, verandah, monsoon, albino, macaw

Sanskrit

macaw

juggernaut, jungle, jute, pundit, nirvana

IDIOMS

An idiom is a group of words used together to mean something different from the same words when they are used on their own. Here are some common examples:

To beat about the bush. To avoid something or to appraoch it in a roundabout way.

On cloud nine. Very happy.

Fifty-fifty. Shared equally.

On the other hand. Alternatively.

To keep something under one's hat. To keep something secret.

For the high jump. In serious trouble.

Keen as mustard. Enthusiastic.

To turn over a new leaf. To change.

One in a million. Special.

Hit the nail on the head. To be exactly right about something.

Nose to the grindstone. Working incessantly.

Flat out. At top speed.

Pour oil on troubled waters. To calm or soothe a difficult situation.

Finger on the pulse. Well informed about what is happening.

Raining cats and dogs. Raining very heavily.

Rub up the wrong way. To irritate or annoy.

Scatter-brained. Unable to concentrate on one thing.

Thick as thieves. Very friendly.

Quick on the uptake. Quick to understand.

To wash one's hands of. To refuse to take responsibility.

Take the bull by the horns. To tackle a problem boldly.

Vanish into thin air. To disappear completely.

Throw down the gauntlet. To set a challenge.

Come a cropper. To fail.

The green-eyed monster. Jealousy.

Kill two birds with one stone. To get two good results from a single action.

Baker's dozen. Thirteen.

THE SPREAD OF ENGLISH

Up to about 400 years ago English was spoken only in a tiny part of the world now called the British Isles. Today the language is spoken in nearly every part of the world. It is now the native language of Great Britain, Ireland, Australia, Canada, New Zealand and the United States. It is widely spoken in South Africa and other parts of Africa as well as in India, Pakistan, Sri Lanka and the West Indies. English is now also accepted as the international language of commerce, science, technology and diplomacy.

English is spoken by at least 400 million people, and is spoken as a first language by 330 million people.

English is used as an official language in the following countries, accounting for a total population of 1.6 billion. In many other countries it is also used as the common second language, or the main business language.

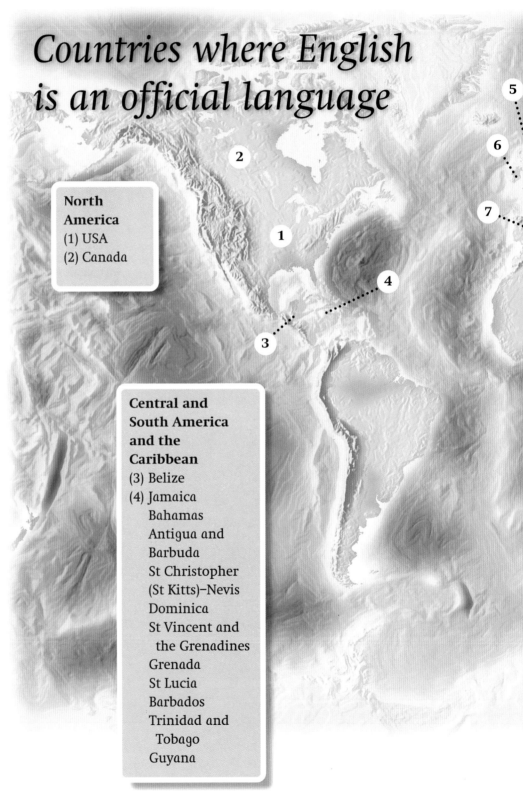

Countries where English is an official language

North America
(1) USA
(2) Canada

Central and South America and the Caribbean
(3) Belize
(4) Jamaica
   Bahamas
   Antigua and
   Barbuda
   St Christopher
   (St Kitts)–Nevis
   Dominica
   St Vincent and
   the Grenadines
   Grenada
   St Lucia
   Barbados
   Trinidad and
   Tobago
   Guyana

Most Jamaicans speak a dialect of English that sounds quite different to standard British or American English. A dialect might use different words and expressions.

Introduction

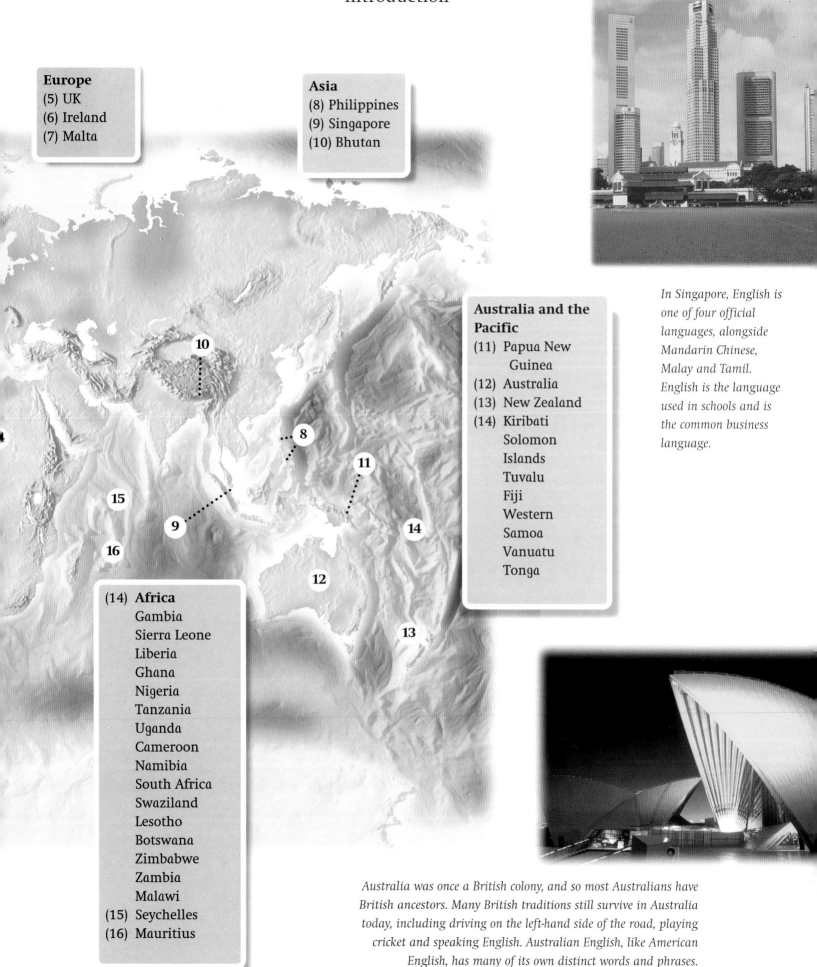

Europe
(5) UK
(6) Ireland
(7) Malta

Asia
(8) Philippines
(9) Singapore
(10) Bhutan

Australia and the Pacific
(11) Papua New Guinea
(12) Australia
(13) New Zealand
(14) Kiribati
Solomon Islands
Tuvalu
Fiji
Western Samoa
Vanuatu
Tonga

(14) **Africa**
Gambia
Sierra Leone
Liberia
Ghana
Nigeria
Tanzania
Uganda
Cameroon
Namibia
South Africa
Swaziland
Lesotho
Botswana
Zimbabwe
Zambia
Malawi
(15) Seychelles
(16) Mauritius

In Singapore, English is one of four official languages, alongside Mandarin Chinese, Malay and Tamil. English is the language used in schools and is the common business language.

Australia was once a British colony, and so most Australians have British ancestors. Many British traditions still survive in Australia today, including driving on the left-hand side of the road, playing cricket and speaking English. Australian English, like American English, has many of its own distinct words and phrases.

HOW TO USE THIS THESAURUS

Headwords
The headword or entry word is the word you look up to find other words with similar meanings (synonyms). These headwords are arranged alphabetically.

Parts of speech
After the headword is the part of speech – noun, verb, adverb, adjective, or preposition.

Synonyms
Synonyms (words with similar meanings) follow the part of speech. They are listed in the order of common usage, rather than alphabetically.

nag VERB pester, annoy, badger, go on about, henpeck.

nail VERB fix, peg, fasten, hammer in.

naive ADJECTIVE innocent, simple, unsophisticated, gullible.

naked ADJECTIVE nude, bare, unclothed.

name NOUN 1 title, label, designation. 2 reputation, character, fame. *He's making a name for himself.*

name VERB call, christen, term, entitle, dub. 2 indicate, specify. *He named the culprit.*

nap VERB sleep, doze, snooze, rest.

narrate VERB tell, describe, recount, relate.

narrow ADJECTIVE fine, thin, slender, limited, tight, cramped. An *opposite word* is wide.

narrow-minded ADJECTIVE biased, bigoted, intolerant. An *opposite word* is broad-minded.

nasty ADJECTIVE 1 bad, dreadful, horrible, offensive, unpleasant, offensive. 2 dirty, filthy, foul. 3 unfriendly, unkind rude, mean, vicious. An *opposite word* is nice.

natter VERB chatter, gossip.

natural ADJECTIVE 1 normal, usual, common. 2 inborn, instinctive, hereditary. 3 frank, open, genuine, unsophisticated, artless. *Opposite words* are 1 unnatural, 2 learned, 3 artificial.

naughty ADJECTIVE bad, unruly, disobedient, mischievous. *Opposite words* are well-behaved, good.

nausea NOUN sickness, queasiness, squeamishness.

nautical ADJECTIVE *See* **naval.**

naval ADJECTIVE maritime, nautical, marine, seafaring.

navigate VERB sail, pilot, steer, guide, direct.

nearly ADVERB almost, not quite, practically, roughly.

neat ADJECTIVE smart, tidy, orderly, spruce. *Opposite words* are untidy, sloppy.

need NOUN necessity, shortage.

need VERB 1 want, require, call for. 2 rely on, depend on, count on.

needy ADJECTIVE poor, needful, penniless, destitute. An *opposite word* is rich.

neglect VERB ignore, overlook, forget. An *opposite word* is look after.

negotiate VERB bargain, haggle, mediate, deal, talk about, discuss.

neighbourhood/neighborhood (US) NOUN district, area, locality, surroundings.

nervous ADJECTIVE anxious, fidgety edgy. An *opposite word* is calm.

nest NOUN burrow, den, lair.

net NOUN mesh, net, trap, snare.

neutral ADJECTIVE 1 impartial, unbiased, fair, even-minded. 2 dull, mediocre.

never ADVERB not ever, at no time, under no circumstances. An *opposite word* is always.

new ADJECTIVE 1 unused, fresh. 2 novel, original, unfamiliar. 3 modern, recent, just out, up-to-date, latest. *Opposite words* are second-hand, old-fashioned, out of date, stale, old.

news NOUN information, report, bulletin, account.

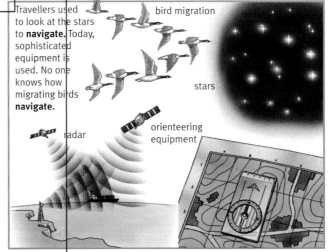

Travellers used to look at the stars to **navigate.** Today, sophisticated equipment is used. No one knows how migrating birds **navigate.**

bird migration

stars

radar

orienteering equipment

Examples
Example sentences are given to show how some words should be used in context.

Opposite words (antonyms)
appear at the end of an entry, after the synonyms, for example *never/always.*

Numbers
Numbers distinguish different meanings of one word. For example, *note* can mean either *letter, message* or *signal, symbol.*

nibble VERB bite, peck, gnaw. *See also* **eat.**

nice ADJECTIVE **1** beautiful, fine, lovely, attractive, pretty, pleasant, good. **2** delicious, tasty, scrumptious **3** friendly, warm, kind, likeable, considerate, good-natured. **4** comfortable, cosy. *A nice, warm bed.* **5** smart (UK), stylish. *A nice new dress.*

nimble ADJECTIVE spry, agile, nippy, lively, swift. *Opposite words are slow, clumsy.*

nip VERB cut, bite, pinch.

nobility NOUN **1** aristocracy, gentry, nobles. **2** dignity, majesty, eminence, worthiness. *Opposite words are* **1** hoi polloi, common people. **2** meanness.

nod VERB **1** beckon, signal, indicate, gesture, agree. **2** doze, sleep.

noisy ADJECTIVE loud, rowdy, deafening, boisterous. *Opposite words are quiet, silent.*

nomadic ADJECTIVE wandering, roving, migratory, itinerant. *The travellers led a nomadic lifestyle.*

none PRONOUN not one, not any, nobody. A word that sounds similar is nun.

nonsense NOUN rubbish, drivel, rot, trash, gobbledegook.

nook NOUN corner, alcove, niche, recess.

normal ADJECTIVE common, ordinary, usual, natural, average. *An opposite word is abnormal.*

nostalgic ADJECTIVE longing, yearning, homesick, wistful, sentimental.

notable ADJECTIVE remarkable, outstanding, famous, notable, momentous. *An opposite word is commonplace.*

note NOUN **1** letter, message. **2** signal, symbol. *A musical note.*

note VERB **1** remark, notice, observe. **2** record, write down.

notice VERB see, note, perceive, detect, observe. *An opposite word is overlook.*

notify VERB inform, tell, announce, declare, advise.

notion NOUN idea, thought, whim. *I had a notion you might think that.*

nought NOUN zero, nil, nothing, naught.

nourish VERB feed, support, sustain. *An opposite word is starve.*

novel ADJECTIVE new, fresh, original, innovative, uncommon, unusual. *Opposite words are trite, familiar, hackneyed.*

novice NOUN beginner, learner, pupil, tyro, apprentice.

now ADVERB **1** instantly, at this moment, immediately. **2** at this time, at present.

nude ADJECTIVE naked, bare, undressed, unclothed, stripped.

nudge VERB elbow, prod, poke, push.

nuisance NOUN bother, pest, trouble, worry, plague.

numb ADJECTIVE insensible, dead, frozen, unfeeling.

number NOUN figure, amount, quantity, total.

numerous ADJECTIVE many, several, abundant. *Opposite words are few, scant.*

nurse VERB care for, mind, tend, look after, nourish.

nut NOUN Some different kinds of nut: almond, brazil, cashew, chestnut, cobnut, coconut, hazelnut, peanut, pecan, pistachio, walnut.

nutty ADJECTIVE foolish. *See also* **mad.**

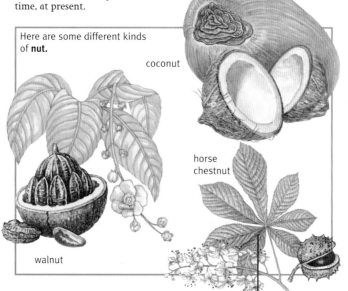

Here are some different kinds of **nut.**

coconut

horse chestnut

walnut

Associated words
These appear either in an illustrated panel or are listed after a headword.
For example, under accommodation are listed all the different kinds of dwelling people live in, from bedsits to mansions.

Words that sound the same (homonyms)
also appear at the end of entries, where appropriate.

Illustrations
On every page, one of the headwords is illustrated , to demonstrate its different meanings.

abandon VERB **1** leave, forsake, desert, quit. *They abandoned the sinking boat.* **2** give up, cancel, forgo, surrender.

abbreviate VERB shorten, reduce, condense, contract, abridge. *Opposite words* are extend, lengthen.

ability NOUN **1** skill, knack, gift, flair, know-how. **2** capability, facility.

able ADJECTIVE skilful/skillfull(US), clever, talented, capable, gifted.

abolish VERB do away with, cancel, destroy, get rid of, erase. *Opposite words* are keep, retain.

about ADVERB around, close to, nearly, almost. *It's about one o'clock.*

about PREPOSITION **1** relating to, concerning, regarding. **2** nearby, surrounding.

abridge VERB See **abbreviate**.

absent ADJECTIVE not present, missing, gone away. An *opposite word* is present.

absolute ADJECTIVE complete, total, perfect, utter, certain.

absurd ADJECTIVE See **funny**.

abundant ADJECTIVE plentiful, full, ample, overflowing. An *opposite word* is scarce.

accelerate VERB speed up, quicken, go quicker, hurry, hasten. *Opposite words* are slow down.

accent NOUN **1** stress, emphasis. **2** pronunciation, tone of voice, brogue. *A Welsh accent.*

accept VERB **1** receive, take. *Accept a present.* **2** admit, acknowledge, tolerate, believe. *I accept that you are right. Opposite words* are refuse and reject.

accident NOUN **1** mishap, disaster, calamity. **2** crash, collision.

accommodation NOUN *See below and also* **house**.

accompany VERB go with, escort, follow.

accomplished ADJECTIVE See **able**.

account NOUN **1** report, description, story, tale, record. *An account of the accident.* **2** record, invoice, bill.

accurate ADJECTIVE precise, exact, correct, right, true, factual. *Opposite words* are innaccurate, wrong.

ache NOUN pain, suffering, throb.

ache VERB hurt, pain, throb.

achievement NOUN accomplishment, attainment, success, exploit, feat. An *opposite word* is failure.

acquaintance NOUN **1** associate, colleague, friend. An *opposite word* is stranger. **2** knowledge, familiarity, understanding. *A slight acquaintance with Russian.*

act NOUN **1** deed, action, achievement, feat. **2** a decree, statute. *An Act of Parliament.*

act VERB **1** work, behave, carry out. *He's acting very strangely today.* **2** perform, imitate, mimic, pretent. *She's acting in the school play.*

action NOUN **1** deed, performance, act, feat. **2** mechanism, motion, functioning. **3** battle, conflict. *He was killed in action.* An *opposite word* is rest.

active ADJECTIVE busy, alert, agile, on the go, brisk. *Opposite words* are idle, lazy.

activity NOUN **1** work, job, occupation, hobby, pastime. **2** liveliness, movement, bustle, action, business.

actual ADJECTIVE real, genuine, correct, certain. *An actual rock from the Moon. Opposite words* are unreal, imaginary.

Here are some different kinds of **accommodation.**

apartments

cottage

stately home

zulu hut

acute ADJECTIVE **1** sharp, shrewd, smart, observant. *An acute eye for detail.* **2** severe, sharp, extreme, intense. *An acute pain in the stomach.*

adapt VERB **1** alter, modify, fit, suit. **2** get used to, adjust, acclimatize.

add VERB **1** attach, join, affix, connect. **2** combine, mix. *Add the ingredients together.* **3** (add up) total, come to. *Opposite words are take away, remove, subtract, deduct.*

additional ADJECTIVE extra, more. *Additional help.*

adequate ADJECTIVE enough, sufficient, ample. An *opposite word is inadequate.*

adjacent ADJECTIVE near, next to.

adjust VERB *See* **adapt, change.**

admire VERB respect, esteem, approve, like, prize, appreciate, value, look at with pleasure. *Opposite words are despise, dislike.*

adopt VERB take care of, choose, follow, select, support.

adore VERB worship, love, idolize, honour/honor (US), revere. *Opposite words are hate, loathe.*

adult NOUN and ADJECTIVE grown-up, mature. An *opposite word is immature.*

advance VERB **1** progress, move forward, further, go on, proceed. An *opposite word is retreat.* **2** lend, give. *Advance some money.*

advantage NOUN help, benefit, asset, gain. *Opposite words are drawback, handicap.*

adventure NOUN exploit, undertaking, venture. *The camping trip was an adventure.*

advertise VERB publicize, promote, plug, make known, hype.

advise VERB suggest, urge, recommend.

affect VERB **1** influence, change, alter, involve, disturb, upset. *The whole village was affected by the floods.* **2** pretend, assume, put on, feign. *An affected manner.*

affection NOUN liking, fondness, warmth, love. *Opposite words are coldness, indifference. A great show of affection.*

affix VERB *See* **attach, fasten.**

afraid ADJECTIVE frightened, alarmed, scared, timid, nervous.

after PREPOSITION following, behind, later. An *opposite word is before.*

again ADVERB once more, another time, anew, often.

age NOUN **1** period of time, date, span, epoch, years. **2** elderliness, senility, maturity. An *opposite word is youth.*

aggressive ADJECTIVE hostile, violent, forceful, pushing. *An aggressive goose. An aggressive sales promotion.*

agile ADJECTIVE alert, nimble, active, lively, sprightly.

agree VERB **1** see eye to eye, accept, harmonize, match. **2** consent, be willing, decide. *They agreed to meet the next day.*

aid VERB help, assist, back, support. *Opposite words are hinder, obstruct.*

aim NOUN purpose, ambition, hope, intention, goal.

aim VERB point, direct at, target.

aircraft NOUN Some different kinds of aircraft: airliner, airship, balloon, biplane, bomber, fighter, glider, helicopter, jet, microlight, monoplane, seaplane, Zeppelin.

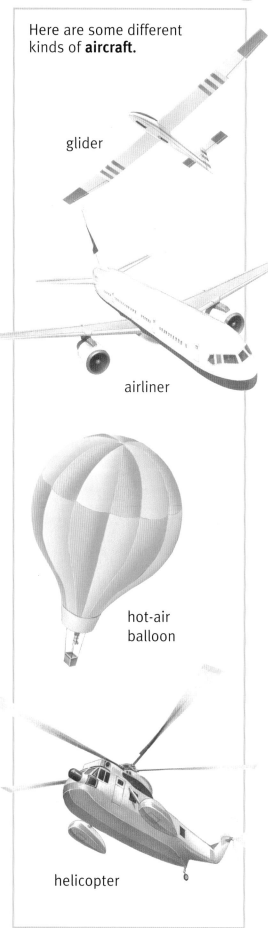

Here are some different kinds of **aircraft.**

glider

airliner

hot-air balloon

helicopter

aisle NOUN corridor, gangway, passageway, path. A word that sounds similar is isle.

alarm NOUN warning signal, siren.

alarm VERB scare, frighten, startle, terrify, distress. *Opposite words* are calm, soothe.

alert ADJECTIVE **1** ready, awake, attentive, on the look out, watchful. **2** active, bright, nimble. *An alert mind. Opposite words are unprepared, stupid.*

alert VERB warn, tell.

alike ADJECTIVE similar, same, resembling, identical. *Opposite words are unlike and different.*

alive ADJECTIVE living, active, in existence, lively, alert. *Opposite words are dead, lifeless, dull.*

all ADJECTIVE every, whole, entire, complete, total. *Opposite words are nothing, none, some.*

allow VERB permit, let, tolerate, authorize. *Dogs are not allowed in the store. An opposite word is forbid.*

ally NOUN *See* **friend.**

alone ADJECTIVE and ADVERB solitary, lonely, lonesome, friendless, on one's own, single-handed. *An opposite word is together.*

aloud ADVERB loudly, clearly, audibly, noisily. *An opposite word is silently. A word that sounds similar is allowed.*

alphabet NOUN Some different kinds of alphabet: Braille, cuneiform, Cyrillic, Devanagari (Hindi), Greek, hieroglyphs.

alter VERB **1** change, vary, revise, amend, adjust, modify, adapt. **2** switch, transfer, exchange, swap, replace. *Opposite words are keep, retain, conserve. A word that sounds similar is altar.*

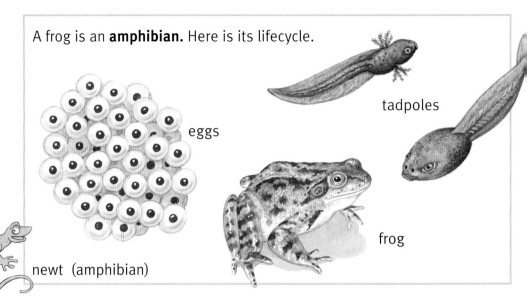

A frog is an **amphibian.** Here is its lifecycle.

tadpoles

eggs

newt (amphibian)

frog

amaze VERB surprise, astound, astonish. An *opposite word* is bore.

amazing ADJECTIVE surprising, astounding, extraordinary, incredible, strange, unusual, odd.

ambition NOUN aim, goal, target, aspiration, objective, wish, commitment, eagerness, drive, enthusiasm. *Opposite words are indifference, diffidence.*

ambush VERB trap, surprise attack, snare.

amend VERB *See* **change** and **alter.**

ammunition NOUN Some different kinds of ammunition: arrow, bomb, bullet, cannonball, hand grenade, mine, rocket, shell, torpedo.

amount NOUN quantity, sum, total, whole, measure, volume.

amphibian NOUN Some different kinds of amphibian: caecilians, frogs, newts, salamanders, toads.

amuse VERB cheer up, entertain, make laugh, divert, interest, please. An *opposite word* is bore.

amusing ADJECTIVE funny, humorous, comical, witty, enjoyable, interesting. *Opposite words are dull, boring.*

ancestor NOUN forebears, predecessors, forefathers. An *opposite word* is descendant.

ancient ADJECTIVE old, aged, antique, prehistoric, primeval. *Opposite words are modern, recent.*

anger NOUN fury, temper, indignation, annoyance, ire, rage.

angry ADJECTIVE cross, furious, mad, annoyed, irate, upset, indignant. *Opposite words are pleased, friendly.*

animal NOUN For different classes of animal *see* **amphibian, bird, fish, insect, mammal, reptile.**

announce VERB declare, reveal, proclaim, state, make known, report, publish, reveal. *Opposite words are stifle, suppress.*

announcement NOUN statement, notification, proclamation, publication, advertisement.

annoy VERB irritate, bother, upset, make angry, trouble, harass.

answer NOUN **1** reply, response. **2** solution, explanation. *What is the answer to the problem?*

antique ADJECTIVE ancient, old, veteran, old-fashioned, archaic. *Antique furniture.*

anxious ADJECTIVE nervous, worried, afraid, uneasy, concerned, jittery.

apart ADVERB separately, away from, singly, independently, cut off from. An *opposite word* is together.

ape NOUN chimpanzee, gorilla, orang-utan, gibbon.

apologize VERB say sorry, express regret.

apparel NOUN *See* **clothes**.

appeal NOUN attraction, allure, fascination, charm.

appeal VERB ask, beg, urge, implore, request, entreat.

appear VERB **1** become visible, come into sight, arrive, turn up. **2** seem, look. *You appear to be sad.*

appetite NOUN hunger, taste, craving, desire, longing.

applaud VERB clap, praise, congratulate, acclaim. An *opposite word* is criticize.

appoint VERB name, nominate, select, choose, designate.

appointment NOUN meeting, engagement, date, rendezvous.

appreciate VERB **1** enjoy, value, relish, like, respect. **2** grow in value, increase, rise.

approach VERB get near, advance, move towards.

appropriate ADJECTIVE suitable, proper, relevant, right. *Opposite words* are inappropriate, unsuitable.

approximately ADVERB nearly, roughly, almost, about, loosely.

apt ADJECTIVE **1** relevant, suitable, fitting. **2** clever, skilful/skillful (US), intelligent. **3** liable, prone, likely to. *She's apt to be a bit aloof.*

arduous ADJECTIVE difficult, hard, strenuous, tough, laborious, harsh. An *opposite word* is easy.

argue VERB discuss, debate, talk over, row, bicker, quarrel, quibble, disagree. An *opposite word* is agree.

There are many ways to create **art.**

sculpture

architecture

painting

argument NOUN dispute, debate, row, disagreement, quarrel.

arid ADJECTIVE *See* dry.

army NOUN troops, soldiers, force, legions, multitude, host.

around PREPOSITION **1** encircling, surrounding, on all sides. **2** about, approximately.

arrange VERB **1** plan, organize, fix, settle. **2** order, group, classify, sort, tidy, position.

arrest VERB seize, capture, catch, take prisoner, hold, detain, stop, block, hinder. An *opposite word* is release.

arrive VERB reach, get to, attain, enter, come, appear, happen.

arrogant ADJECTIVE scornful, superior, patronizing, condescending, disdainful, insolent, supercilious. An *opposite word* is modest.

art NOUN Some different kinds of art: painting, drawing. sketching, sculpture, pottery, woodcarving, metalwork, engraving, printing, needlework, photography, weaving.

artificial ADJECTIVE synthetic, fake, false, bogus, unnatural, fictitious. Some *opposite words* are genuine, real.

artist NOUN Some different types of artist: painter, photographer, potter, printer, sculptor, weaver.

ascend VERB go up, rise, climb scale, mount. An *opposite word* is descend.

ashamed ADJECTIVE sorry, embarrassed, guilty, sheepish, mortified, shame-faced, humbled, abashed.

ask VERB **1** enquire, find out, beg, demand, query, request. **2** invite. An *opposite word* is answer.

asleep ADJECTIVE sleeping, napping, snoozing, resting, dozing.

assassinate VERB murder, kill, slaughter, slay.

assault VERB attack, strike, hit, set upon, beat up, invade, charge. An *opposite word* is defend.

assist VERB *See* **help.**

assistant NOUN helper, partner, colleague, aide, accomplice.

associate VERB **1** mix, mingle, join in. *Associate with thieves.*
2 connect, link, relate, combine, couple. *Associate sun and warmth.*

association NOUN group, club, organization, society, company, partnership, union, confederation.

astonish VERB amaze, astound, surprise, alarm, stun, shock.

athletic ADJECTIVE fit, strong, muscular, energetic, active, good at sports, sporty.

attach VERB fasten, tie, fix, join, connect, stick, link, unite. An *opposite word* is detach.

attack VERB assault, charge, mug, set on, storm, bomb, raid, invade. *Opposite words* are retreat, withdraw.

attain VERB reach, achieve, accomplish, acquire, grasp. An *opposite word* is fail.

attempt VERB try, endeavour/ endeavor (US), struggle, have a go, undertake, tackle.

attend VERB **1** visit, be present, go to. *Attend a meeting.* **2** accompany, escort, look after, nurse. **3** listen to, pay attention, heed.

attentive ADJECTIVE
1 careful, mindful, alert, heedful. **2** considerate, kind, polite. *Opposite words* are inattentive, inconsiderate.

Here are some **athletic** sports.

high jump

running

javelin

hurdling (athletic)

attitude NOUN position, point of view, outlook, disposition, bearing.

attract VERB **1** appeal, fascinate, enchant, interest, lure, tempt.
2 pull, drag, entice.

attractive ADJECTIVE lovely, beautiful, handsome, pretty, good-looking, gorgeous, charming, tempting, nice. *Opposite words* are plain, ugly, unattractive.

audience NOUN listeners, onlookers, spectators, viewers, fans.

austere ADJECTIVE severe, stern, rigid, harsh, strict, stark, grim, bleak, formal. *Opposite words* are lenient, informal.

available ADJECTIVE obtainable, accessible, on sale, handy. An *opposite word* is unavailable.

average ADJECTIVE normal, usual, ordinary, moderate, mediocre, medium, standard, everyday, fair, so-so, all right, not bad. An *opposite word* is exceptional.

avid ADJECTIVE keen, eager, enthusiastic, earnest, hungry, greedy, grasping.

awake ADJECTIVE alert, attentive, watchful, aware, conscious. An *opposite word* is asleep.

aware ADJECTIVE conscious, informed, knowing, on the ball. An *opposite word* is unaware, ignorant.

awful ADJECTIVE dreadful, terrible, vile, fearful, horrible, ghastly.

awkward ADJECTIVE **1** clumsy, inept, sloppy, unskilful, gawky. *Awkward with her hands.* **2** fiddly, difficult. *Awkward to clean.*
3 embarrassed, uncomfortable. *An awkward silence.* **4** difficult, unhelpful. *Don't be so awkward.*

Bb

baby NOUN infant, child, tot, toddler. *See* **small**.

back NOUN rear, end, stern, posterior. *The back of the room.* An *opposite word* is front.

back VERB **1** reverse, go backwards. **2** support, aid, endorse, help, champion. *We backed the project.*

bad ADJECTIVE **1** evil, wicked, wrong, dangerous, vile. *Bad dreams.* **2** harmful, damaging, unhealthy. *Smoking is bad for you.* **3** naughty, disobedient, ill-behaved. **4** rotten, sour. *Bad apples.* **5** unpleasant, nasty, offensive. *A bad smell.* **6** serious, severe, dreadful. *A bad cold. A bad accident.* **7** shoddy, inferior, poor, careless. *A bad drawing. Opposite words* are good, harmless, healthy.

badge NOUN crest, symbol, emblem, trademark.

bad-mannered ADJECTIVE impolite, rude, discourteous, boorish. *Opposite words* are polite, well-mannered.

bad-tempered ADJECTIVE angry, irritable, grumpy, snappy.

baggage NOUN luggage, bags, suitcases, gear.

bake VERB *See* **cook**.

balance VERB weigh, steady, poise, counteract.

bald VERB **1** hairless, bare, uncovered. **2** plain, direct, stark.

ball NOUN **1** sphere, globe. *See* **shape**. **2** dance, party.

ban VERB forbid, stop, prohibit, bar, banish, outlaw. *Opposite words* are allow, permit.

band NOUN **1** strip, belt, ribbon, zone. *A rubber band.* **2** orchestra, group. *Strike up the band.* **3** gang, group, troop. *A band of robbers.*

bang NOUN **1** blast, explosion, crash, boom. **2** bump, hit, knock. *A bang on the door.*

bang VERB hit, beat, thump, pound, hammer.

banish VERB expel, exclude, exile, deport, cast out, send away, dismiss, outlaw. An *opposite word* is admit.

bank NOUN **1** shore, edge, embankment, coast, mound, pile. **2** treasury, fund, deposit, savings.

banner NOUN flag, standard, streamer, ensign.

bar NOUN **1** barricade, barrier, obstacle. **2** counter, pub, inn. **3** block, slab. *A bar of soap.* **4** rod, stick, rail. *Bars of a cage.*

bar VERB stop, block, prevent, seal off, bolt, lock, hinder. **2** ban, forbid, exclude.

barbaric ADJECTIVE fierce, savage, cruel, brutal, uncivilized, wild, rude. *Barbaric manner.*

bare ADJECTIVE **1** naked, unclothed, nude. **2** barren, empty. A word with a similar sound is bear.

barely ADVERB hardly, scarcely, only just, almost.

bashful ADJECTIVE shy, modest. An *opposite word* is confident.

basically 1 ADVERB fundamentally, essentially. **2** importantly, principally. *Basically, the main thing is to finish the work in time.*

basin NOUN bowl, sink, dish.

bathe VERB swim, wet, immerse, wash, soak, cleanse.

batter VERB **1** beat, hit, clout, pound. **2** ill-treat, assault, hurt, bruise, crush, destroy.

battle NOUN fight, struggle, war, raid, conflict, contest, clash, strife, combat, brawl, scuffle.

bay NOUN **1** gulf, inlet, bight. **2** alcove, niche, recess.

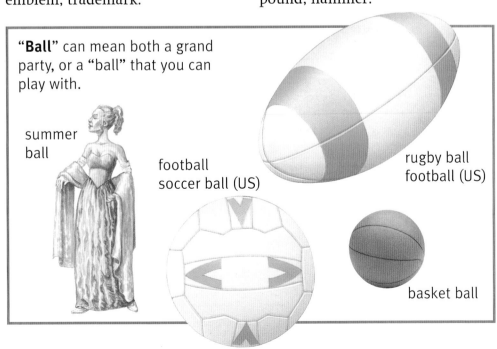

"**Ball**" can mean both a grand party, or a "ball" that you can play with.

summer ball

football soccer ball (US)

rugby ball football (US)

basket ball

Bb

school bell (bell)

beach NOUN coast, shore, seaside, sands, seashore. A similar sounding word is beech.

beam NOUN **1** gleam, ray. **2** plank, board, girder, joist.

beam VERB **1** gleam, shine, glow, radiate. **2** smile, grin.

bear VERB **1** put up with, tolerate, stand, endure, suffer. **2** carry, lift, support, haul. A word with a similar sound is bare.

beat VERB **1** hit, strike, whip, flog, smack. **2** throb, thump, pulsate. **3** overcome, conquer. *They beat us at football.*

beast NOUN animal, brute, creature, monster.

beastly ADJECTIVE brutal, cruel, unpleasant, nasty. *A beastly person.*

beautiful ADJECTIVE lovely, pretty, handsome, gorgeous, attractive, sweet, cute, elegant, glamorous, nice. An *opposite word* is ugly.

beauty NOUN loveliness, charm, elegance.

beckon VERB call, summon, signal, wave, gesture.

become VERB change into, turn into, be transformed.

bed NOUN Some kinds of bed: **1** berth, bunk, divan, couch, four-poster. **2** floor, bottom. *The sea-bed.*

beg VERB ask, plead, entreat, request, implore.

belief NOUN **1** trust, faith. **2** creed, principle. **3** conviction, opinion.

believe VERB **1** accept, trust, depend on, count on, maintain. **2** think, feel, reckon. *Opposite words* are disbelieve, doubt.

belittle VERB play down, minimize, underestimate, scorn, laugh at.

bell NOUN Some different kinds of bell: bicycle bell, church bell, doorbell. How bells sound: chime, clang, peal, ring, tinkle and toll.

belongings NOUN possessions, property.

belt NOUN band, strap, sash, strip, zone.

bend VERB curve, turn, incline, bow, twist, buckle. An *opposite word* is straighten.

beneath PREPOSITION under, underneath, below, lower than.

bestow VERB See **give**.

bet VERB stake, wager, gamble.

betray VERB mislead, double-cross, deceive, delude, play false.

beware VERB take care, be careful, look out, steer clear.

bewilder VERB confuse, muddle, baffle, puzzle, perplex. An *opposite word* is clarify.

bewitched VERB charmed, enchanted, spellbound, captivated.

biased VERB prejudiced, one-sided, bigoted, unfair, angled. *Opposite words* are impartial, fair.

bicker VERB quarrel, argue, disagree, wrangle.

bicycle NOUN The different parts of a bicycle: bell, brake, chain, gear, handlebars, hub, lamp, pedal, pump, saddle, spokes, wheel.

big ADJECTIVE **1** enormous, great, heavy, huge, vast, immense, massive. **2** important, serious. *A big day in her life. Opposite words* are small, little, tiny.

bigoted NOUN prejudiced, narrow-minded, intolerant. *See also* **biased**.

bill NOUN **1** account, receipt, charges, invoice. **2** law, legislation, proposal. **3** beak.

bind VERB fasten, attach, tie up, secure. *An opposite word* is untie.

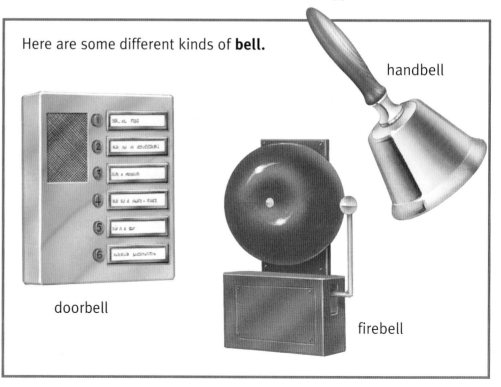

Here are some different kinds of **bell**.

handbell

doorbell

firebell

bird NOUN Some different kinds of bird: **birds of prey**: eagle, falcon, hawk, kestrel, kite, owl. **songbirds**: robin, thrush, lark. **flightless birds**: emu, kiwi, ostrich, penguin. **game birds**: grouse, partridge, pheasant. **water birds**: duck, goose, heron, pelican. **sea birds**: gull, cormorant, puffin. **tropical birds**: canaries cockatoos, parrots. **birds kept on farms as poultry**: chicken, duck, goose, turkey, quail.

birth NOUN creation, start, origin, beginning, delivery, nativity. An *opposite word* is death. A word with a similar sound is berth.

bit NOUN piece, scrap, shred, crumb, morsel, fragment, chip, portion.

bite VERB See **eat**.

bitter VERB **1** acid, sour, sharp, harsh. *Bitter medicine.* **2** fierce, angry, savage. *Bitter enemies.* **3** sarcastic. *Bitter remarks.* An *opposite word* is sweet.

bizarre VERB See **strange**.

blade NOUN Some things that have blades: axe, dagger, knife, razor, scalpel, scissors, scythe, sword. Also: oars and a blade of grass.

blame VERB accuse, condemn, find fault with, scold, reproach, rebuke, chide, criticize.

blameless ADJECTIVE innocent, faultless, guiltless, sinless. An *opposite word* is guilty.

bland ADJECTIVE smooth, tasteless, soft, mild, gentle, kind, insipid, boring, dull. *Opposite words* are harsh, bitter, lively.

blank ADJECTIVE empty, vacant, void, bare, unmarked, unused. An *opposite word* is full.

blare VERB blast, boom, clang, roar, crash, shriek, thunder, hoot.

There are many species of **bird**.

eagle

cockatoo

penguin

peacock

blast VERB explode, burst, erupt, bang, boom, split.

blaze VERB burn, flare, flash.

bleak VERB **1** gloomy, dismal, cheerless, desolate, dreary. *A bleak future.* **2** bare, desolate, windswept, barren.

blend VERB mix, combine, whisk, stir together. An *opposite word* is separate.

blessed ADJECTIVE holy, sacred, revered, favoured/favored (US), lucky.

blessing NOUN advantage, godsend, boon, gain, benefit.

blind ADJECTIVE **1** unseeing, sightless, eyeless. **2** ignorant, oblivious, unaware. *Blind to her unhappiness. Opposite words* are sighted, aware.

bliss NOUN See **happiness, joy**.

blizzard NOUN See **storm**.

block NOUN lump, chunk, mass. *A block of ice.*

block VERB obstruct, bar, stop, hinder, impede, clog, seal off.

bloom NOUN flower, blossom, bud.

bloom VERB grow, develop, thrive, flourish. *Opposite words* are wither, fade, decay.

blossom NOUN See bloom.

blow NOUN hit, smack, clout, bang, bash. *A blow to the head.*

blow VERB **1** puff, pant, breathe, gust, blast. **2** sound, play.

blow up VERB **1** explode, go off, burst. **2** inflate, pump up. *Blow up the balloon.*

blue VERB **1** azure, sapphire, indigo, cyan. **2** sad, glum, unhappy, depressed, miserable. *Opposite words* are happy, cheerful. A word that sounds similar is blew.

blunder NOUN mistake, error, howler, stupidity, gaffe.

blunt ADJECTIVE **1** dull, unsharpened. **2** direct, plain, abrupt, forthright, frank. *Opposite words* are **1** sharp. **2** tactful.

blurred ADJECTIVE dimmed, smeared, fuzzy, hazy, obscure, indistinct, foggy, out of focus. An *opposite word* is clear.

blurt-out VERB say, let slip, reveal, blab.

Bb

board NOUN **1** plank, strip, beam, table. **2** panel, committee. *A board of directors.* A word with a similar sound is bored.

boast VERB brag, show off, swank, talk big, swagger.

boat NOUN vessel, bark, ship. Some different types of boat or ship: **rowing boats:** dinghy, kayak, gondola, raft. **sailing boats:** dhow, catamaran, clipper, galleon, junk, sampan, yacht. **steam ships:** ferry, liner, submarine, trawler, tanker. **motorboats:** cabin cruiser, lifeboat, speedboat. **warships:** aircraft carrier, battleship, cruiser, destroyer, frigate, minesweeper.

body NOUN **1** (dead) corpse, cadaver, carcass, trunk. **2** group, collection, corporation, party, band, council, committee.

bog NOUN marsh, swamp, quagmire, morass.

bogus ADJECTIVE fake, spurious, false, sham, phoney, artificial.

boil VERB *See* **cook**.

boisterous ADJECTIVE noisy, loud, stormy, lively, rowdy, wild.

bold ADJECTIVE **1** brave, daring, valiant, fearless, courageous, adventurous, confident. **2** strong, striking, eye-catching. *Opposite words* are timid, restrained.

book NOUN Some different kinds of book: album, annual, atlas, autobiography, diary, dictionary, directory, encyclopedia, exercise book, guidebook, handbook, manual, notebook, novel, scrapbook, thesaurus.

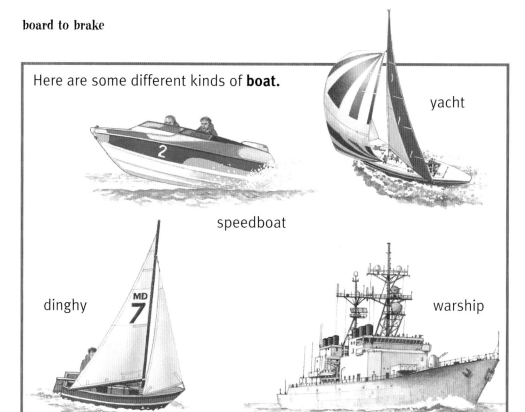

Here are some different kinds of **boat.**

yacht

speedboat

dinghy

MD 7

warship

rowing boat

boom NOUN **1** blast, explosion, thunder, roar, rumble. **2** growth, expansion, boost, improvement, upturn. *A boom in exports.*

boot NOUN *See* **shoe**.

border NOUN *See* **edge**.

boring ADJECTIVE dull, dreary, tedious, monotonous, uneventful, tiresome, uninteresting. *The play was really boring. Opposite words* are interesting, original.

boss NOUN chief, employer, leader, governor, manager, supervisor.

bossy ADJECTIVE demanding, high-handed, autocratic, dictatorial, domineering, arrogant.

bother VERB annoy, distress, pester, irritate, trouble, harass, disturb, hassle, upset.

bottom NOUN **1** base, foot, foundation. **2** seabed. **3** backside, rear, behind, buttocks.

bough NOUN *See* **branch**. A word that sounds similar is bow (see above).

boulder NOUN stone, slab, rock.

bounce VERB rebound, spring, leap, bound. *The ball bounced on the floor.*

bound VERB leap, jump, spring, vault. *The rabbits bounded away.*

boundary NOUN border, verge, edge, frontier, limit.

bow VERB **1** bend, nod, buckle, incline. *He bowed his head.* **2** give in, surrender, submit. *He bowed to her wishes.* A word with a similar sound is bough (see below).

bowl NOUN basin, sink, dish, vessel.

box NOUN **1** crate, carton, case, chest, trunk. **2** (slang) television.

box VERB **1** enclose, pack. *She boxed the apples in a wooden crate.* **2** fight, punch, hit, clout, spar.

brag VERB *See* **boast**.

brainy ADJECTIVE clever, smart (US), intelligent, intellectual, talented. *An opposite word* is stupid.

brake VERB slow down, check, curb, halt.

branch NOUN **1** bough, shoot, sprig, twig, arm. **2** department, division, section.

branch out VERB expand, develop, enlarge, extend, diversify.

brand NOUN stamp, trademark, make, mark, logo, label, tag, class, kind.

brash ADJECTIVE overconfident, hasty, reckless, cocky, bold, rude.

brave ADJECTIVE daring, bold, fearless, audacious, valiant. An *opposite word* is cowardly.

brawny VERB *See* **strong**.

bread NOUN Some different kinds of bread: loaf, roll, bagel, chapati, ciabatta, crispbread, croissant, focaccia, matzo, rye, soda, wholemeal.

break NOUN rest, interval, half-time, gap, opening.

break VERB **1** smash, crack, fracture, snap, split, shatter, splinter, destroy, demolish, wreck, ruin. *Break a record. Opposite words* are fix, mend, repair. **2** interrupt. *Break a journey.* A word that sounds similar is brake.

break in VERB **1** interrupt, butt in. **2** invade, burgle.

break loose/out VERB escape, flee.

break up VERB **1** split, divide. **2** end, adjourn, stop.

breathe VERB exhale, inhale, emit, respire. Some ways we can breathe: puff, pant, gasp, wheeze, gulp.

breed NOUN kind, type, variety, pedigree, stock, race.

breed VERB reproduce, bear, hatch, propagate, create, generate, nurture, make.

breeze NOUN *See* **wind**.

bribe NOUN incentive, inducement.

bridge NOUN Some different kinds of bridges: arched, beam, drawbridge, footbridge, suspension, cantilever, viaduct.

brief ADJECTIVE short, little, concise, terse, pithy, crisp, curt. An *opposite word* is lengthy.

bright ADJECTIVE **1** sparkling, radiant, shining, luminous, brilliant, gleaming, clear. **2** clever, intelligent, keen, smart, ingenious. An *opposite word* is dull.

brilliant ADJECTIVE shining, radiant, dazzling, glittering, sparkling, bright. **2** gifted, talented, outstanding, witty, clever. *Opposite words* are **1** dull. **2** unimportant.

brim NOUN full to the brim, edge, brink, rim, border.

bring VERB carry, take, convey, bear, fetch, get, lead.

bring about VERB cause, make happen, achieve.

bring up VERB rear, train, educate.

brink NOUN edge, border, boundary, limit.

brisk ADJECTIVE alert, fast, quick, rapid, agile, keen, energetic, nimble, refreshing, invigorating.

brittle ADJECTIVE fragile, frail, delicate, weak, breakable, crisp. *Opposite words* are flexible, supple.

broad ADJECTIVE wide, large, roomy, extensive. An *opposite word* is narrow.

broken-down ADJECTIVE worn-out, dilapidated, not working.

broken-hearted ADJECTIVE unhappy, grief-stricken, inconsolable, miserable, sad.

brook NOUN *See* **river**.

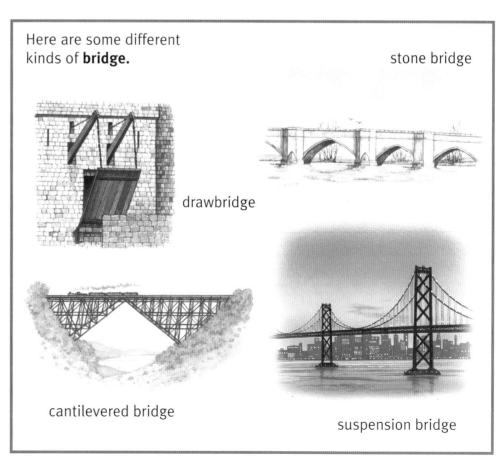

Here are some different kinds of **bridge.**

stone bridge

drawbridge

cantilevered bridge

suspension bridge

brush NOUN broom. Some different types of brush: toothbrush, clothes brush, paintbrush, hairbrush.

brush aside VERB ignore, dismiss, disregard.

brush up VERB revise, relearn, review.

brusque ADJECTIVE abrupt, gruff, blunt, rude. An *opposite word* is polite.

brutal VERB cruel, ruthless, merciless, savage, callous, hard, bestial. *Opposite words* are kind, humane.

bubbles NOUN foam, droplets, lather, suds, froth.

bubbly VERB fizzy, sparkling, foaming, effervescent, lively. An *opposite word* is flat.

budge VERB move, shift, push, roll, stir, dislodge.

build VERB construct, erect, assemble, put up, raise, fabricate. An *opposite word* is destroy.

building NOUN construction, erection, structure, edifice. Some different kinds of building: **1** apartment block/apartment building (US), block of flats (UK), bungalow, castle, chalet, chateau, cottage, dwelling, house, mansion, villa. **2** basilica, cathedral, chapel, church, mosque, synagogue, temple. **3** college, hospital, library, museum, police station, prison, school, town hall/city hall. **4** cafe, hotel, inn, pub, restaurant. **5** shop, store, warehouse. **6** barn, cowshed, stable, windmill. **7** factory, office block/office building (US).

bulge NOUN swelling, bump, projection, lump.

Leaning Tower of Pisa (building)

bully VERB torment, threaten, intimidate, browbeat, oppress, frighten, boss.

bump VERB hit, knock, bang, strike, jolt, collide.

bump into VERB meet, come across.

bunch NOUN bundle, batch, lot, cluster, collection.

bundle NOUN bunch, group, mass, parcel, package, roll. *A bundle of newspapers.*

bungle VERB botch, blunder, fumble, mess up, mismanage.

buoyant ADJECTIVE floating, afloat, light-hearted, carefree.

burden NOUN **1** load, weight, encumbrance **2** responsibility, trouble, hardship.

burglar NOUN robber, thief, housebreaker.

burn VERB **1** blaze, flare, smoulder. **2** scorch, singe, char, toast. **3** cremate (a body), incinerate, kindle.

bury VERB inter, hide, conceal, immerse. An *opposite word* is unearth. A similar sounding word is berry.

burst VERB explode, erupt, break open, blow up, crack, spout, gush, pop.

business NOUN **1** trade, job, occupation, work, profession, employment. **2** commerce, trading, industry. **3** firm, company, organization, office.

busy VERB employed, active, occupied, working, tied up, industrious, on the go. *Opposite words* are idle, lazy

buy VERB purchase, procure, obtain, get. An *opposite word* is sell.

Buildings are all sorts of sizes and shapes.

a building site

museum

Arabian palace

Cc

cabin NOUN **1** hut, shed, shack, shelter. **2** berth, compartment.

cable NOUN flex, rope, line, wire, lead.

cafe NOUN restaurant.

cake NOUN pastry, gateau, tart.

cake VERB cover, coat, encrust, harden, solidify.

calamity NOUN disaster, tragedy, catastrophe, accident, mishap, misfortune.

calculate VERB count, reckon, compute, work out, estimate.

call VERB **1** name, baptise, christen, term, style, dub. **2** cry, cry out, shout, yell, exclaim. **3** summon, invite, assemble muster. An *opposite word* is dismiss. **4** telephone, phone, ring. **5** visit.

call for VERB request, demand, need.

call off VERB cancel, stop.

calling NOUN profession, vocation, job, work, business, trade.

callous ADJECTIVE hard, unfeeling, harsh, hard-bitten, indifferent. *Opposite words* are caring, tender.

calm ADJECTIVE **1** peaceful, quiet, cool, patient, unruffled, laid back. **2** smooth, peaceful, mild, windless, still, tranquil. *A calm sea crossing. Opposite words* are disturbed, upset, stormy.

cancel VERB stop, abandon, call off, postpone, give up, drop, quash, repeal.

candid ADJECTIVE open, frank, blunt, truthful, straightforward.

canoe NOUN *See* **boat** and **ship**.

cap NOUN *See* **hat**.

capable ADJECTIVE able, efficient, competent, clever, skilled, gifted, qualified, suited. *Opposite words* are incompetent and incapable.

capacity NOUN **1** volume, space, size. *A seating capacity of 1000.* **2** ability, capability, aptitude. *A capacity for remembering facts.*

captain NOUN leader, commander, boss. *See also* **chief**.

captive NOUN *See* **prisoner**.

capture VERB seize, take, catch, grab, trap, arrest. *Opposite words* are free, release, liberate.

car NOUN automobile, vehicle.

carcass NOUN corpse, body, cadaver, shell, remains.

care NOUN **1** worry, anxiety, trouble. **2** attention, protection.

care VERB **1** mind, be bothered about. **2** mind, watch out, beware, heed. *Take care!* **3** look after, nurse, mind, protect. *Take care of her!*

care for VERB be fond of, like, love.

careful ADJECTIVE **1** cautious, wary, watchful. **2** thorough, precise, thoughtful. *Opposite words* are careless, forgetful, neglectful, thoughtless, negligent.

careless ADJECTIVE *See* **careful**.

caress VERB hug, cuddle, stroke, embrace, touch, kiss.

carol NOUN *See* **song**.

carriage NOUN *See* **transport**.

carry VERB convey, bring, take, move. **2** lift, support, bear.

cart NOUN *See* **vehicle**.

carve VERB cut, chisel, sculpt. *See also* **cut**.

case NOUN *See* **box**.

castle NOUN fort, fortress, chateau.

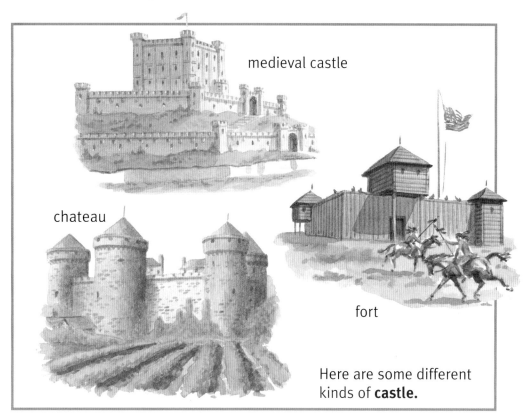

medieval castle

chateau

fort

Here are some different kinds of **castle**.

Here are some different aspects of **character.**

sad

happy

naughty

cartoon character

casual ADJECTIVE **1** informal. *Casual clothes.* **2** uninterested. *Casual manner.* **3** accidental, chance, random. *Casual meeting. Opposite words* are **1** formal. **2** interested. **3** planned.

catastrophe NOUN disaster, calamity, blow, misfortune, fiasco.

catch VERB capture, grab, seize, grasp, snatch, take hold of, arrest, stop, trap, get. *Opposite words* are release, let go, free.

cause NOUN **1** reason, motive, source, origin. **2** purpose, object, undertaking. *A good cause.*

cause VERB bring about, produce, create, result in.

cautious ADJECTIVE careful, watchful, prudent, wary. An *opposite word* is careless.

cease VERB stop, end, finish, break off, terminate, conclude. An *opposite word* is begin.

cell NOUN prison, room, den, dungeon. A word that sounds similar is sell.

cellar NOUN vault, basement, crypt, store.

cemetery NOUN graveyard, churchyard, burial-ground, necropolis.

centre/center (US) NOUN middle, heart, nucleus, core.

cereal NOUN grain, corn. Some different kinds of cereal: barley maize, oats, rice, rye, wheat.

certain ADJECTIVE **1** sure, positive, definite, unquestionable, confident. An *opposite word* is doubtful. **2** particular, regular, fixed. *At certain times of the year.*

challenge VERB dare, defy, brave, threaten, question.

champion NOUN **1** guardian. An *opposite word* is loser. **2** protector, defender, supporter. *A champion of the poor.*

chance NOUN **1** opportunity, occasion, opening. *A chance to get on.* **2** accident, luck, fortune, fluke. *By pure chance.* **3** risk, hazard. *Take a chance.*

change VERB adjust, alter, make different, modify, amend, revise, convert, vary, replace, swap.

chant VERB *See* **sing.**

chaos NOUN turmoil, disorder, confusion, anarchy, bedlam.

character NOUN **1** letter, sign, symbol, emblem, hieroglyph. **2** nature, personality, quality, feature, reputation. **3** person, individual, part, role.

charge NOUN cost, price.

charge VERB attack, assault, storm.

charming ADJECTIVE appealing, attractive, pleasant, fascinating, delightful, nice. *Opposite words* are repulsive, ugly.

chase VERB follow, pursue, run after, hunt, tail, shadow, drive.

chaste ADJECTIVE modest, pure.

chastise VERB *See* **punish.**

chat VERB talk, gossip.

chatter VERB *See* **chat.**

cheap ADJECTIVE **1** inexpensive, bargain, cut-price, low-cost. **2** paltry, inferior, shoddy, tatty. *Opposite words* are **1** expensive. **2** superior.

cheat VERB swindle, defraud, con, diddle, trick, fool.

check VERB **1** examine, inspect, test, look over. **2** stop, restrain, curb, hinder. *Check your feelings.*

cheeky ADJECTIVE impertinent, saucy, rude, insolent.

cheerful ADJECTIVE happy, glad, contented, bright, merry, jolly. *Opposite words* are sad, gloomy.

cherish VERB treasure, care for, hold close, prize, value.

chest NOUN **1** case, coffer, trunk, casket. **2** bosom.

chew VERB *See* **eat**.

chide VERB *See* **punish**.

chief ADJECTIVE main, principal, prime, key, important. *Opposite words* are unimportant, minor.

chief NOUN boss, leader, governor, commander, lord, master, ruler.

chilly ADJECTIVE **1** cool, cold, crisp, fresh. **2** unfriendly, unwelcoming. An *opposite word* is warm.

chip NOUN piece, fragment, sliver.

choke VERB **1** strangle, throttle, suffocate, smother, gag. **2** block.

choose VERB pick, select, vote for, prefer, settle on. A word that sounds similar is chews.

chop VERB hack, hew, fell. *See also* **cut**.

chubby ADJECTIVE *See* **fat**.

chuckle VERB laugh, titter, giggle.

chum NOUN *See* **friend**.

chunk NOUN lump, piece, block.

church NOUN cathedral, chapel, temple, meeting-house.

churlish ADJECTIVE rude, uncivil, brusque, sullen, morose.

circle NOUN **1** ring, hoop, disk, band. **2** company, group, set, fellowship. *A circle of friends.*

circulate VERB broadcast, spread, publicize, publish, diffuse.

civil ADJECTIVE **1** polite, courteous, well-mannered. **2** public, state, political. *Civil rights. Opposite words* **1** are impolite, rude, churlish.

civilize VERB educate, tame, train, cultivate, polish, improve.

claim VERB ask for, call for, demand, require, request.

clamour/clamor (US) NOUN *See* **noise**.

clap VERB **1** applaud, cheer. **2** smack, hit.

clarify VERB **1** make clear, explain, define, elucidate. **2** purify, refine.

clash VERB **1** disagree, conflict, quarrel. **2** clatter, crash. *See also* **sound**.

clasp VERB grasp, hold, embrace, clutch.

class NOUN **1** group, set, category, rank. **2** form, grade (US).

classify VERB sort, set in order, group, arrange, categorize, file.

clean ADJECTIVE spotless, sparkling, unsoiled, unstained, immaculate, fresh, unused, blank. An *opposite word* is dirty. Some different ways to clean things: brush, dust, mop, polish, rinse, scrub, sweep. *The kitchen looked very clean.*

clear ADJECTIVE **1** fine, sunny, bright, cloudless. *Clear weather.* **2** obvious, plain, evident, simple, straightforward. **3** transparent, clean. **4** empty, bare, unobstructed. **5** audible, distinct. *Opposite words* are **1** dull, dim. **2** obscure, vague. *Everything seems clear.*

clever ADJECTIVE bright, intelligent, brainy, brilliant, sharp, skilled, gifted, talented. *Opposite words* are stupid, foolish.

A **church** is a place of worship.

cathedral

altar

temple

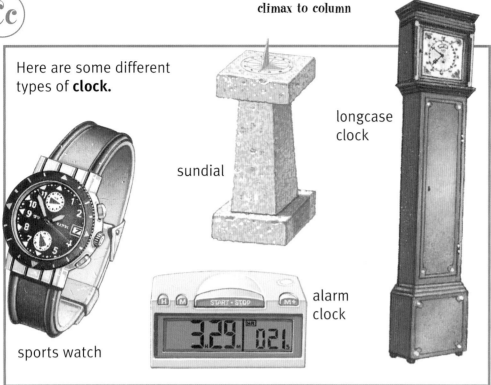

Here are some different types of **clock.**

sundial

longcase clock

alarm clock

sports watch

climax NOUN peak, apex, high point, culmination.

climb VERB mount, ascent, scale, go up.

cling VERB adhere, stick, attach, embrace, grasp, clasp, hold.

clip VERB trim, prune. *See also* **cut.**

cloak NOUN *See* **clothes.**

clock NOUN watch, timepiece, chronometer. Different types of clocks and watches (all are used to tell the time): alarm clock, atomic clock, cuckoo clock, digital clock, fob watch, hourglass, longcase clock, stopwatch, sundial, water clock.

clog VERB block up, dam up, choke, obstruct, stop up.

close ADJECTIVE **1** nearby, adjacent, neighbouring/neighboring (US), imminent. An *opposite word* is far. **2** intimate, friendly. *Close friends.* **3** mean, stingy, niggardly. **4** stuffy, muggy, heavy. *The weather is close.* **5** careful, thorough. *A close look at the picture.*

close VERB shut, end, cease, finish, lock, fasten.

cloth NOUN material, fabric, stuff.

clothes NOUN clothing, gear, outfit, garments, attire. Some different kinds of clothes: belt, blouse, cardigan, dress, dressing gown, frock, gloves, jacket, jeans, jumper, nightie, overcoat, parka, poncho, raincoat, scarf, shirt, socks, suit, tie, trousers/pants (US), t-shirt. **headgear** *See* **hats. shoes** *See* **shoes. underwear** vest/undershirt (US), knickers/underpants (US), slip.

cloud NOUN haze, mist, fog, nebula. Different kinds of cloud: altocumulus, altostratus, cirrus, cirrocumulus, cirrostratus, cumulus, cumulonimbus, nimbostratus, stratocumulus, stratus.

cloudy ADJECTIVE hazy, overcast, dim, obscure, dull, murky, blurred. An *opposite word* is clear.

clumsy ADJECTIVE awkward, ungainly, gawky, gauche, blundering, unwieldy, lumbering. An *opposite word* is graceful.

cluster NOUN bunch, clump, group, collection.

clutch VERB *See* **clasp.**

clutter NOUN mess, muddle, jumble, disorder.

coach NOUN *See* **vehicle.**

coach VERB *See* **teach.**

coarse ADJECTIVE **1** rough, unrefined, unpolished. **2** rude, uncivil, bawdy, vulgar. An *opposite word* is refined. A word that sounds similar is course.

coast NOUN shore, seaside, beach.

coax VERB persuade, urge, wheedle, entice, soft-soap.

coffer NOUN *See* **box.**

coil VERB curl, twist, loop, wind.

cold ADJECTIVE **1** cool, chilly, unheated, fresh, frosty, nippy, raw, wintry. **2** frigid, unfriendly. An *opposite word* is warm.

collapse VERB fall down, drop, break down, crumple, fail.

colleague NOUN workmate, partner, companion, associate.

collect VERB gather together, amass, accumulate, save, hoard. An *opposite word* is scatter.

collide VERB bang into, crash into, smash into, hit.

colossal ADJECTIVE gigantic, huge, enormous, massive, immense, vast. An *opposite word* is tiny.

colour/color (US) NOUN tint, shade, hue, tinge, dye, pigment.

colourful/colorful (US) ADJECTIVE **1** bright, rich, vivid, brilliant, flashy. **2** interesting, exciting.

column NOUN post, pillar. Types of column: Corinthian, Doric, Egyptian, Ionic.

Cc

combat VERB oppose, resist, contest, battle, fight.

combine VERB unite, join, put together, mix, blend, merge. An *opposite word* is separate.

come VERB arrive, appear, reach, get to, approach, draw near.

come across VERB find by chance, discover, meet.

come by VERB get, obtain.

come down VERB drop, decrease, fall, decline.

come off VERB happen, take place.

come round VERB **1** visit. **2** recover, awake.

comfort NOUN rest, ease, enjoyment, consolation.

comfort VERB soothe, console, calm.

comfortable ADJECTIVE **1** restful, snug, luxurious, nice. **2** happy, at ease. *A comfortable bed.*

comforting ADJECTIVE cheering, consoling.

comic ADJECTIVE funny.

command VERB **1** order, tell, instruct, direct. **2** to control, be in charge of, manage, rule.

commence VERB begin, start.

comment VERB remark, observe, point out, mention, criticize.

commit VERB carry out, perform, enact, be guilty of.

common ADJECTIVE **1** everyday, regular, usual, ordinary, normal. **2** vulgar, coarse, loutish. *Opposite words* are **1** unusual, rare.

commotion NOUN upset, turmoil, upheaval, disturbance, bustle, bother. An *opposite word* is calm.

communicate VERB **1** contact, talk, write, telephone. **2** tell, reveal, declare, proclaim, announce.

communications NOUN Some different kinds of communication: advertising, braille, circular, fax, Internet, letter, memo, mobile phone, newspaper, radio, satellite, semaphore, telephone, television.

community NOUN society, district, hamlet, village, locality, group, partnership, fellowship.

compact ADJECTIVE small, neat, solid, dense, concise, condensed, terse.

companion NOUN *See* **friend**.

company NOUN **1** firm, business, association, syndicate. **2** society, companionship, party, crowd, group.

comparable ADJECTIVE similar, like, equal, alike. *Opposite words* are incomparable, different.

compare VERB liken, compare, contrast.

compassion NOUN pity, kindness, sympathy. An *opposite word* is indifference.

compel VERB force, order, make, urge, browbeat.

compete VERB contest, rival, strive, emulate.

competent ADJECTIVE capable, clever, able, qualified, skilled, trained. An *opposite word* is incompetent.

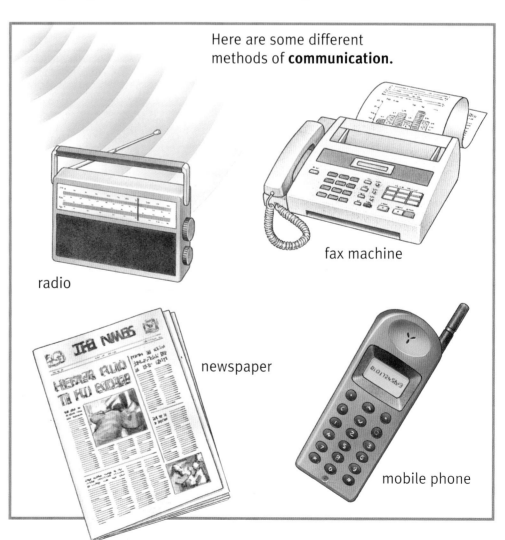

Here are some different methods of **communication.**

radio

fax machine

newspaper

mobile phone

competition NOUN contest, match, rivalry, emulation, tournament.

compile VERB put together, amass, gather, combine, compose, arrange.

complain VERB grumble, grouse, protest, object, whine.

complete ADJECTIVE **1** whole, total, entire, full. *A complete jigsaw.* **2** utter, absolute. *Complete nonsense.*

complete VERB finish, accomplish, achieve, carry out, conclude, end.

complex ADJECTIVE involved, difficult, hard, complicated, confused, intricate. An *opposite word* is simple.

complex NOUN organization, structure, network.

complicated ADJECTIVE *See* **complex.**

component NOUN part, element, ingredient, piece.

comprehend VERB understand, grasp, fathom, know, appreciate, take in, perceive.

comprehensive ADJECTIVE complete, thorough, extensive, general.

comprise VERB consist of, contain, be made up of, include, form part of. *Great Britain comprises England, Scotland and Wales.*

compulsory ADJECTIVE obligatory, forced, necessary. An *opposite word* is optional.

computer NOUN personal computer, PC, word processor, microprocessor, laptop, calculator. Some words connected with computers: bit, bug, byte, cursor, CD, data, file, floppy disk, hacker, hard disk, hardware, keyboard, memory, microchip, modem, monitor, mouse, peripheral, printer, printout, program, RAM, ROM, software, virus.

comrade NOUN *See* **friend.**

conceal VERB hide, mask, camouflage, cover, secrete. *Opposite words* are reveal, show, display.

conceited ADJECTIVE arrogant, bigheaded, smug, self-important, boastful, vain.

concentrate VERB **1** think about, pay attention to, heed, focus on. **2** condense, reduce.

concept NOUN idea, notion, theory, thought, plan.

concern NOUN **1** matter, affair, consequence. *No concern of yours.* **2** company, business, organization, firm.

concern VERB **1** trouble, disturb, upset, worry. **2** interest, affect, involve, be of importance to, touch. *Road safety concerns all of us.*

concerned ADJECTIVE worried, anxious, upset.

concerning PREPOSITION regarding, about, respecting.

concise ADJECTIVE brief, condensed, short, pithy, compact. *Opposite words* are rambling, diffuse, wordy.

conclude VERB *See* **end.**

condemn VERB blame, judge, convict, punish. *Condemn to death.* **2** disapprove, criticize.

condense VERB reduce, compress, concentrate, shorten, abridge, abbreviate.

condition NOUN **1** state, plight, situation, case. **2** terms, requirement. *Conditions of the treaty.* **3** health, fitness, shape.

conduct NOUN behaviour/behavior (US), attitude, manner, bearing. *Bad conduct.* **2** management, guidance, control, leadership. *Conduct of affairs.*

conduct VERB lead, guide, direct, command, control.

conference NOUN meeting, convention, forum, get-together.

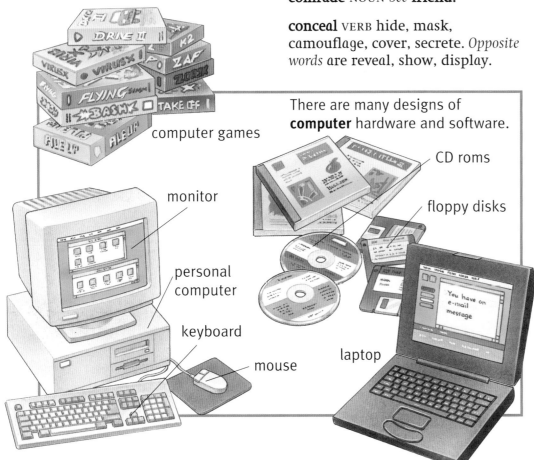
computer games

There are many designs of **computer** hardware and software.

CD roms

monitor

floppy disks

personal computer

keyboard

mouse

laptop

You have an e-mail message

confess VERB admit, own up, acknowledge, tell, declare, admit, concede. An *opposite word* is deny.

confident ADJECTIVE sure, certain, positive, assured, fearless, bold, composed. *Opposite words* are nervous, uncertain, diffident.

confiscate VERB seize, take away, commandeer, appropriate. An *opposite word* is restore.

conflict NOUN **1** struggle, fight, battle. **2** difference, disagreement. *A conflict of interests.*

confront VERB meet, face, encounter, address, challenge.

confuse VERB **1** puzzle, bewilder, perplex, baffle, mislead. **2** mix up, muddle, jumble.

confusing ADJECTIVE muddling, puzzling, perplexing.

confusion NOUN **1** disorder, mess, upheaval, disarray. **2** misunderstanding.

congested ADJECTIVE crowded, jammed, blocked, packed.

congregate VERB meet, assemble, come together, gather, converge.

connect VERB join, unite, link, combine. *Opposite words* are disconnect, separate.

conquer VERB overcome, beat, defeat, vanquish, overrun, crush, trounce, thrash.

conqueror NOUN winner, victor, champion.

consent NOUN permission, agreement, approval.

consent VERB allow, permit, agree, approve.

consequence NOUN **1** outcome, result, effect, upshot. **2** importance, influence. *Of little consequence.*

conserve VERB keep, preserve, safeguard, protect, save. An *opposite word* is squander.

consider VERB think about, ponder, reflect, contemplate, examine, muse.

considerate ADJECTIVE thoughtful, kind, helpful, polite. An *opposite word* is selfish.

consist of VERB comprise, be made up of, contain, be composed of.

console VERB comfort, sympathize with, soothe. *Opposite words* are burden, upset.

conspire VERB plot, intrigue, scheme.

constant ADJECTIVE **1** endless, never-ending, continuous, ceaseless, incessant, unchanging. **2** stable, loyal, true, trustworthy. *A constant companion.*

construction NOUN building, structure, erection, assembly, creation.

constructive ADJECTIVE helpful, useful, productive.

consult VERB discuss, confer, question.

consume VERB **1** use, eat, devour, waste, squander. **2** destroy, ravage. *Consumed by fire.*

contain VERB include, comprise, hold, enclose.

container NOUN Some different kinds of container: basin, bucket, cup, glass, jug, pail, vase.

contempt NOUN scorn, disdain, derision. An *opposite word* is respect.

contented ADJECTIVE happy, satisfied, pleased, cheerful. An *opposite word* is unhappy.

contest NOUN competition, match, fight.

continent NOUN Africa, Asia, Australasia, Europe, North America, South America.

continual ADJECTIVE endless, ceaseless, non-stop, constant, incessant. An *opposite word* is occasional.

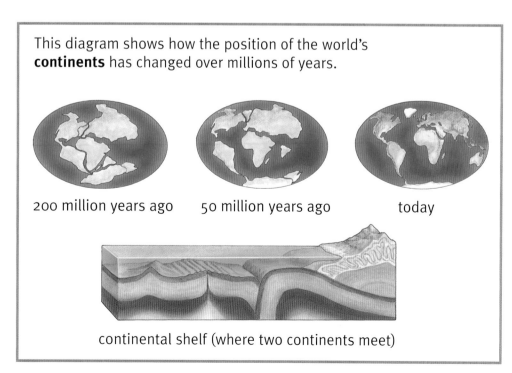

This diagram shows how the position of the world's **continents** has changed over millions of years.

200 million years ago   50 million years ago   today

continental shelf (where two continents meet)

continue VERB carry on, last, endure, persist, go on, remain. *Opposite words* are stop, discontinue.

continuous ADJECTIVE uninterrupted, unbroken, non-stop, constant.

contract NOUN agreement, treaty, pact, deal, understanding.

contract VERB reduce, condense, shrink, lessen, abbreviate. An *opposite word* is expand.

control VERB manage, command, restrain, direct, guide, supervise.

convenient ADJECTIVE **1** appropriate, suitable. *A convenient time to visit.* **2** handy, helpful, useful.

conversation NOUN talk, chat, discussion.

convert VERB change, alter, adapt, modify.

convey VERB carry, take, transport, bear, escort.

convict NOUN prisoner, criminal, felon, captive.

convict VERB condemn, pass judgement, sentence, find guilty.

convince VERB persuade, satisfy, prove, win over, demonstrate.

cook VERB Some different ways of cooking: bake, barbecue, boil, broil, fry, grill, poach, roast, stir-fry, stew, toast. Some things we use for cooking: bowl, casserole, colander, food processor, frying-pan, grater, kettle, ladle, pan, peeler, ramekin, rolling pin, saucepan, sieve, spoon, tureen, whisk, wok.

cool ADJECTIVE *See* **cold.**

cooperate VERB collaborate, help, assist, join forces, participate, work together, combine. An *opposite word* is oppose.

Here are some different types of **costume.**

Santa Claus outfit

matador

angel costume

duck costume

cope VERB manage, deal with, grapple, handle, make do.

copy VERB **1** imitate, mimic, ape. **2** duplicate, reproduce, photocopy, trace, Xerox. **3** fake, forge.

cord NOUN rope, string, line, twine, flex. A word with a similar sound is chord.

corn NOUN maize, sweet corn. *See also* **cereal.**

corpse NOUN carcass, dead body, cadaver.

correct ADJECTIVE true, right, actual, accurate, faultless. *Opposite words* are wrong, incorrect.

corridor NOUN passageway, aisle, gallery.

corrode VERB rust, decay, erode, waste away, crumble, waste.

corrupt ADJECTIVE crooked, dishonest, fraudulent, depraved, immoral, bad, wicked.

cost NOUN **1** expense, amount, charge, price. **2** loss, damage, penalty, sacrifice. *At the cost of his good reputation.*

costly ADJECTIVE expensive, dear, precious, valuable, rich. An *opposite word* is cheap.

costumes NOUN outfit, dress, fancy dress, attire, uniform, robes.

cottage NOUN *See* **house.**

count VERB add up, total, reckon, number, list, estimate.

counterfeit ADJECTIVE forged, sham, mock, fake, bogus, feigned, spurious. *Opposite words* are real, genuine, authentic.

couple NOUN pair, two, brace, duo.

courage NOUN bravery, valour/valor (US), daring, pluck, guts. An *opposite word* is cowardice.

course NOUN **1** way, road, track, trail. **2** syllabus, studies. A word with a similar sound is coarse.

courteous ADJECTIVE polite, civil, well-mannered, considerate. *Opposite words* are rude, inconsiderate.

cover VERB **1** hide, camouflage, secrete, bury, screen, cloak, veil. **2** include, incorporate, embrace. *Covers the cost of insurance.*

coward NOUN funk, weakling, wimp, chicken.

coy ADJECTIVE shy, bashful, timid, demure. An *opposite word* is brash.

crack NOUN gap, split, crevice, break, flaw, fissure.

crack VERB break, burst, snap, split, splinter.

crack up VERB collapse, go to pieces.

craft NOUN **1** skill, talent, ability, expertise, handicraft. **2** boat, vessel, aircraft, spacecraft.

crafty ADJECTIVE clever, cunning, deceitful, sly, guileful.

cram VERB fill, stuff, ram, squeeze.

crash VERB **1** shatter, break, splinter, dash. **2** collide, bump into. **3** fall down, topple. *See also* **sound**.

crate NOUN *See also* **box**.

crawl VERB **1** creep, glide, slither. **2** grovel.

crazy ADJECTIVE **1** mad, insane, lunatic, idiotic, demented, deranged, foolish. **2** ridiculous, absurd, weird, impractical. *A crazy idea.* **3** keen, fanatical, enthusiastic. *Crazy about football. Opposite words are* sane, sensible.

creak VERB grate, grind, scrape, squeak.

crease VERB or NOUN pleat, fold, wrinkle, groove, crumple.

create VERB make, form, originate, devise, think up, invent, bring into being, compose, concoct. *An opposite word is* destroy.

creative ADJECTIVE inventive, artistic, imaginative, original.

credible ADJECTIVE believable, reliable, trustworthy, likely.

creep VERB **1** crawl, slither. **2** grovel, cringe.

crew NOUN team, gang, party, company, band.

Here are some jobs which are **creative** in different ways.

painter

actor

writer

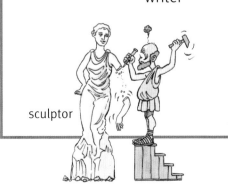

sculptor

crime NOUN felony, offence, wrong, misdemeanour/misdemeanor (US), law-breaking, treason.

criminal NOUN offender, felon, law-breaker, wrongdoer, convict, culprit, crook. Some different kinds of criminal: arsonist, burglar, embezzler, hijacker, kidnapper, murderer, mugger, pickpocket, robber, thief.

crippled ADJECTIVE *See* **disabled**.

crisis NOUN emergency, danger, problem, calamity.

crisp ADJECTIVE **1** brittle, crunchy, firm. *Crisp bacon. Opposite words are* soft, soggy. **2** brusque, terse, clear, incisive. *A crisp remark.*

criticize VERB **1** judge, examine, review, estimate, assess. **2** knock, condemn, find fault. *An opposite word is* praise.

crockery NOUN pots, dishes, earthenware. Some different kinds of crockery: bowl, cup, jug, mug, plate, pot, saucer, tureen.

crony NOUN *See* **friend**.

crook NOUN *See* **criminal**.

crooked ADJECTIVE **1** bent, curved, bowed, askew, twisted. *An opposite word is* straight. **2** dishonest, underhand.

cross ADJECTIVE (old-fashioned, US) grumpy, bad-tempered, snappy, short. *See also* **angry**.

cross VERB go across, traverse, bridge, pass over.

cross out VERB delete, draw a line through.

crowd NOUN mass, group, throng, gang, mob, assembly, company, flock, swarm, herd.

crucial ADJECTIVE critical, urgent, vital, decisive. *An opposite word is* unimportant.

crude ADJECTIVE **1** raw, rough, unrefined, unpolished. **2** coarse, rude, vulgar. An *opposite word* is refined.

cruel ADJECTIVE harsh, fierce, heartless, merciless, vicious, brutal, cold-hearted, barbarous. *Opposite words* are kind, gentle.

crumble VERB decay, disintegrate, break up, powder.

crumple VERB crease, wrinkle, crush.

crunch VERB *See* **eat**.

crush VERB **1** squash, squeeze, compress, mash, grind, crumple. **2** conquer, overcome, overrun, subdue, quash.

cry VERB **1** sob, weep, shed tears. **2** shout, call out, yell, exclaim, scream, shriek. Some other ways we cry: blubber, snivel, whimper.

cuddle VERB hug, embrace, hold, fondle, nestle.

cue NOUN hint, sign, signal, suggestion. A word with a similar sound is queue.

culprit NOUN *See* **criminal**.

cultivate VERB **1** grow, farm, till. **2** educate, train, encourage, help.

cultivated ADJECTIVE refined, educated, cultured, civilized. *Opposite words* are crude, primitive, neglected.

cunning ADJECTIVE sly, shrewd, wily, artful, astute, canny, clever. *Opposite words* are naive, artless, gullible.

curb VERB restrain, hold back, control, bridle. *Opposite words* are encourage, incite.

cure NOUN remedy, drug, medicine, antidote, treatment.

cure VERB **1** heal, remedy, restore, relieve, fix.

curious ADJECTIVE **1** inquisitive, interested, nosy, prying. **2** strange, odd, peculiar, queer, funny.

curl VERB twist, coil, wind, bend, curve, loop.

currency NOUN money, coins.

current NOUN **1** stream, water course, flow, drift, trend. **2** present, up to date, modern, common, widespread. *Opposite words* are out of date, obsolete. A word with a similar sound is currant.

curtail VERB shorten, cut, abridge, clip, trim, lop. An *opposite word* is lengthen.

curve VERB bend, twist, coil, wind, arch.

custom NOUN habit, tradition, usage, practice, rite.

cut VERB slice, crop, reduce. Some different ways of cutting: amputate, carve, chisel, chop, cleave, clip, crop, hack, hew, lacerate, mow, prune, saw, sculpt, sever, shave, slash, split, stab, trim, wound.

cute ADJECTIVE **1** charming, pretty, attractive. **2** clever, cunning.

cutlery NOUN Some items of cutlery: dessertspoon, fork, knife, soupspoon, spoon, tablespoon, teaspoon.

cutting ADJECTIVE bitter, sharp, sardonic, sarcastic.

cynical ADJECTIVE scornful, sneering, pessimistic, scoffing, sour, morose, contemptuous.

Here are some different ways we can **cultivate** the land.

grassland

terraces cut into the hillside

hothouse flowers

rows of crops

Dd

daft ADJECTIVE silly, soppy, stupid, foolish. *See also* **crazy**.

dainty ADJECTIVE delicate, neat, small, pretty, fine. An *opposite word* is coarse.

damage VERB harm, hurt, injure, vandalize, deface, wreck, destroy, demolish.

damp ADJECTIVE moist, humid, dank, soggy. An *opposite word* is dry.

dance NOUN ball, caper, hop. Some different kinds of dance: ballet, ballroom, country, folk dancing, line dancing, jive, morris dancing, old tyme dancing, tap. Some different dances: bolero (Spain), bossa nova (Brazil), czarda (Hungary), flamenco (Spain), limbo (Caribbean), mazurka (Poland), tarantella (Italy). Modern ballroom dances: cha cha, carioca, foxtrot, mambo, paso doble, quickstep, rumba, tango, waltz.

danger NOUN risk, threat, peril, hazard.

dangerous ADJECTIVE unsafe, hazardous, perilous, risky, harmful. *Opposite words* are safe, secure.

dangle VERB hang, sway, swing, tempt.

dank ADJECTIVE *See* **damp**.

dare VERB venture, risk, brave, challenge, defy.

daring ADJECTIVE fearless, brave, adventurous, bold, intrepid, doughty, plucky. *Opposite words* are timid, cowardly.

dark ADJECTIVE **1** murky, dingy, overcast, shadowy, sunless, cloudy. *A dark room.* **2** gloomy, dismal, grim, mournful, sorrowful. *Dark looks. Opposite words* are bright, cheerful.

dart VERB dash, hurtle, charge, rush, spring.

dash VERB **1** dart, rush, race. **2** hurl, throw, cast.

date NOUN **1** time, age, epoch, period. **2** appointment, engagement.

dated ADJECTIVE out of date, old-fashioned, obsolete, archaic.

dawdle VERB loiter, linger, lag, hang about/hang around (US), dally. An *opposite word* is hurry.

day NOUN daytime, daylight. The *opposite word* is night. The days of the week are Monday, Tuesday, Wednesday, Thursday, Friday, Saturday, Sunday. *What day is it today?*

dazed ADJECTIVE confused, bewildered, dazzled, stunned. *He was dazed after the crash.*

dazzle VERB **1** amaze, overwhelm, astonish, surprise. *The young actress was dazzled by her success.* **2** blind, confuse, blur. *The rabbit was dazzled by the headlights.*

dazzling ADJECTIVE sparkling, bright.

dead NOUN **1** lifeless, deceased. **2** dull, cold, frigid, cheerless. *Opposite words* are **1** alive. **2** lively.

deal VERB **1** trade, transact, traffic. **2** share out, divide, distribute. *Deal out the cards.* **3** handle, attend to, cope with. *She doesn't like dealing with spiders.*

dealer NOUN merchant, trader, retailer, shopkeeper. *A secondhand car dealer.*

dear ADJECTIVE **1** expensive, costly, pricey. An *opposite word* is cheap. **2** darling, beloved, pet, precious. *She's a dear child.* A word that sounds similar is deer.

debate NOUN discussion, dialogue, talk, argument, dispute, controversy. *The debate continued throughout the day.*

Here are some different types of **dance.**

modern dance

belly dance

ballet dance

debris NOUN rubbish, remains, ruins, junk.

decapitate VERB behead, execute, guillotine.

decay VERB rot, decompose, go bad, waste away, perish, disintegrate, wither, putrefy.

deceive VERB mislead, cheat, trick, betray, fool, con, swindle.

decent ADJECTIVE proper, respectable, fit, seemly.

deceptive ADJECTIVE misleading, deceiving, false, seeming.

decide VERB resolve, determine, elect, choose to.

decipher VERB solve, explain, unravel, figure out.

declare VERB assert, state, announce, maintain, claim.

decompose VERB See **decay**.

decorate VERB **1** adorn, embellish, trim, ornament, paint, paper. **2** honour/honor (US), reward. *Decorated with medals.*

decrease VERB diminish, dwindle, decline, go down, lessen, reduce. An *opposite word* is increase.

decree NOUN law, order, edict, act, edict, command.

decrepit ADJECTIVE weak, aged, tottering, worn-out, dilapidated.

deduct VERB take away, subtract, withdraw, remove.

deed NOUN act, achievement, action, feat.

deep ADJECTIVE **1** profound. **2** mysterious, difficult, wise, learned, sagacious. *Deep thoughts.* An *opposite word* is shallow.

deface VERB disfigure, deform, damage, spoil, vandalize.

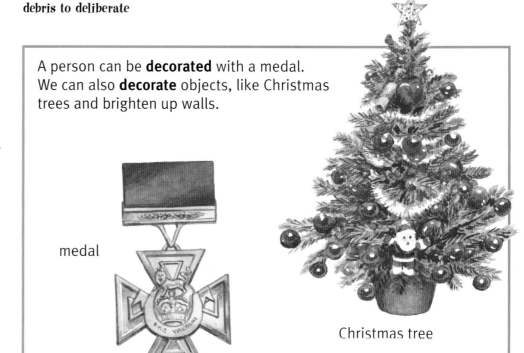

A person can be **decorated** with a medal. We can also **decorate** objects, like Christmas trees and brighten up walls.

medal

Christmas tree

defeat VERB conquer, overcome, beat, vanquish, get the better of, thwart.

defect NOUN flaw, blemish, imperfection, fault, failing, weakness.

defect VERB desert, abandon, rat on.

defective ADJECTIVE faulty, imperfect, deficient, not working. An *opposite word* is perfect.

defence/defense (US) NOUN **1** guard, protection, fortification, barricade, bulwark. An *opposite word* is attack. **2** justification, explanation.

defend VERB guard, protect, shield, resist, stand up for. An *opposite word* is attack.

defer VERB delay, put off, postpone, procrastinate.

deficient ADJECTIVE lacking, wanting, incomplete, inadequate. An *opposite word* is superfluous.

home decorating (decoration)

define VERB explain, describe, clarify, specify.

definite ADJECTIVE **1** certain, positive, decided, fixed. **2** clear, obvious, precise, exact. An *opposite word* is vague.

definition NOUN **1** explanation description, meaning. **2** clarity, distinctness, sharp focus.

deformed ADJECTIVE misshaped, disfigured, mutilated, distorted, contorted, warped.

defraud VERB swindle, cheat, trick, dupe, cheat, con.

defy VERB disregard, flout, spurn, ignore, scorn, challenge. An *opposite word* is obey.

dejected ADJECTIVE depressed, downcast, despondent, dispirited, gloomy, glum, blue.

delay VERB **1** dawdle, hang about/hang around (US), linger, loiter. **2** put off, postpone, defer. 3 hinder, obstruct, hold up. *Fog delayed the train.* An *opposite word* is **1** hurry.

delete VERB rub out, erase, cancel.

deliberate ADJECTIVE **1** careful, cautious. **2** planned, intentional.

delicate ADJECTIVE **1** frail, dainty, fragile. An *opposite word* is rough. **2** weak, unhealthy, ailing. *Delicate health.* An *opposite word* is strong.

delicious ADJECTIVE tasty, palatable, scrumptious, appetizing, delightful, enjoyable.

delighted ADJECTIVE pleased, happy, charmed.

delightful ADJECTIVE enjoyable, charming, enchanting, pleasant, agreeable. An *opposite word* is horrid.

deliver VERB **1** convey, carry, hand over, transfer, yield, grant, surrender. **2** free, release.

deluge NOUN flood, inundation, downpour, overflow. An *opposite word* is drought.

demand VERB **1** request, ask, require, beg, want. **2** require, involve. *Demanding a lot of hard work.*

demented ADJECTIVE *See* **crazy.**

demolish VERB destroy, raze, wreak, smash, pull down, knock down, dismantle.

demon NOUN devil, fiend, evil-spirit, monster, rogue.

demonstrate VERB **1** show, prove, establish, exhibit. **2** protest, march.

den NOUN Places where wild animals live: a rabbit's burrow, a lion's den, a squirrel's drey, a fox's earth, a hare's form, a wolf's lair, an otter's lodge, a bird's nest, a badger's sett.

denounce VERB condemn, blame, accuse, defame, brand, attack. An *opposite word* is commend.

dense ADJECTIVE **1** thick, compact, compressed. **2** stupid, dull. *He appeared to be very dense.*

deny VERB refute, contradict, reject, not agree, gainsay. *Deny the truth.*

depart VERB leave, go away, set out, quit, vanish. An *opposite word* is arrive.

department NOUN section, part, branch, division.

depend on VERB **1** rely on, count on, trust. **2** revolves round, turns on, hinges on. *It depends on the weather.*

depict VERB portray, sketch, paint, draw, outline, describe. *The poem depicts a tree.*

deplorable ADJECTIVE **1** sad, regrettable, distressing. **2** scandalous, disgraceful, shocking.

deplore VERB condemn, denounce, regret.

deposit VERB **1** put, place, lay down. **2** save, bank, entrust.

depressed ADJECTIVE miserable, unhappy, dejected, gloomy, upset. *See also* **sad.**

depression NOUN **1** slump, stagnation, decline. **2** dip, hollow, dent. **3** gloominess, dumps, unhappiness. *Opposite words* are **1** boom. **2** concavity. **3** cheerfulness.

deprive VERB deny, refuse, take away, rob, strip, divest. An *opposite word* is provide.

deride VERB laugh at, jeer, mock, scoff, knock. An *opposite word* is praise.

derive VERB **1** get, obtain, gain. **2** spring from, arise, originate, stem from.

descent NOUN **1** fall, drop, plunge. **2** slope, decline. *Opposite words* are ascent, rise.

Here are some different methods of **descent.**

parachutist

abseiler

deep sea diver

descendant NOUN offspring, family, issue, progeny. *Opposite words* are forebears, ancestors.

describe VERB define, explain, tell, narrate, relate, portray, characterize, detail, depict, specify.

descriptive ADJECTIVE graphic, colourful/colorful (US), illustrative.

desert NOUN wasteland, wilderness, solitude.

desert VERB abandon, leave, quit, forsake, renounce, defect.

deserted ADJECTIVE barren, desolate, wild, forsaken, empty. *A deserted village.*

deserve VERB merit, be worthy of, justify, earn, be entitled to, warrant.

design NOUN **1** plan, drawing, draught, sketch, pattern, outline, scheme. **2** aim, goal, purpose.

desire VERB want, fancy, wish for, long for, crave, yearn after, ask for.

despair NOUN despondency, misery, hopelessness, desperation, distress. An *opposite word* is hope.

desperate ADJECTIVE **1** hopeless, despondent, despairing, serious. *A desperate situation.* **2** reckless, rash, daring, foolhardy. *A desperate action.*

despise VERB look down on, dislike, disdain, spurn, scorn, detest, abhor.

despite PREPOSITION notwithstanding, in spite of, regardless of.

dessert NOUN sweet, pudding (UK). Some different kinds of dessert and pudding: apple dumpling, cake, cassata, crème brûlée, crepe suzette, gateau, pavlova, pie, profiteroles, sorbet/sherbet (US), strudel, sundae, zabaglione. *What is for dessert?*

Here are some images that you might see in the **desert.**

bedouin people

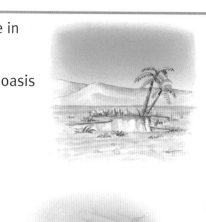

oasis

snake

"Dessert" sounds like "desert" but actually means a pudding or sweet!

destitute ADJECTIVE needy, penniless, poverty-stricken, down and out, bankrupt. An *opposite word* is wealthy.

destroy VERB **1** demolish, break, knock down, wreck, raze, pull down, smash, ruin, devour. **2** kill off, wipe out, exterminate, eliminate, eradicate. *A powder for destroying fleas. Opposite words* are build, create.

detach VERB separate, undo, unfasten, disconnect, divide, remove. An *opposite word* is attach.

detail NOUN component, portion, part, item, feature.

detailed ADJECTIVE thorough, exhaustive, comprehensive, exact. *A detailed account of the accident.*

detain VERB keep, delay, stop, retain, hold back, check.

detect VERB **1** discover, expose, reveal. **2** notice, observe, spy.

deteriorate VERB decline, worsen, go downhill, weaken, degenerate. An *opposite word* is improve.

detest VERB See **hate.**

devastate VERB wreck, ravage, lay waste, ransack. *See also* **destroy.**

develop VERB improve, progress, grow, expand, get better, evolve, flourish.

device NOUN tool, implement, gadget, instrument, apparatus, contrivance, contraption.

devise VERB scheme, contrive, invent, plot. *Devising a plan for winning the lottery.*

devoted ADJECTIVE loyal, trusted, loving, dedicated, faithful, true.

devour VERB destroy, ravage. *See also* **eat.**

diagram NOUN plan, drawing, sketch, graph, chart.

dictate VERB speak, utter, say, read out, command, instruct, order, decree.

die VERB expire, pass away, perish, decease. An *opposite word* is live. A word that sounds similar is dye.

different ADJECTIVE dissimilar, unlike, opposite, contrasting, clashing. **2** varied, various, mixed, assorted. *Different kinds of nut.* **3** distinct, separate, original, unusual.

difficult ADJECTIVE hard, complex, complicated, intricate, tricky, tough, laborious, demanding. *Opposite words are easy, simple.*

difficulty NOUN problem, snag, trouble, predicament, plight, dilemma.

diffident ADJECTIVE *See* **bashful**.

dig VERB **1** tunnel, burrow, excavate, delve. **2** investigate.

dilapidated ADJECTIVE broken-down, ruined, ramshackle, battered, crumbling, uncared for.

dilemma NOUN quandary, predicament, problem, plight, difficulty.

dilute VERB water down, make weaker, thin, lessen.

dim VERB dark, shadowy, obscure, blurred, misty, cloudy, murky, unfocused, faint, vague. *An opposite word is clear.*

diminish VERB reduce, lessen, decrease, become smaller, shrink. *An opposite word is increase.*

din NOUN noise, uproar, racket, clatter. *See also* **sound**.

dine VERB *See* **eat**.

dingy ADJECTIVE drab, dull, dreary, dirty, grimy, shabby. *An opposite word is bright.*

dinosaur NOUN Some different kinds of dinosaur: Apatsaurus, Ankylosaurus, Brachiosaurus, Camptosaurus, Diplodocus, Hadrosaurus, Stegosaurus, Tyrannosaurus.

direct ADJECTIVE straightforward, frank, candid, outspoken.

direct VERB **1** show, point, guide, conduct. **2** manage, control. **3** tell, command, order.

direction NOUN **1** course, road, way, bearing. **2** control, management, guidance.

directly ADVERB straightaway, immediately, soon, presently.

dirt NOUN filth, muck, grime, mud, mire.

dirty ADJECTIVE filthy, grubby, grimy, mucky, foul, unclean, polluted, smutty. *An opposite word is clean.*

disabled ADJECTIVE handicapped, incapacitated, disadvantaged, maimed, crippled, lame, impaired, immobilized. *The opposite word is able-bodied.*

disagree VERB quarrel, differ, oppose, argue, dispute, squabble.

disagreeable ADJECTIVE **1** crabby, surly, bad-tempered. *A disagreeable woman.* **2** nasty, offensive, repulsive. *A disagreeable smell.* *An opposite word is pleasant.*

disappear VERB vanish, fade away, depart, leave, recede. *An opposite word is appear.*

disappoint VERB let down, displease, fail, frustrate, deceive, betray. *Sorry to disappoint you. An opposite word is please.*

dinosaur eggs

disaster NOUN catastrophe, calamity, misfortune, accident, blow, fiasco.

discard VERB throw away, get rid of, scrap, reject, dump, shed. *Discard the outer wrapping. An opposite word is keep.*

disclose VERB uncover, reveal, expose, show, divulge, tell, betray. *They refused to disclose their location.*

discontinue VERB stop, cease, interrupt, abandon. *An opposite word is continue.*

discord NOUN disagreement, strife, wrangling, contention.

discount NOUN reduction, cut, deduction, rebate.

Here are some different kinds of **dinosaur.**

troodon

hypachrosaurus

yangchuanosaurus

ouranosaurus

discover VERB **1** find, come across, come upon, uncover. **2** learn, detect, track down.

discrimination NOUN **1** judgement, assessment, discernment, insight, perception. **2** prejudice, bias, bigotry. *Racial discrimination.*

discuss VERB talk about, consider, argue about, debate.

disease NOUN illness, disorder, ailment, infection, malady, sickness, complaint. *She is suffering from a rare disease.*

disguise VERB camouflage, hide, mask, pretend to be, dress up.

disgusting ADJECTIVE offensive, revolting, repellent, loathsome, distasteful. An *opposite word* is pleasant.

dislike VERB loathe, hate, detest, abhor, disapprove of. An *opposite word* is like.

dismal ADJECTIVE gloomy, dreary, drab, depressing, cheerless. An *opposite word* is cheeful.

dismay NOUN fright, fear, alarm, concern, distress.

dismiss VERB sack (UK), fire, send away, discharge, release. An *opposite word* is retain.

disobey VERB rebel, defy, ignore, disregard. An *opposite word* is obey.

disorder NOUN upheaval, mess, muddle, confusion, untidiness. *See also* **disease**.

dispense VERB distribute, hand out, share out, supply, administer.

display VERB show, exhibit, flaunt, parade.

dispute NOUN disagreement, argument, discussion, debate, quarrel, squabble. An *opposite word* is agreement. *There was some dispute over the money.*

disrupt VERB disturb, upset, put into disorder.

dissolve VERB melt, thaw, evaporate, disintegrate, break up, fade away.

distant ADJECTIVE far away, remote. *The distant sound of traffic.*

distinct ADJECTIVE **1** clear, lucid, obvious, plain. *A distinct smell of rubber.* **2** separate, contrasting, different, detached, independent. *Two distinct groups.*

distress VERB upset, trouble, bother, worry, harass, frighten. *The news distressed them.*

distribute VERB allot, share out, hand out, dispense, circulate. An *opposite word* is collect.

disturb VERB upset, worry, trouble, bother, annoy, interrupt, pester, disorder, frighten, move.

dither VERB hesitate, waver, oscillate.

dive VERB plunge, leap, nose-dive, jump, drop.

divert VERB **1** amuse, entertain, please. **2** distract, deflect, switch, reroute.

divide VERB **1** distribute, allot, share, dispense, deal out. **2** split, separate, cleave, fork, branch.

divulge VERB disclose, reveal, expose, show, release, uncover, betray.

do VERB **1** perform, accomplish, carry out, complete, end, finish. *She is doing her homework.* **2** make, deal with, prepare, producing, creating. **3** be enough, suffice. *Will this do? Opposite words* are neglect, undo.

dodge VERB avoid, evade, elude, duck, side-step.

dog NOUN hound, cur, pup, whelp, mongrel, bitch. Some different breeds of dog: beagle, boxer, bull-terrier, bulldog, chow, cocker-spaniel, collie, corgie, dachshund, foxhound, German shepherd, greyhound, Jack Russell, labrador, pekingese, poodle, retriever, setter, springer spaniel, St Bernard, Yorkshire terrier, whippet.

donate VERB give, present, contribute, subscribe to.

doubtful ADJECTIVE uncertain, undecided, dubious, unsure. An *opposite word* is certain.

Here are some different breeds of **dog.**

bulldog

alsation

golden retriever

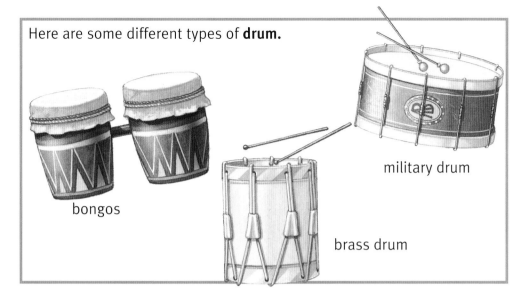

Here are some different types of **drum.**

bongos

military drum

brass drum

dowdy ADJECTIVE drab, dreary, dull, frumpish, unfashionable. *Opposite words* are smart (UK) or fashionable.

downfall NOUN defeat, collapse, destruction.

down-hearted ADJECTIVE downcast, gloomy, miserable, unhappy, sad, depressed, dejected, despondent. An *opposite word* is cheerful.

drag VERB tow, pull, draw, tug, heave. An *opposite word* is push.

dramatic ADJECTIVE stirring, thrilling, exciting, flamboyant, important.

drastic ADJECTIVE violent, extreme, powerful, harsh, severe, far-reaching.

draw VERB **1** sketch, trace, depict. **2** haul, tug, tow, pull. **3** attract, entice, persuade. **4** equal, be even. *The teams drew 1-1.*

dreadful ADJECTIVE terrible, awful, frightening, shocking, bad, tragic. *A dreadful accident.*

dreary ADJECTIVE See **dowdy.**

drench VERB soak, wet, immerse, steep, douse (or dowse).

drift VERB float, move off, wander, stray.

drill VERB **1** teach, train, coach, discipline. **2** pierce, bore, perforate, penetrate.

drink NOUN imbibe, sip, swig, lap, swallow, gulp, quaff. Some different kinds of drink: chocolate, coffee, cola, juice, lemonade, milk, tea, water.

drip VERB dribble, trickle, drop, ooze, flow, slobber, drool.

drive VERB **1** direct, control, steer, operate, propel. **2** force, send, push, hurl, impel.

drizzle VERB See **rain.**

droll ADJECTIVE See **funny.**

droop VERB sag, flop, dangle, hang, wilt, wither. An *opposite word* is flourish.

drop VERB **1** lower, let fall, dump, shed, discard. **2** fall, descend, sink, plunge, cascade. **3** decrease, diminish, go down. *Dropping sales.* **4** abandon, desert, leave.

drum kit

drowsy ADJECTIVE sleepy, tired, heavy, soporific. An *opposite word* is alert.

drum VERB beat, tap, rap, bang. Some different kinds of drum: bass, bongo, snare, timpani (kettledrums).

dry ADJECTIVE **1** arid, parched, waterless, thirsty. **2** boring, tedious.

duck NOUN drake (male), duckling (baby).

dull ADJECTIVE **1** boring, tedious, uninteresting, drab. **2** muffled. *A dull sound.* **3** gloomy, dingy, grey. *Dull weather.* **4** slow, stupid. *Opposite words* are **1** exciting, **3, 4** bright.

dumb ADJECTIVE **1** silent, soundless, speechless, mute. **2** foolish.

duplicate NOUN copy, double, replica, reproduction, facsimile, photocopy.

durable ADJECTIVE lasting, endurable, reliable, strong, sturdy. *Opposite words* are weak, fragile.

dusk NOUN twilight, sunset, nightfall, evening, gloaming, eventide.

dusty ADJECTIVE powdery. *See also* **dirty.**

duty NOUN **1** obligation, responsibility, task, job, work. **2** tax. *Duty free.*

dwell VERB See **live.**

dwindle VERB diminish, decrease, get smaller, shrink.

dye VERB colour/color (US), stain, tint, hue, pigment. A word with a similar sound is die.

dynamic ADJECTIVE energetic, active.

eager ADJECTIVE keen, enthusiastic, zealous, impatient, ardent. An *opposite word* is reluctant.

early ADJECTIVE and ADVERB **1** soon, recent, forward, advanced, premature. **2** primeval. *Early humans.*

earn VERB receive, get, gain, deserve, merit, acquire.

earnest ADJECTIVE **1** serious, solemn. *Earnest looks.* **2** determined, conscientious, sincere.

easy ADJECTIVE **1** simple, uncomplicated, smooth, trouble-free, obvious, effortless, straightforward. **2** carefree, restful, relaxed, comfortable.

eat VERB **1** consume, swallow, feed. **2** erode, wear away, corrode. Some of the different ways we can eat: chew, chomp, devour, gobble, gulp, guzzle, masticate, munch, nibble, scoff, tuck in, wolf down.

ebb VERB recede, fall back, wane, decline, subside. An *opposite word* is flow.

eccentric ADJECTIVE strange, odd, peculiar, weird, erratic, abnormal, quirkish, wayward. *Opposite words* are ordinary, normal.

edge NOUN border, margin, boundary, rim, side, periphery.

edible ADJECTIVE eatable, wholesome, good, palatable.

edifice NOUN *See* **building**.

educate VERB teach, train, instruct, tutor, coach, bring up. *Some examples of different places* where people are educated: academy, business school, college, kindergarten, playgroup, public school, school, Sunday school, technical college, university.

effective ADJECTIVE **1** useful, efficient, productive. **2** functioning, operative.

efficient ADJECTIVE able, effective, capable, competent, working well, skilful/skillful (US). An *opposite word* is inefficient.

effort NOUN **1** toil, trouble, work, exertion. **2** endeavour/endeavor (US), attempt. *Try to make an effort.*

elaborate NOUN complex, intricate, complicated, ornate, detailed, carefully planned. An *opposite word* is simple.

elect VERB choose, pick, opt for, vote for.

elegant ADJECTIVE smart, chic, elegant, stylish, graceful, refined. An *opposite word* is coarse.

eliminate VERB abolish, do away with, remove, delete, get rid of, exclude.

eloquent ADJECTIVE articulate, expressive, flowing.

embarrassed ADJECTIVE ashamed, upset, shy, awkward, distressed.

embrace VERB **1** hug, hold, caress, fondle, clasp. **2** include, contain.

emerge VERB come out, appear, surface. An *opposite word* is disappear.

emergency NOUN crisis, difficulty, extremity, plight, dilemma, predicament.

eminent ADJECTIVE famous, distinguished, celebrated, prominent, outstanding, well-known.

emotion NOUN feeling, passion, sentiment, excitement, agitation.

emphasize VERB stress, accentuate, accent, underline, highlight.

employ VERB **1** engage, hire, recruit. **2** use, adopt, apply.

Here are some **edible** objects.

bread and cheese

chocolate cake

banana

fruit

employee NOUN worker, member of staff, servant, hand.

employment NOUN work, occupation, job, trade, profession, vocation, calling.

empty ADJECTIVE unoccupied, unfilled, deserted, vacant, void, clear, blank, hollow. *Opposite words are occupied, full.*

enchant VERB entrance, bewitch, enthral, fascinate, charm, delight. An *opposite word* is bore.

encourage VERB exhort, urge on, support, inspire, aid, boost. An *opposite word* is discourage.

end NOUN **1** conclusion, ending, finish, termination. **2** purpose, aim, goal. **3** tip, point.

end VERB **1** finish, conclude, terminate, close, cease, stop, achieve. **2** abolish, destroy. An *opposite word* is begin.

endeavour/endeavor (US) VERB attempt, try, strive, aim, struggle, essay.

endless ADJECTIVE unending, ceaseless, continuous, perpetual, unlimited.

energetic ADJECTIVE active, lively, vigorous, enthusiastic, forceful. An *opposite word* is sluggish.

energy NOUN strength, power, force, might, drive, vitality, muscle.

engaging ADJECTIVE charming, attractive, delightful, agreeable. An *opposite word* is repulsive.

engine NOUN **1** machine, motor. **2** locomotive. Some different engines: diesel, fuel injection, internal combustion, ramjet, steam, turbine, turbojet, Wankel.

enjoy VERB like, love, delight in, appreciate. An *opposite word* is dislike.

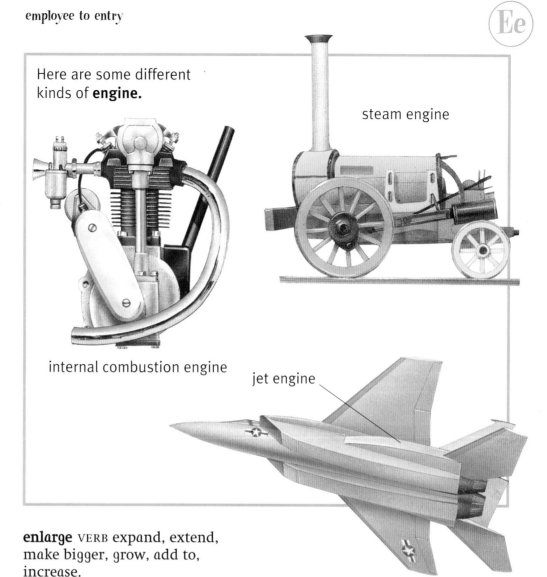

Here are some different kinds of **engine.**

steam engine

internal combustion engine

jet engine

enlarge VERB expand, extend, make bigger, grow, add to, increase.

enormous ADJECTIVE huge, vast, gigantic, massive, colossal, tremendous. *The blue whale was enormous.*

enough ADJECTIVE sufficient, adequate, plenty, abundant. *Is there enough food?*

enquire VERB *See* **ask**.

enter VERB **1** go into, come into, board, invade, penetrate. **2** record, register, inscribe.

entertain VERB **1** amuse, divert, cheer. **2** receive guests. **3** consider. *Entertaining an idea.*

entertainers NOUN Some different types of entertainers: acrobat, clown, comedian, dancer, DJ, magician, musician, singer. *We hired a group of entertainers.*

entertaining ADJECTIVE interesting, amusing, fun. An *opposite word* is boring.

entertainment NOUN amusement, diversion, enjoyment, fun, distraction.

enthusiasm NOUN eagerness, fervour/fervor (US), zeal, passion.

entire ADJECTIVE complete, whole, intact. An *opposite word* is partial.

entrance NOUN doorway, gate, opening, way in, entry. *Opposite words* are exit, way out.

entrance VERB *Look at* **enchant**.

entry NOUN **1** *entry into the club* admittance. access. *Look also at* **entrance** (NOUN). **2** record, note. *The last entry in the book.*

Here are some different ways to **exercise.**

swimming

stretching

cycling

environment NOUN surroundings, neighbourhood/neighborhood (US), setting, habitat.

envy VERB covet, desire, crave, be jealous of.

episode NOUN **1** part, instalment/installment (US), chapter. **2** incident, occurrence, happening.

epoch NOUN period, age, era.

equal ADJECTIVE **1** alike, matching, the same, equivalent. *Equal lengths of wood.* **2** even, level, regular. **3** fit, up to, suitable, able. *Are you equal to the job?*

equipment NOUN gear, apparatus, outfit, tackle, tools.

eradicate VERB *See* **destroy.**

erase VERB rub out, delete, remove, blot out, eradicate.

erect ADJECTIVE upright. rigid, firm, vertical.

erect VERB build, construct, put up, set up, raise. An *opposite word* is demolish.

errand NOUN job, task, chore, mission, assignment.

error NOUN mistake, fault, slip, blunder, fallacy.

escape VERB **1** flee, get away, break free, abscond. **2** avoid, dodge, elude.

essential ADJECTIVE necessary, vital, important, needed, crucial. An *opposite word* is superfluous.

establish VERB set up, organize, found, place, institute, fix, secure. *Opposite words* are abolish, uproot.

estate NOUN property, land, possessions, inheritance.

esteem VERB admire, value, prize.

estimate VERB assess, work out, value, appraise, reckon, calculate.

eternal ADJECTIVE endless, everlasting, incessant, ceaseless, continuous, unending, infinite.

evacuate VERB leave, abandon, depart, quit, forsake, empty. *Opposite words* are fill, occupy.

evade VERB avoid, escape, elude, dodge. An *opposite word* is face.

evaporate VERB vanish, disappear, melt away, dissolve, vaporize. An *opposite word* is appear.

even ADJECTIVE **1** calm, placid, steady, equal. *Even tempered.* **2** flat, smooth, level. *An even surface.*

even ADVERB still, yet.

event NOUN happening, incident, occurrence, occasion.

evidence NOUN facts, proof, testimony, information, sign.

evil ADJECTIVE wicked, wrong, harmful, bad, sinful. An *opposite word* is good.

exact ADJECTIVE **1** accurate, correct, faultless. **2** careful, painstaking. An *opposite word* is faulty.

exaggerate VERB overemphasize, magnify, amplify, embroider. An *opposite word* is underestimate.

examination NOUN test, inspection, inquiry, investigation, search, survey, check-up.

examine VERB inspect, test, scrutinize, question, interrogate.

excavate VERB dig, delve, unearth, burrow, scoop up.

exceed VERB beat, surpass, outstrip.

excel VERB outdo, surpass, shine at, exceed.

excellent ADJECTIVE outstanding, first-class, superb, superlative, marvellous/marvelous (US). An *opposite word* is inferior.

exercis

exchange VERB trade, swap, replace, substitute.

excitement NOUN commotion, agitation, action, activity, unrest, suspense, ferment. An *opposite word* is calm.

exciting ADJECTIVE thrilling, inspiring, stimulating, rousing, exhilarating. An *opposite word* is dull.

exclaim VERB cry out, shout, proclaim, declare.

exclude VERB shut out, forbid, expel, evict, keep out.

excursion NOUN outing, trip, journey, tour, expedition.

excuse VERB 1 pardon, forgive, overlook. 2 let off, exempt, relieve, free.

execute VERB carry out, do, achieve, accomplish. 2 kill, put to death, hang, electrocute.

exercise VERB 1 use, employ, utilize. 2 train, practise/practice (US), work out.

exhausted ADJECTIVE 1 tired, dog-tired, worn-out, weary. 2 empty, used up, consumed.

exhibition NOUN show, display, exposition.

exist VERB live, be, continue, survive, be present.

expect VERB 1 forecast, foresee, await, hope, look out for, anticipate. 2 require, insist on, demand. *We expect your cooperation.*

expel VERB banish, exile, eject, exclude, throw out, deport, evict, bar.

expensive ADJECTIVE dear, costly, precious, high-priced. An *opposite word* is cheap.

experience NOUN undergo, encounter, endure, feel, suffer.

experienced ADJECTIVE skilled, practised/practiced (US), expert, trained, accomplished.

explain VERB make clear, show, describe, spell out, elucidate.

explore VERB search, investigate, look around, hunt, probe, pry.

explosion NOUN blast, bang, eruption, detonation.

expose VERB reveal, disclose, uncover, show, lay bare. 2 betray.

express VERB say, speak, utter, state, assert. 2 show, signify, stand for.

express ADJECTIVE fast, rapid, quick.

extend VERB stretch, expand, lengthen, reach, continue, prolong. An *opposite word* is contract.

exterior ADJECTIVE external, outside, outer. The *opposite word* is internal.

exterminate VERB destroy, get rid of, wipe out, kill, eliminate.

extinct ADJECTIVE dead, defunct, vanished, exterminated, ended. An *opposite word* is living.

extra ADJECTIVE 1 additional, more. 2 spare, surplus, excess.

extract VERB remove, pull out, draw out, select. *Extract a tooth.*

extraordinary ADJECTIVE outstanding, remarkable, amazing, unusual, strange, incredible. An *opposite word* is commonplace.

extravagant ADJECTIVE wasteful, reckless, expensive, flamboyant, lavish.

eye NOUN Parts of the eye: cornea, eyebrow, eyelid, eyelash, iris, lens, optic nerve, pupil, retina, sclera.

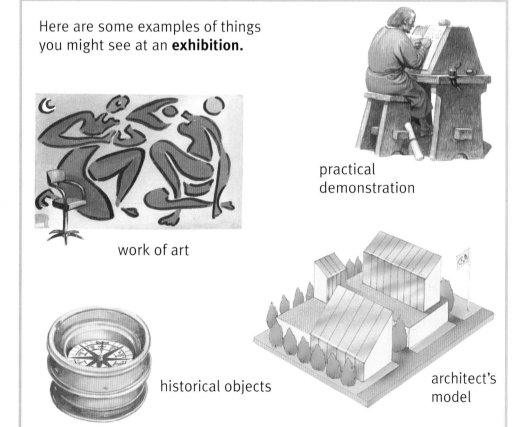

Here are some examples of things you might see at an **exhibition.**

work of art

practical demonstration

historical objects

architect's model

Ff

fable NOUN **1** story, tale, legend, parable. **2** lie, falsehood.

fabric NOUN textile, cloth, material, stuff.

face NOUN countenance, visage, aspect, look.

face VERB **1** meet, encounter. **2** be opposite, overlook.

fact NOUN information, datum, evidence, event, happening, truth, deed, reality. An *opposite word* is fiction.

factory NOUN works, plant, mill, floor.

fad NOUN craze, fashion, mania, trend.

fade VERB pale, bleach, diminish, dwindle, weaken, disappear, discolour/discolor (US).

fail VERB **1** neglect, omit, forget. *Failed to appear.* **2** be unsuccessful. **3** collapse, fall, go wrong, flop. *Failed the test.* An *opposite word* is succeed.

failing NOUN fault, weakness, flaw, defect, shortcoming.

faint ADJECTIVE **1** dim, weak, feeble, hazy, indistinct. An *opposite word* is clear. **2** giddy, dizzy, feeble.

fair ADJECTIVE **1** blond, light-coloured/colored (US), pale. **2** just, even-handed, right, unbiased, equal. **3** bright, sunny. *Fair weather.*

fair NOUN carnival, market, fete.

faithful ADJECTIVE reliable, loyal, trustworthy. *Opposite words* are faithless, false.

fake ADJECTIVE false, bogus, forged, spurious, mock.

fall VERB **1** drop, dip, plunge, sink, descend. **2** collapse, crash, topple, tumble. *The wall fell down.* **3** decrease, decline, diminish. *The temperature is falling.* An *opposite word* is rise.

false ADJECTIVE **1** inaccurate, untrue, wrong, incorrect. **2** dishonest, disloyal, faithless. **3** *See also* **fake**.

fame NOUN renown, distinction, stardom, celebrity, glory, repute. An *opposite word* is oblivion.

familiar ADJECTIVE **1** common, well-known, normal, usual. *A familiar face.* **2** intimate, friendly, easy.

family NOUN ancestors, tribe, race, relations.

famine NOUN shortage, scarcity, hunger, want, starvation. An *opposite word* is plenty.

famous ADJECTIVE renowned, well-known, celebrated. An *opposite word* is unknown.

fan NOUN admirer, follower, enthusiast, supporter.

fanatical ADJECTIVE enthusiastic, extreme, wild, frenzied.

fancy VERB **1** like, wish for, long for, yearn for, be attracted to. *Something you fancy.* **2** imagine, dream, suppose, think.

fantastic ADJECTIVE amazing, wonderful, incredible, tremendous, strange, good. An *opposite word* is ordinary.

far ADJECTIVE distant, remote, out of the way. An *opposite word* is near.

far ADVERB much, greatly, decidedly. *She's far better today.*

farm VERB cultivate, grow, till, husband. Some words associated with farms and farming: arable land, barn, combine harvester, cowshed, croft, crops, dairy farming, farmhouse, fish farming, harrow, harvest, irrigate, livestock, organic farming, pig farming, pigsty, plough/plow (US), reap, sow, stable, thresh, till.

There are many different types of **farm**.

dairy farm

arable farm

fascinating ADJECTIVE interesting, engrossing, absorbing, attractive.

fashion NOUN **1** style, vogue, craze, mode, trend. **2** way, method, manner.

fashion VERB make, mould/mold (US), create.

fast ADJECTIVE quick, speedy, swift, hurried, rapid, brisk. An *opposite word* is slow.

fast ADVERB **1** rapidly, speedily, like lightning. **2** tightly, firm, securely. *Hold fast to the rope.*

fasten VERB do up, attach, tie up, secure, bind. An *opposite word* is release.

fat ADJECTIVE plump, stocky, well-built, stout, chubby, overweight, corpulent, obese. *Opposite words* are thin, slender, skinny.

fatigue ADJECTIVE tiredness, exhaustion, weariness.

fault NOUN **1** mistake, error, blunder, flaw, weakness, defect, imperfection, failing. **2** blame, responsibility. *Whose fault is it?*

fault VERB criticize. *Find fault with.* An *opposite word* is perfection.

favourite/favorite (US) ADJECTIVE preferred, best-liked, chosen.

fear NOUN terror, dread, fright, alarm, panic, distress. *A fear of heights.* An *opposite word* is courage.

fearless ADJECTIVE brave, courageous, gallant. An *opposite word* is fearful.

feat NOUN brave action, deed, exploit, achievement, accomplishment. A word with a similar sound is feet.

feeble ADJECTIVE weak, frail, delicate, puny, powerless. An *opposite word* is strong.

A **festival** is a time for celebration.

Chinese dragon

carnival

Easter basket

Shinto festival

feed VERB nourish, foster, supply, provide, nurture, eat.

feel VERB **1** touch, handle, stroke, caress, grope. **2** experience, suffer from, notice, perceive, think, consider. *She feels the heat.*

feeling NOUN **1** sense, sensation, instinct. **2** emotion, sympathy, passion, pity, concern, warmth. **3** belief, opinion. *Strong feelings about cruelty.*

felon NOUN *See* **criminal**.

female ADJECTIVE feminine, womanly. The *opposite word* is male.

fence NOUN barrier, hedge, wall, railing, paling.

ferocious ADJECTIVE fierce, savage, vicious, cruel, barbaric, wild. An *opposite word* is harmless.

fertile ADJECTIVE productive, fruitful, plentiful, abundant, rich. An *opposite word* is barren.

festival NOUN feast, holiday, celebration, jubilee, anniversary.

fetch VERB carry, bring, get, collect, convey.

feud NOUN row, quarrel, dispute, disagreement, squabble, vendetta.

few ADJECTIVE not many, scarce, scanty, rare. An *opposite word* is many.

fiasco NOUN *See* **disaster**.

fib NOUN lie, falsehood, untruth. The *opposite word* is truth.

fiddle VERB **1** tinker, play about with, fidget. **2** swindle, cheat.

fidget VERB fret, fuss, be nervous, wriggle, fiddle.

field NOUN paddock, meadow, playing field, ground, plot.

fierce ADJECTIVE *See* **ferocious**.

fiery ADJECTIVE passionate, hot, excitable, fervent, ardent, violent, heated. An *opposite word* is cool.

fight VERB **1** combat, battle, strive, struggle, wage war, row, quarrel, brawl, squabble. **2** wrestle, box. **3** oppose, resist.

fighter NOUN **1** combatant, warrior. **2** boxer, wrestler.

figure NOUN **1** number, numeral, digit, cipher, symbol, outline.

fill VERB cram, load, stuff, pack, replenish. An *opposite word* is empty.

filter VERB sieve, sift, refine, strain, purify.

filthy ADJECTIVE See **dirty**.

final ADJECTIVE closing, last, latest, concluding. An *opposite word* is first.

find VERB discover, come upon, recover, locate, track down. An *opposite word* is lose. A word with a similar sound is fined.

fine ADJECTIVE **1** excellent, good, splendid, attractive, great. *A fine building.* **2** thin, slender, delicate, powdery, fragile. *Fine bones; fine sugar.* **3** bright, sunny, dry. *A fine day.* **4** all right, OK. *That's fine by me.*

finish VERB **1** complete, end, stop, accomplish. **2** use up, eat, consume. *Who finished all the chocolate?*

fire VERB **1** ignite, kindle, light. **2** let off, shoot, discharge, detonate. **3** dismiss.

firm ADJECTIVE steady, solid, secure, fixed, rigid.

firm NOUN company, business, concern.

first-rate ADJECTIVE supreme, excellent, matchless, superb, first class. An *opposite word* is inferior.

fish NOUN Some different types of fish: cod, Dover sole, eel, goldfish, haddock, hake, halibut, herring, mackerel, plaice, salmon, sardine, shark, sole, trout, tuna. Parts of a fish: dorsal fin, gill, lateral line, mandible, pectoral fin, tail fin.

fishy ADJECTIVE suspicious, dubious, doubtful.

fit ADJECTIVE **1** well, healthy, strong, robust. **2** apt, suitable, able, competent, qualified. *Opposite words* are **1** unhealthy, **2** unsuitable, incompetent.

fit VERB assemble, put together, adjust, adapt, alter.

fix NOUN dilemma, predicament, jam, hole, plight.

fix VERB **1** fasten, connect, attach, secure, stick, establish, settle. **2** repair, mend, adjust.

fizzy ADJECTIVE sparkling, bubbly, carbonated, gassy.

flabby ADJECTIVE soft, sagging, floppy, drooping, limp. An *opposite word* is firm.

flag NOUN ensign. Some different kinds of flag: banner, bunting, ensign, jack, pennant, standard, streamer.

flag VERB droop, tire, weaken.

flair NOUN talent, gift, knack, ability, aptitude.

flake NOUN slice, sliver, chip, shaving, scale.

flap VERB flutter, wave, shake, beat.

flash VERB **1** flare, flicker, gleam, sparkle. **2** speed, dash, fly. *Flashed past.*

flat ADJECTIVE **1** level, plain, even, smooth, horizontal. **2** dull, lifeless, insipid, tame, boring. *Opposite words* are **1** hilly **2** exciting.

flatter VERB praise, compliment, humour/humor (US), butter up.

flavour/flavor (US) NOUN taste, savour/savor (US), tang, relish, seasoning.

flaw NOUN See **fault**.

flee VERB run away, escape, bolt, vanish, scarper, make off. An *opposite word* is stay.

fleeting ADJECTIVE passing, brief, transient, momentary. An *opposite word* is lasting.

flexible ADJECTIVE bendy, pliable, bendable, stretchy, supple, elastic, adjustable. An *opposite word* is rigid.

flicker VERB twinkle, flash, flutter, waver, sparkle. *The stars flickered in the summer sky.*

flimsy ADJECTIVE fragile, frail, meagre/meager (US), insubstantial, thin, weak. *It was a flimsy excuse.* An *opposite word* is sturdy.

fling VERB See **throw**.

flip VERB toss, flick, spin, pitch.

flippant ADJECTIVE frivolous, light-hearted, facetious, impertinent, pert. An *opposite word* is serious.

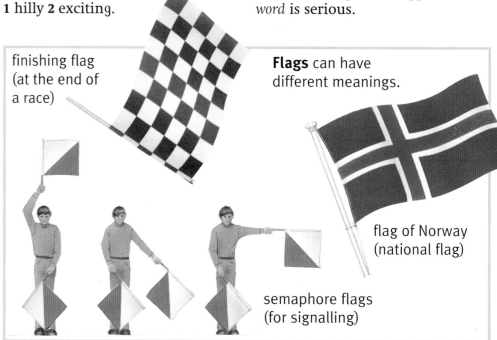

finishing flag (at the end of a race)

Flags can have different meanings.

flag of Norway (national flag)

semaphore flags (for signalling)

float VERB waft, drift, hover, glide
An *opposite word* is sink.

flock NOUN gathering, collection, set. *See also* **group**.

flourish VERB thrive, do well, succeed, prosper, blossom. An *opposite word* is fail.

flow VERB run, pour, stream, glide, lap, trickle, dribble, stream.

flower NOUN bloom, blossom. A word that sounds similar is flour. Parts of a flower: anther, calyx, ovary, petal, stalk, stamen, stigma, style. Types of arrangement: bouquet of flowers, corsage, posy, wreath.

fluent ADJECTIVE articulate, eloquent, glib, facile, flowing.

fluid ADJECTIVE watery, liquid, runny, molten, flowing.

flutter VERB wave, beat, flap, flit, shake.

fly VERB glide, soar, rise up, ascend, hover, sail, swoop.

foam NOUN froth, lather, surf, suds.

fog NOUN mist, cloud, smog, haze.

fold VERB crease, bend, double.

follow VERB **1** pursue, come after, trail, track, go along. **2** come next, succeed, supersede. *May follows April.* **3** understand, comprehend. An *opposite word* is **1** precede.

food NOUN nourishment, grub, nutriment, rations, fare, nosh, provisions, refreshments.

foolhardy ADJECTIVE reckless, rash, bold, irresponsible. *What a foolhardy thing to do!* An *opposite word* is cautious.

foolish ADJECTIVE idiotic, stupid, daft, silly, unwise, senseless, inept, crazy. An *opposite word* is wise.

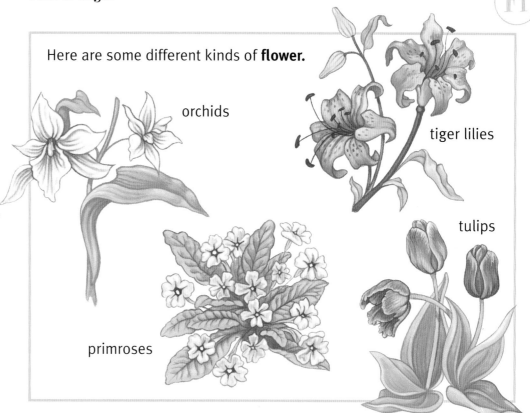

Here are some different kinds of **flower.**

orchids

tiger lilies

tulips

primroses

forbid VERB ban, prohibit, stop, disallow, veto. An *opposite word* is allow.

forbidding ADJECTIVE threatening, menacing, hostile, grim, stern, awesome. *Opposite words* are attractive, inviting.

force VERB make, compel, order, coerce, push, drive, urge.

forecast VERB predict, foresee, foretell, prophesy, expect.

foreign ADJECTIVE strange, alien, outlandish, imported, overseas.

forgery NOUN fake, counterfeit, dud, copy, imitation.

forget VERB overlook, omit, neglect, leave behind. An *opposite word* is remember.

forgetful ADJECTIVE absent-minded, neglectful, inattentive, thoughtless. *Opposite words* are attentive, heedful.

forgive VERB pardon, excuse, let off, absolve. *Can you forgive me?* An *opposite word* is blame.

form NOUN **1** shape, appearance, outline, pattern. **2** method, system, practice, variety, kind of. *A different form of voting.*

forsake VERB abandon, desert, reject, jilt.

forthright ADJECTIVE frank, candid, straightforward, direct.

fortify VERB strengthen, reinforce, confirm, protect.

fortunate ADJECTIVE lucky, happy, successful, favourable/favorable (US).

found VERB set up, start, originate, establish, create. *Founded in 1888.*

fountain NOUN well head, spring, source, spray, spout, jet.

fraction NOUN part, division, piece, fragment.

fracture VERB
See **break**.

fragile ADJECTIVE frail, weak, flimsy, delicate, brittle. *Opposite words* are sturdy, tough.

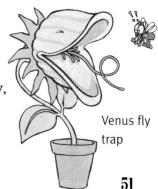

Venus fly trap

fragment NOUN piece, bit, chip, morsel, scrap, sliver, segment.

fragrance NOUN scent, smell, aroma, odour/odor (US).

frail ADJECTIVE *See* **fragile**.

frank ADJECTIVE candid, open, honest, direct, forthright. *Opposite words are devious, evasive.*

fraud NOUN deception, deceit, dishonesty, forgery, swindle.

freak ADJECTIVE strange, abnormal, unusual. *A freak storm.*

free ADJECTIVE **1** unoccupied, vacant, available. *Is this chair free?* **2** liberated, at large, independent. *A free country.* **3** no charge, gratis.

free VERB release, liberate, let loose, dismiss, acquit. An *opposite word* is jail.

freeze VERB ice up, refrigerate, chill, congeal. An *opposite word* is thaw.

frequent ADJECTIVE **1** many, numerous, repeated, regular. **2** common, usual, everyday. *Opposite words are infrequent, rare. Frequent trains.*

fresh ADJECTIVE **1** new, unused, different. **2** lively, energetic, refreshed. *Opposite words are old, stale, tired.*

friction NOUN **1** chaffing, abrasion, grating, rubbing. **2** hostility, discord, ill-feeling, quarrelling.

friend NOUN mate, pal, chum, partner, companion, acquaintance, ally, colleague. *An opposite word is enemy.*

frighten VERB alarm, startle, daunt, terrify, scare, shock.

frill NOUN edging, border, ruffle.

fringe NOUN edging, trimming, edge, border.

frivolous ADJECTIVE trivial. *See also* **flippant**.

frontier NOUN border, boundary, margin, limit.

froth NOUN foam, lather, bubbles, suds.

frugal ADJECTIVE economical, sparing, thrifty, stingy, meagre/meager (US). *Opposite words are wasteful, extravagant, generous.*

fruit NOUN crop, harvest, produce. *Citrus fruit, soft fruit, tropical fruit.*

fruitful ADJECTIVE productive, fertile, abundant, plentiful, successful. *An opposite word is barren.*

frustrate VERB thwart, hinder, foil, defeat, baffle, block, disappoint.

fry VERB *See* **cook**.

fuel NOUN Some different kinds of fuel: wood, coal, coke, diesel, electricity, gas, hydroelectric power, nuclear power, oil, peat, petrol/gasoline (US), paraffin/kerosene (US).

fugitive NOUN refugee, deserter, runaway.

fulfil/fulfill (US) VERB achieve, accomplish, complete, conclude.

full ADJECTIVE packed, filled, loaded, bulging, complete.

fun NOUN enjoyment, amusement, pleasure, sport, recreation, jollity.

function NOUN **1** purpose, use, part, role. **2** meeting, gathering, party. *A business function.*

function VERB operate, go, run, drive. *How do computers function?*

fundamental ADJECTIVE basic, essential, rudimentary, important, crucial. *Opposite words are minor, unimportant.*

funeral NOUN burial, cremation, interment.

funny ADJECTIVE **1** amusing, comic, humorous, ridiculous, witty, laughable, droll. **2** strange, weird, peculiar, odd, curious.

furious ADJECTIVE *See* **angry**.

furtive ADJECTIVE stealthy, sly, secretive, clandestine, sneaky.

fury NOUN rage, ferocity, anger, frenzy, passion.

fuse NOUN blend, join, weld.

futile ADJECTIVE useless, pointless, fruitless, in vain.

fuzzy ADJECTIVE misty, blurred, hazy, unclear.

Here are some different kinds of **fruit.**

cherries

lemon and lime

grapes

strawberries

bananas

pirate (galleon)

Gg

gabble VERB chatter, prattle, babble.

gadget NOUN device, instrument, tool, contraption.

gag NOUN joke, jest.

gag VERB choke, silence, throttle, stifle.

gain VERB earn, get, acquire receive, obtain, win. An *opposite word* is lose.

gale NOUN *See* **storm**.

galleon NOUN *See* **boat**, **ship**.

gallery NOUN museum, arcade, corridor, passage.

gallop VERB run, speed, race.

gamble VERB bet, risk, wager, chance, hazard.

game ADJECTIVE courageous, brave, gallant, valiant.

game NOUN **1** pastime, sport, amusement, play, entertainment, recreation, contest. Some different kinds of game: badminton, baseball, basketball, cards, chess, cricket, football, golf, hockey, ice hockey, pool, table tennis. **2** prey, quarry.

gang NOUN band, group, mob, clique.

gaol (UK) NOUN jail, prison, lock-up, clink, nick, penitentiary.

gap NOUN hole, space, opening, chink, break, crevice.

garbage NOUN *See* **rubbish**.

garden NOUN plot, allotment, orchard. Some things used in gardening: fork, hoe, rake, secateurs, shears, shovel, spade, trowel, watering-can, wheelbarrow.

garish ADJECTIVE gaudy, loud, vulgar, flashy, showy. An *opposite word* is tasteful.

garment NOUN dress, attire. *See also* **clothes**.

garnish VERB decorate, embellish adorn.

gas NOUN vapour/vapor (US), fumes, smoke. Some different kinds of gas: ammonia, carbon dioxide, carbon monoxide, ether, helium, hydrogen, nitrous oxide (laughing gas), methane, neon, oxygen, ozone.

gash NOUN slash, cut, slit, wound.

gasp VERB pant, puff, choke.

gate NOUN portal, doorway, barrier, entrance, way in, way out.

gather VERB **1** collect, accumulate, put together. *Gather facts.* **2** pick, pluck. *Gather apples.* **3** come together, congregate, assemble. *Gather round the fire.* **4** understand, deduce, infer. *We gather you'll be away.*

gathering NOUN meeting, assembly, collection.

gaudy ADJECTIVE cheap, tawdry. *See also* **garish**.

gaunt ADJECTIVE thin, haggard, skinny, emaciated. An *opposite word* is robust.

gay ADJECTIVE bright, attractive, vivid, jolly. *Gay designs.*

gaze VERB stare, contemplate, look steadily at.

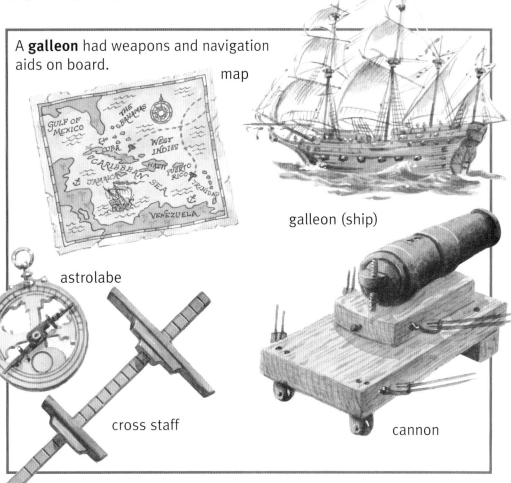
A **galleon** had weapons and navigation aids on board.
map
galleon (ship)
astrolabe
cross staff
cannon

gem NOUN jewel, precious stone, treasure.

general ADJECTIVE **1** usual, widespread, common. *What's the general feeling about it?* **2** vague, inaccurate, broad.

generous ADJECTIVE **1** kind, giving, unselfish, open-handed, charitable. *Opposite words are stingy or mean (UK).* **2** big, large, abundant, copious.

genius NOUN brilliance, cleverness, talent, flair, ability.

gentle ADJECTIVE **1** kind, tender, mild, good-hearted. **2** smooth, moderate, slight. *Some gentle exercise.* **3** pleasant, soft, peaceful, restful. *An opposite word is harsh.*

genuine ADJECTIVE real, authentic, natural. *An opposite word is false.*

gesture NOUN signal, motion, nod, movement, indication.

get VERB **1** obtain, gain, win, earn, secure. **2** become, turn, grow. **3** fetch, bring, collect. **4** arrive, come, reach. *When did you get here?* **5** understand. *Did you get the joke?* **6** receive. *We got a big welcome.*

ghastly ADJECTIVE horrible, awful, hideous, dreadful.

ghostly ADJECTIVE spooky, eerie, shadowy, haunted, weird.

giant ADJECTIVE huge, enormous, gigantic, colossal, immense, big. *An opposite word is tiny.*

gibberish NOUN nonsense, drivel, gabble.

giddy ADJECTIVE **1** dizzy, unsteady, light-headed. **2** flighty, wild, reckless.

gift NOUN **1** present, donation, offering. **2** talent, ability, flair, aptitude, bent.

gigantic ADJECTIVE See **giant**.

giggle VERB titter. *See also* **laugh**.

gingerly ADJECTIVE cautiously, carefully, delicately, tentatively.

give VERB **1** offer, hand over, present. **2** contribute, donate. **3** deliver, convey, pass on. **4** supply, issue, grant, distribute, hand out. **5** make, do. *He gave a deep chuckle.* **6** present, perform. *She gave a talk.* **7** bend, yield. *Opposite words are retain, keep.*

glad ADJECTIVE pleased, happy, delighted. *An opposite word is sad.*

glamour/glamor (US) NOUN appeal, attraction, charm, fascination.

glance VERB See **look**.

glare VERB **1** frown, glower, scowl. *See also* **look**. **2** dazzle, shine, glitter.

glaring ADJECTIVE obvious, blatant, barefaced, terrible. *A glaring mistake.*

glaze VERB gloss, varnish, polish, enamel.

gleam VERB sparkle, flash, glow, glitter, glint.

glen NOUN See **valley**.

glib ADJECTIVE easy, smooth, slick, talkative, facile.

glide VERB slide, soar, sail, skim, float, drift. *The seaplane glided to a stop.*

glider NOUN See **aircraft**.

glimmer VERB gleam, shine, glow, flicker, glitter.

glimpse VERB see, spot, spy, catch sight of.

glisten VERB glimmer, gleam, shine.

glitter VERB shine, sparkle, flash, glisten, glimmer, gleam, scintillate. *The treasure glittered in the morning light.*

gloat VERB exult, revel, crow, triumph, relish.

global ADJECTIVE worldwide, international, general.

globe NOUN ball, sphere, orb, planet.

gloomy ADJECTIVE **1** depressing, dismal, dark, dreary. **2** unhappy, sad, miserable, glum.

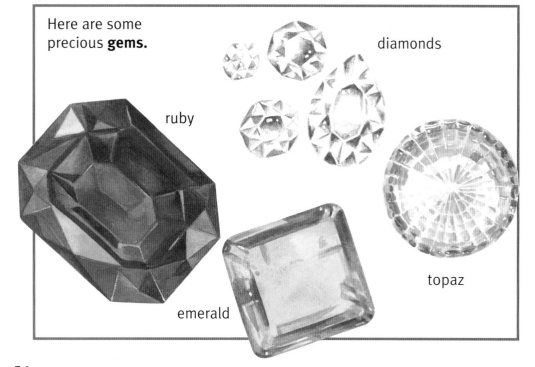

Here are some precious **gems.**

diamonds

ruby

emerald

topaz

Gg

glorious ADJECTIVE **1** brilliant, splendid, bright, beautiful, superb. **2** famous, noted, noble, exalted. An *opposite word* is inglorious.

glory NOUN **1** fame, honour/honor (US), praise, greatness. **2** beauty, splendour/splendor (US), brilliance. **3** praise, worship.

glossy ADJECTIVE shiny, polished, burnished, sheeny.

glow VERB **1** gleam, shine, burn, smoulder. **2** flush.

glower VERB *See* **glare**.

glue NOUN and VERB gum, adhesive, paste, cement.

glum ADJECTIVE sad, depressed, sullen, morose, miserable. *See also* **gloomy**. *Opposite words* are happy, cheerful, elated.

glut NOUN surplus, excess, abundance, plenty. *Opposite words* are scarcity, famine.

gnaw VERB nibble, bite, chew. *See also* **eat**.

go VERB **1** leave, depart, set out. **2** escape, flee, run away. *When does the plane go?* **3** become, grow, turn, get. *He went pale with fear.* **4** continue, extend, lead, reach. *Most rivers go to the sea.* **5** belong, fit. *The nut goes with the bolt.* **6** travel, journey. **7** work, operate, function. *The car won't go.* An *opposite word* is stop.

goal NOUN aim, ambition, target, purpose.

good ADJECTIVE **1** correct, faultless, perfect, excellent, admirable. **2** caring, generous, honest, loyal, reliable. **3** kind, considerate, virtuous. **4** obedient, well-behaved, polite. **5** skilled, clever, capable, talented. **6** interesting, exciting, thrilling, entertaining. *Opposite words* are **1** bad; **3** unkind, wicked; **5** incompetent.

Things which are burning, or very hot, **glow** brightly.

glow worm

candle flame

volcanic lava

goods NOUN belongings, property, merchandise, cargo.

gorge VERB *See* **eat**.

gorgeous ADJECTIVE superb, magnificent, brilliant, splendid, beautiful. *It's a gorgeous afternoon, let's have a picnic. Opposite words* are ugly, plain.

gossip VERB talk, tittle-tattle, chatter, tell tales.

govern VERB rule, manage, control, run, supervise, direct.

government NOUN rule, management, administration, authority, state, parliament. Some different kinds of government: aristocracy, autocracy, democracy, despotism, federation, matriarchy, meritocracy, monarchy, oligarchy, patriarchy, plutocracy, republic, technocracy, theocracy, totalitarianism.

gown NOUN robe. *See also* **clothes**.

grab VERB seize, clutch, take hold of, snatch, grasp.

graceful ADJECTIVE elegant, flowing, natural, attractive. *A graceful ballerina danced across the stage.* An *opposite word* is clumsy.

gracious ADJECTIVE polite, kindly, friendly, gentle, generous, urbane. *Opposite words* are ungracious, churlish.

grade NOUN rank, position, degree, status, category, class.

grade VERB sort, group, classify, rank, assess.

gradient NOUN slope, incline, ascent, descent.

gradual ADJECTIVE slow, continuous, steady, little by little. *Opposite words* are abrupt, sudden.

grand ADJECTIVE impressive, important, splendid, superb, magnificent, majestic, imposing. *Opposite words* are common, inferior.

grant VERB **1** give, donate, bestow, award. **2** allow, consent to, permit. *Opposite words* are **1** withhold. **2** refuse, deny.

grasp VERB **1** hold, clasp. *See also* **grab**. **2** understand. *I'm not sure I grasped exactly what you are trying to say. See also* **comprehend**.

grateful ADJECTIVE thankful, indebted, appreciative. *We're grateful for the opportunity.* An *opposite word* is ungrateful.

grave ADJECTIVE **1** serious, solemn, thoughtful. *A grave moment.* **2** important, essential. *Grave news.*

greasy ADJECTIVE fatty, oily, slimy, slippery.

great ADJECTIVE **1** large, huge, tremendous, immense. **2** important, spectacular, splendid, grand. **3** classic, famous, well-known, leading. *A great work of art.* **4** excellent, wonderful, marvellous/marvelous (US).

greedy ADJECTIVE **1** gluttonous, ravenous, piggish. **2** grasping, selfish, avaricious.

greet VERB salute, hail, welcome, meet.

grief NOUN sadness, sorrow, distress, heartache, woe, misery, suffering, unhappiness. An *opposite word* is happiness.

grieve VERB mourn, sorrow, lament. An *opposite word* is rejoice.

grill NOUN *See also* **cook**.

grim ADJECTIVE **1** serious, harsh, solemn. *It was grim news.* **2** frightening, horrid, gruesome, unpleasant.

grime NOUN smut, dust. *See also* **dirt**.

grin VERB smile, beam, smirk, simper, laugh.

grind VERB **1** crush, pulverize, crunch. **2** sharpen, whet.

grip VERB seize, clasp, grasp, clutch, hold. *He gripped the door handle tightly.*

groan NOUN and VERB moan, sigh, whine, wail, lament, grumble. A word that sounds similar is grown.

groom VERB tidy, smarten, clean, brush, preen.

grope VERB hold, feel, handle, touch, fumble.

ground NOUN **1** earth, soil, clay. **2** base, foundation.

grounds NOUN **1** justification, cause, excuse, reason. **2** dregs, sediment. **3** land, estate, territory, parkland.

group NOUN division, section, collection, assortment.

grow VERB **1** develop, expand, enlarge, get bigger, get taller, increase. *The town is growing.* **2** become. *It grew late.* **3** plant, raise, cultivate, germinate, sprout.

growl VERB snarl, grumble, threaten.

grubby ADJECTIVE *See* **dirty**.

gruesome ADJECTIVE horrible, hideous, nasty, disgusting, grisly.

gruff ADJECTIVE **1** rough, harsh, hoarse. *A gruff voice.* **2** rude, grumpy, curt, churlish.

grumble VERB complain, moan, protest, carp.

grumpy ADJECTIVE bad-tempered, snappish, surly, sullen. An *opposite word* is affable.

guarantee VERB promise, vouch for, warrant, assure, make sure.

guard VERB protect, shield, defend, watch over, look after, shelter.

guess VERB **1** estimate, surmise, conjecture, reckon. **2** think, suppose, assume.

guest NOUN visitor, caller.

guide VERB lead, direct, conduct, manage, control, escort. An *opposite word* is mislead.

guilty ADJECTIVE blameworthy, responsible, wrong, wicked. An *opposite word* is innocent.

gulf NOUN bay, gap, rift, breach, chasm.

gulp VERB *See* **drink**.

gun NOUN some different types of gun: bazooka, blunderbuss, cannon, carbine, firearm, musket, machine-gun, pistol, revolver, rifle.

guzzle VERB *See* **eat**.

Here are some tools that are used to **groom** a horse.

horse braids

brush

bridegroom

curry comb

hoof-cleaning tool

horse and groom

Hh

sombrero (hat)

habit NOUN
1 custom, usage, tradition, practice, way, addiction. 2 mannerism.

haggle VERB bargain, barter, argue.

hairy ADJECTIVE furry, hirsute, shaggy, bushy, woolly.

hall NOUN vestibule, foyer, lobby, corridor, entrance, auditorium, concert-hall. A word that sounds similar is haul.

halt VERB stop, pull up, wait, cease, end. An *opposite word* is start.

halve VERB divide, bisect, dissect, split in two.

hammer VERB beat, hit, pound, bang, knock.

hamper VERB hinder, prevent, obstruct, get in the way, impede, restrict, curb. An *opposite word* is help.

hand NOUN mitt. Parts of a hand: finger, fingernail, fist, knuckle, palm, thumb, wrist.

hand VERB give, pass, transmit, deliver.

handicap NOUN disability, disadvantage, hindrance, drawback, restriction.

handle VERB 1 feel, hold, fondle, touch. 2 manage, control, manipulate, look after, wield.

handsome ADJECTIVE 1 good-looking, attractive, elegant. An *opposite word* is ugly. 2 generous. liberal, ample. *Opposite words* are mean (UK), niggardly.

handy ADJECTIVE 1 useful, helpful, convenient, accessible, to hand, compact. 2 skilful, practical.

hang VERB 1 dangle, sag, droop, suspend, drape. 2 execute.

hanker VERB crave, long for, want, desire, yearn, thirst for.

haphazard ADJECTIVE accidental, chance, random, slapdash. *Opposite words* are deliberate, orderly.

happen VERB occur, take place, come about, transpire.

happy ADJECTIVE merry, cheerful, joyful, delighted, glad, pleased, contented. *Opposite words* are sad, unhappy. 2 lucky, fortunate, appropriate.

harass VERB pester, annoy, tease, badger, disturb, bother, hassle.

harbour/harbor (US) NOUN port, docks, quay, haven, mooring, anchorage.

hard ADJECTIVE 1 solid, rigid, dense, stiff, tough. 2 difficult, complicated, baffling, complex, intricate. 3 severe, harsh, cruel. *A hard punishment.* 4 exhausting, tiring, tough, arduous. *Opposite words* are 1 soft. 2 easy. 3 gentle. merciful. 4 relaxing.

hardly ADVERB just, barely, not quite, only just. *I can hardly stay awake.*

hardy ADJECTIVE strong, rugged, robust, sturdy, tough. An *opposite word* is weak.

harm VERB injure, hurt, damage, spoil, abuse, ill-treat.

harmful ADJECTIVE damaging, dangerous, injurious, unhealthy. An *opposite word* is harmless.

harsh ADJECTIVE 1 rough, grating, rasping, jarring. *A harsh noise.* 2 hard, cruel, pitiless, strict. 3 glaring, dazzling, bright.

hasten VERB hurry, speed up, rush, dash, fly. *Opposite words* are dawdle, loiter.

hasty ADJECTIVE hurried, speedy, brisk, impulsive, careless, sloppy. *Opposite words* are slow, careful.

hat NOUN headgear, millinery. Some different kinds of hats and headgear: balaclava, bearskin, beret, biretta, boater, bonnet, bowler, cap, cloche, crown, fez, helmet, kepi, mitre, shako, skullcap, sombrero, tricorn, trilby, tiara, turban.

Here are some different kinds of **hat.**

hard hat

decorative hat

military hat

hate VERB dislike, loathe, detest, despise. *Opposite words are like, love.*

haul VERB drag, pull, tow, heave, tug. *An opposite word is push. A word that sounds similar is hall.*

have VERB **1** own, possess. *I have a new bike.* **2** contain, consist of, be made up of, include. *The castle has a hundred rooms.* **3** get, obtain, receive. *How many Christmas cards did you have?* **4** allow, put up with, tolerate. *She wouldn't have the dog in the house.* **5** produce, give birth to. *The cat had eight beautiful kittens.* **6** experience, go through, enjoy. *We had a lovely time at the coast.*

havoc NOUN chaos, disturbance, upset, disorder, mayhem.

hazy ADJECTIVE misty, cloudy, foggy, blurred, dim, indistinct. *An opposite word is clear.*

head ADJECTIVE leading, main, principal.

head NOUN **1** skull, mind, brains. **2** top, summit, peak, apex. **3** leader, boss, chief, commander, ruler.

heady ADJECTIVE thrilling, exciting.

heal VERB cure, make better, restore, remedy. *Words that sound similar are heel, he'll.*

health NOUN fitness, strength, wellbeing, soundness. *Opposite words are illness, sickness.*

healthy ADJECTIVE fit, well, sound, robust. *An opposite word is ill.*

heap NOUN pile, mound, mass, collection. *A heap of stones.*

hear VERB listen, eavesdrop, pay attention. *A word that sounds similar is here.*

heart NOUN centre/center (US), middle, core, kernel, nucleus. **2** kindness, sympathy, feeling.

heartless ADJECTIVE cruel, pitiless, callous, harsh, brutal, unkind. *Opposite words are kind, merciful.*

hearty ADJECTIVE **1** enthusiastic, warm, friendly, sincere. **2** large, nourishing, ample. *A hearty meal.*

heat NOUN warmth, fervour, fever, excitement.

heat VERB warm, boil, cook. *See also* **cook**.

heave VERB *See* **haul**.

heavy ADJECTIVE **1** weighty, ponderous, bulky. **2** hard, difficult. *An opposite word is light.*

hectic ADJECTIVE busy, frenetic, frenzied, heated, feverish. *An opposite word is calm.*

hedge NOUN fence, barrier, boundary.

heed VERB pay attention to, observe, follow, obey.

heir NOUN inheritor, offspring, child.

help VERB **1** aid, assist, give a hand, serve. **2** improve, make better. *Opposite words are hinder, hamper.*

helpful ADJECTIVE **1** useful, beneficial, worthwhile. **2** kind, friendly, considerate, caring. *Opposite words are* **1** useless, **2** unhelpful.

helpless ADJECTIVE weak, powerless, incapable.

hem NOUN edge, margin, border.

hence ADVERB therefore, thus, accordingly.

herb NOUN plant, seasoning, flavouring/flavoring (US). Some different kinds of herb: basil, bay leaf, camomile, chives, fennel, mint, oregano, rosemary, sage, tarragon, thyme.

heritage NOUN **1** inheritance, legacy, bequest. **2** tradition, culture.

heroic ADJECTIVE brave, valiant, courageous, gallant, fearless. *Opposite words are cowardly, bashful.*

hesitate VERB delay, pause, waver, falter, hold back, demur. *An opposite word is decide.*

hew VERB *See* **cut**.

hide VERB conceal, cover, put away, veil, mask, disguise. *Opposite words are show, find.*

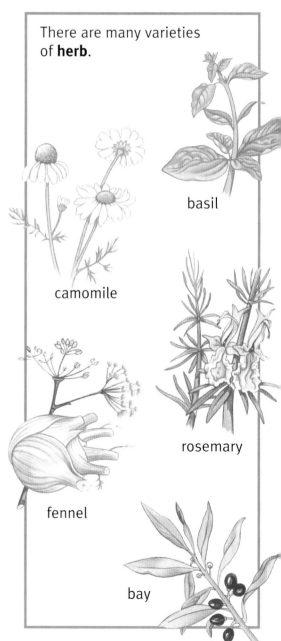

There are many varieties of **herb**.

basil

camomile

rosemary

fennel

bay

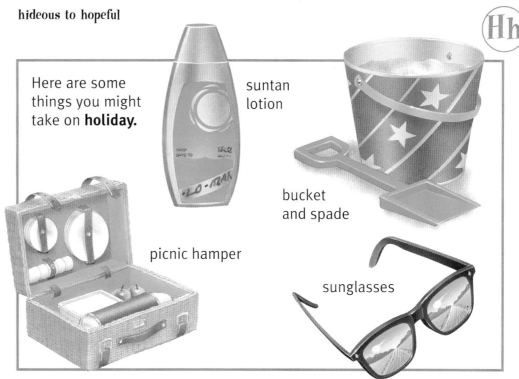

Here are some things you might take on **holiday.**

suntan lotion

bucket and spade

picnic hamper

sunglasses

hideous ADJECTIVE ugly, ghastly, frightful, horrible, repulsive. An *opposite word* is beautiful.

high ADJECTIVE **1** tall, lofty, elevated, towering. **2** eminent, important, distinguished. **3** shrill, sharp, piercing.

highbrow ADJECTIVE intellectual, clever, cultivated, brainy. An *opposite word* is lowbrow.

highly ADVERB very, extremely, decidedly.

highly-strung ADJECTIVE sensitive, nervous, tense.

high-powered ADJECTIVE dynamic, go-ahead, forceful.

highway NOUN *See* **road.**

hike VERB ramble. *See also* **walk.**

hilarious ADJECTIVE funny, amusing, entertaining, hysterical. An *opposite word* is serious.

hill NOUN mound, rise, elevation, peak, slope, height, knoll.

hinder VERB check, impede. *See also* **hamper.**

hint VERB suggest, mention, insinuate, allude to.

hire VERB rent, lease, charter, let, book. A word that sounds similar is higher.

hit VERB **1** beat, thrash, whip, cane, flog. **2** punch, clout, sock, clobber, batter, wallop. **3** tap, touch, tip, knock. *She tapped on the window.* **4** collide with, crash into, smash into, bump into.

hoard VERB collect, amass, save, accumulate. An *opposite word* is squander. A word that sounds similar is horde.

hoarse ADJECTIVE husky, raucous, croaking, gruff, rough. A word that sounds similar is horse.

hoax NOUN prank, trick, joke, deception, spoof, con.

hobble VERB limp, totter, stagger, stumble, shuffle.

hobby NOUN pastime, interest, recreation, pursuit, sideline.

hoist VERB raise, lift, elevate.

hold VERB **1** clutch, grip, grasp, seize. An *opposite word* is release. **2** possess, admit. **3** contain. *The box holds a lot.* **4** think, believe, judge, reckon. **5** imprison, arrest, detain.

hole NOUN opening, cavity, crater, gap, puncture, tear, split, burrow. A word that sounds similar is whole.

holiday NOUN vacation, festival, anniversary, leave, time off.

hollow ADJECTIVE **1** sunken, concave, empty. **2** insincere, sham, artificial. *It was nothing but a hollow promise.* An *opposite word* is sincere.

hollow NOUN dip, depression, cavity, hole.

home NOUN **1** house, dwelling, residence, abode. **2** institution, asylum. *They're building a home for the elderly.*

holiday

homonym NOUN homonyms are words with the same spelling but different meanings, as in bank (a place money is kept) and bank (the side of a river).

homophone NOUN homophones are words that have the same sound but a different spelling and a different meaning: ail/ale, allowed/aloud, altar/alter, bail/bale, band/banned, bare/bear, be/bee, beach/beech, been/bean, berry/bury, billed/build, blew/blue, boar/bore, boarder/border, bough/bow, brake/break, bread/bred, buy/by/bye.

honest ADJECTIVE truthful, sincere, genuine, direct, straight, candid. *Opposite words* are dishonest, deceitful.

hooligan NOUN lout, ruffian, thug, yob (UK), hoodlum.

hop VERB leap, jump, spring, dance, hobble, limp.

hope VERB wish, long for, look forward to, await, desire, yearn, believe. An *opposite word* is despair.

hopeful ADJECTIVE expectant, optimistic, confident, cheerful. An *opposite word* is pessimistic.

hopeless ADJECTIVE **1** despairing, pessimistic, despondent. **2** useless, no good. **3** unattainable.

horde NOUN crowd, mob, gang, swarm, throng, host. A word that sounds similar is hoard.

horizontal ADJECTIVE flat, level, straight, plane.

horrible ADJECTIVE nasty, unpleasant, disgusting, horrid, frightful, frightening, terrible. *Opposite words* are pleasant, wonderful.

horrify VERB terrify, alarm, shock, appal, outrage, disgust. *Opposite words* are please, reassure.

horror NOUN fear, dread, fright, terror, loathing, revulsion, disgust.

horse NOUN hack, mount, charger, cob, nag, stallion, mare, filly, colt.

hospital NOUN clinic, nursing home, sanitorium, infirmary.

hostile ADJECTIVE unfriendly, aggressive, unsympathetic, adverse, bellicose. An *opposite word* is friendly.

hot ADJECTIVE **1** warm, scalding, boiling, sweltering, scorching, sizzling, blazing. *A hot fire.* An *opposite word* is cold. **2** peppery, pungent. *A hot sauce.*

hotel NOUN inn, boarding house, guest house, bed and breakfast, motel, hostel.

hound VERB chase, pursue, harry, persecute.

house NOUN building, dwelling, home, residence.

hovel NOUN shack, cabin, hut, dump, shanty.

hover VERB fly, float, flutter, rift, linger, hang around.

however CONJUNCTION still, yet, nonetheless, nevertheless, notwithstanding.

howl VERB hoot, shriek, cry, scream, wail.

huddle VERB cluster, crowd, flock, gather, snuggle.

hue NOUN *See* **colour/color**.

hug VERB cuddle, embrace, hold, cling to.

huge ADJECTIVE colossal, gigantic. *See also* **big**.

hum VERB drone, purr, buzz, murmur.

humane ADJECTIVE kind, merciful, forgiving, compassionate, sympathetic. *Opposite words* are cruel, harsh.

humble ADJECTIVE meek, modest, submissive, simple, unassuming. An *opposite word* is proud.

humiliate VERB mortify, degrade, embarrass, crush, deflate. An *opposite word* is dignify.

hump NOUN lump, bulge, bump, mound.

hunch NOUN suspicion, notion, feeling, intuition, premonition.

hunger NOUN **1** famine, starvation, appetite. **2** greed, desire, yearning, thirst.

hunt VERB **1** chase, stalk, pursue, track down, hound. **2** look for, search, probe, seek.

hurdle NOUN fence, barrier, obstacle, handicap, snag.

hurl VERB throw, fling, propel, chuck, toss, cast, pitch.

hurry VERB hasten, speed, dash, race, run, scurry, fly. *Opposite words* are delay, dawdle.

hurt VERB **1** harm, damage, wound, injure. **2** ache, pain, throb. *Her ankle hurts.* **3** upset, distress, offend. *You've hurt their feelings.*

hush VERB silence, quieten, soothe. An *opposite word* is arouse.

hush-hush ADJECTIVE secret.

hut NOUN shed, cabin, shanty, shack.

hymn NOUN religious song, psalm. A word that sounds similar is him.

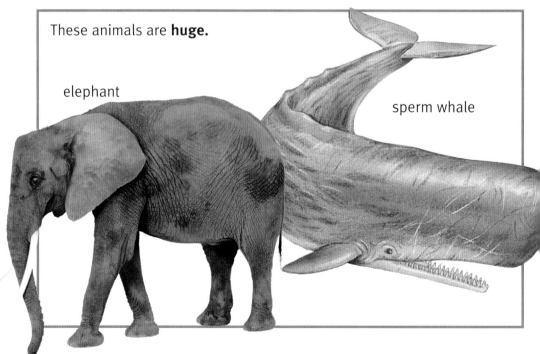

These animals are **huge.**

elephant

sperm whale

Ii

icon NOUN picture, image, symbol.

icy ADJECTIVE chilly, cold, freezing, frosty. An *opposite word* is warm.

idea NOUN thought, notion, suggestion, plan, opinion, belief.

ideal ADJECTIVE perfect, complete, model, excellent, best.

identical ADJECTIVE same, indistinguishable, duplicate, matching. An *opposite word* is different.

identify VERB know, recognize, distinguish, discern, pick out.

idiom NOUN turn of phrase, expression. '*Kick the bucket*' *is an idiom.*

idiot NOUN fool, moron, dunce, halfwit, imbecile, simpleton.

idle ADJECTIVE lazy, indolent, unoccupied, inactive, unemployed. An *opposite word* is busy.

idol NOUN **1** image, god, statue. **2** favourite/favorite (US), hero, heroine, darling.

ignite VERB light, set fire to, kindle, spark off.

ignorant ADJECTIVE **1** stupid, unintelligent, illiterate, uneducated, clueless. **2** unaware, oblivious.

ignore VERB disregard, disobey, overlook, neglect, pay no attention to. *Opposite words* are heed, observe.

ill ADJECTIVE **1** unwell, sick, poorly, under the weather, infirm. **2** harmful, damaging.

ill-treat VERB injure, abuse, harm.

illegal ADJECTIVE unlawful, forbidden, banned, prohibited, illicit. *Opposite words* are legal, lawful.

illegible ADJECTIVE unreadable, indecipherable, indistinct. *His handwriting is almost illegible.*

illness NOUN sickness, ailment, disease, complaint, disorder, disability, malady. An *opposite word* is health.

illuminate VERB shed light on, enlighten, explain, elucidate, clarify. An *opposite word* is darken.

illustration NOUN picture, drawing, sketch, decoration, representation, example. *The illustrations in this book are terrific.*

image NOUN picture, likeness, representation, statue, concept, idea.

imaginary ADJECTIVE unreal, made-up, fictitious, imagined, make-believe, illusory, fanciful. An *opposite word* is real.

imagination NOUN fancy, idea, vision, creativity, inspiration.

imagine VERB **1** picture, dream, fancy, invent, make up, envisage. **2** think, believe, suppose.

imitate VERB copy, ape, parody, simulate, reproduce, follow, caricature, impersonate, forge.

immature ADJECTIVE raw, crude, unripe, unformed, young, childish, puerile. *Opposite words* are mature, ripe.

immediately ADVERB straightaway, at once, without delay, forthwith.

immense ADJECTIVE huge, vast, enormous, vast, massive. *Opposite words* are tiny, minute.

immerse VERB plunge, submerge, dip, dunk, douse, souse.

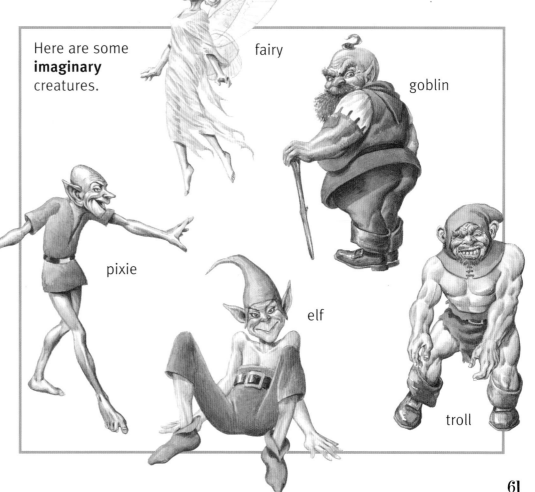

Here are some **imaginary** creatures.

fairy

goblin

pixie

elf

troll

61

imminent ADJECTIVE impending, looming, approaching, threatening.

immortal ADJECTIVE eternal, everlasting, undying, ever-living. An *opposite word* is mortal.

immune ADJECTIVE resistant, invulnerable, spared, free.

impact NOUN **1** effect, influence, repercussions. *The impact of new technology.* **2** collision, crash, bang, shock, blow.

impartial ADJECTIVE objective, unbiased, disinterested, neutral, fair. *Opposite words* are prejudiced, biased.

impassive ADJECTIVE calm, unruffled, composed, indifferent, unmoved. *Opposite words* are moved, emotional.

impatient ADJECTIVE eager, anxious, fidgety, restless, hasty intolerant, bad-tempered. An *opposite word* is patient.

impede VERB hinder, obstruct, get in the way of, interrupt, block, stop.

impending ADJECTIVE imminent, threatening, approaching, coming.

impenetrable ADJECTIVE **1** dense, thick, solid, impassable. **2** mysterious, incomprehensible, baffling, puzzling.

imperfect ADJECTIVE faulty, defective, flawed, unsound, damaged. An *opposite word* is perfect.

impersonal ADJECTIVE formal, official, remote, aloof. An *opposite word* is friendly.

impertinent ADJECTIVE rude, impudent, insolent. An *opposite word* is polite.

impetuous ADJECTIVE hasty, impulsive, rash, reckless.

imply VERB hint, insinuate, suggest, intimate.

import VERB bring in, introduce.

important ADJECTIVE **1** basic, chief, essential, main. *Important dates in history.* **2** famous, well-known, notable, great. *An important Hollywood star.* **3** big, major, significant, special. *An important anniversary. Opposite words* are minor, petty, insignificant, unimportant.

imposing ADJECTIVE impressive, magnificent, stately.

impossible ADJECTIVE unworkable, inconceivable, hopeless, impracticable, absurd. An *opposite word* is possible.

impractical ADJECTIVE unworkable, unrealistic, unusable, idealistic.

impression NOUN **1** mark, stamp, brand. **2** feeling, idea, a vague idea. opinion. *I have the impression she's unhappy.* **3** impersonation, imitation, take-off. *He did a good impression of the teacher.*

impressive ADJECTIVE splendid, magnificent, wonderful, overpowering.

imprison VERB jail, lock up, incarcerate, confine. An *opposite word* is release.

improve VERB correct, get better, make better, develop, amend, perfect.

improvise VERB make up, extemporize, invent, ad-lib.

impudent ADJECTIVE saucy, impertinent, cocky, insolent. An *opposite word* is polite.

impure ADJECTIVE contaminated, unclean, polluted, dirty, indecent. *Opposite words* are pure, chaste.

inaccessible ADJECTIVE remote, isolated, unreachable, unobtainable. An *opposite word* is accessible.

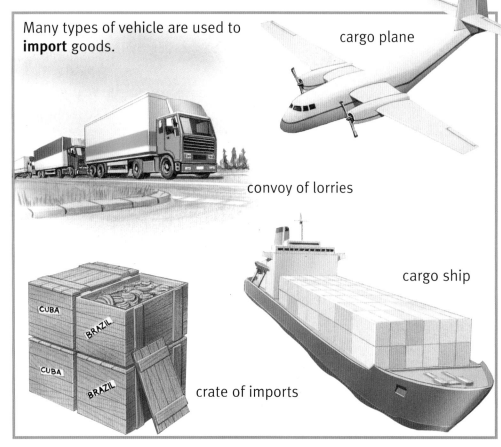

Many types of vehicle are used to **import** goods.

cargo plane

convoy of lorries

cargo ship

crate of imports

inaccurate ADJECTIVE wrong, incorrect, faulty, imprecise, inexact.

inarticulate ADJECTIVE unintelligible, incoherent, tongue-tied.

inaudible ADJECTIVE silent, noiseless, faint, muffled, indistinct. *Opposite words* are audible, loud.

incapable ADJECTIVE unable, helpless, unfit, weak, incompetent. *Opposite words* are capable, qualified.

incentive NOUN spur, motive, encouragement, bait, inducement.

incessant ADJECTIVE unending, interminable, continual, ceaseless, non-stop. *Opposite words* are spasmodic, periodic.

incident NOUN event, happening, occurrence, experience.

incline VERB tend, lean, slope, veer, favour/favor (US), be disposed.

include VERB contain, consist of, comprise, hold, enclose. *Opposite words* are exclude, omit.

incomparable ADJECTIVE superb, unequalled/unequaled (US), matchless, superlative, unrivalled/unrivaled (US). An *opposite word* is ordinary.

incompetent ADJECTIVE incapable, helpless, inept, unqualified, useless.

incorrect ADJECTIVE faulty, mistaken, wrong, erroneous, untrue, inaccurate.

increase VERB expand, extend, enlarge, boost, add to, swell, enhance, develop. *Opposite words* are decrease, diminish.

incredible ADJECTIVE unbelievable, amazing, extraordinary, far-fetched.

independent ADJECTIVE free, self-governing, self-reliant, separate, self-sufficient.

indicate VERB show, point to, denote, suggest, symbolize.

indifference NOUN disregard, negligence, unconcern, apathy, lack of interest.

indispensable ADJECTIVE essential, vital, necessary, needed. An *opposite word* is unnecessary.

indulge VERB pander to, give in to, yield, gratify, pamper, satisfy, humour/humor (US), spoil. An *opposite word* is deny.

inefficient ADJECTIVE incompetent, unworkable, wasteful, time-consuming. An *opposite word* is efficient.

inevitable ADJECTIVE unavoidable, doomed, inescapable, destined, certain, sure. An *opposite word* is uncertain.

infallible ADJECTIVE unfailing, unerring, sure, dependable, trustworthy.

infamous ADJECTIVE notorious, disreputable, shameful, disgraceful, wicked. An *opposite word* is honourable/honorable (US).

infatuated ADJECTIVE besotted, crazy about, smitten, fascinated.

infectious ADJECTIVE contagious, catching, polluting, virulent. *Infectious disease.*

inferior ADJECTIVE mediocre, second-rate, shoddy, minor, subordinate, secondary, lesser. An *opposite word* is superior.

infinite ADJECTIVE unending, endless, eternal, boundless, limitless, immeasurable, vast. *Opposite words* are finite, limited.

inflexible ADJECTIVE unbending, rigid, stiff, fixed, stubborn, adamant. *Opposite words* are yielding, supple, pliable. *An inflexible arrangement.*

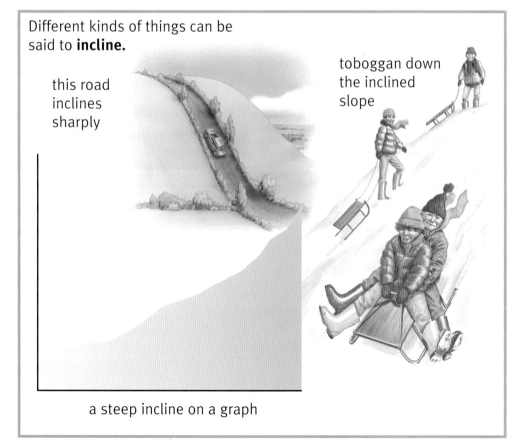

Different kinds of things can be said to **incline.**

this road inclines sharply

toboggan down the inclined slope

a steep incline on a graph

Ii

inflict VERB burden, impose, deliver, give, put. An *opposite word* is spare.

influence VERB affect, impress, inspire, sway, persuade, manipulate.

ant

inform VERB tell, notify, let know, instruct, communicate, relate. An *opposite word* is conceal.

informal ADJECTIVE casual, relaxed, easy-going, unceremonious, simple, friendly. *Opposite words* are formal, conventional.

information NOUN news, knowledge, intelligence, advice, facts, data.

infuriate VERB anger, enrage, vex, madden, annoy. An *opposite word* is calm.

ingenious ADJECTIVE clever, cunning, shrewd, resourceful, inventive. An *opposite word is* unimaginative.

inhabit VERB live in, occupy, dwell, reside.

initial ADJECTIVE first, beginning, introductory, original. An *opposite word* is final.

initiative NOUN resourcefulness, drive, energy, ambition, go, innovativeness.

inject VERB insert, inoculate, vaccinate.

injure VERB harm, damage, hurt, wound, maltreat.

injustice NOUN unfairness, discrimination, oppression, prejudice. *Opposite words* are fairness, justice.

innocent ADJECTIVE **1** blameless, guiltless, sinless, faultless, pure. **2** naive, simple, unworldly, gullible, harmless. **1** *An innocent remark.* **2** *An innocent young child.*

innovation NOUN change, novelty, variation.

inquisitive ADJECTIVE curious, prying, nosy, enquiring, snooping.

insanity NOUN madness, mental illness, craziness, lunacy, mania.

inscribe VERB engrave, etch, carve, cut, incise, stamp, write, dedicate.

insect NOUN Some different kinds of insect: ant, bee, beetle, butterfly, cricket, earwig, fly, gnat, grasshopper, ladybird/ladybug (US), mosquito, moth, wasp.

insert VERB put in, implant, introduce, inject, interleave.

insincere ADJECTIVE false, two-faced, deceptive, hypocritical, devious, faithless. *Opposite words* are sincere, frank.

insinuate VERB hint at, suggest, imply, intimate.

insipid ADJECTIVE tasteless, flavourless/flavorless (US), flat, bland, weak, dull, lifeless. *Opposite words* are tasty, spicy, lively.

inspect VERB look over, check, examine, investigate, supervise.

inspire VERB excite, provoke, hearten, cheer, stimulate, stir, arouse, spur.

instal/install (US) VERB fix, set, position, establish, set up.

instantly ADVERB immediately, without delay, at once, now.

institute VERB found, start, establish, originate. *Opposite words* are abolish, discontinue.

instruct VERB **1** order, command, direct, tell, inform. **2** teach, train, educate, coach, tutor.

instrument NOUN tool, utensil, device, contraption, appliance, implement.

insulate VERB protect, pad, cocoon, shield, isolate, disconnect.

insult NOUN abuse, offence/offense (US), rudeness, slander, snub.

intact ADJECTIVE whole, complete, unharmed, sound. An *opposite word* is broken.

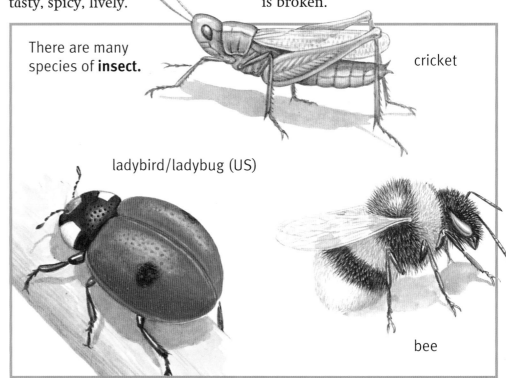

There are many species of **insect.**

cricket

ladybird/ladybug (US)

bee

integrity NOUN honour/honor (US), honesty, goodness, uprightness. *Opposite words* are dishonesty, disrepute.

intelligent ADJECTIVE clever, astute, bright, quick, brainy, smart, alert. *Opposite words* are unintelligent, foolish.

intense ADJECTIVE **1** strong, great, very, extreme. *Intense heat.* **2** eager, ardent, passionate. An *opposite word* is moderate.

intercept VERB interrupt, stop, seize, catch, arrest. *Intercepted by the police.*

interesting ADJECTIVE fascinating, amazing, intriguing, entertaining, amusing, exciting, thrilling. *Opposite words* are dull, monotonous, boring.

interfere VERB pry, intrude, butt in, snoop, meddle, cut, disturb.

interior ADJECTIVE internal, inside, secret, hidden.

interlude NOUN *See* **interval**.

internal ADJECTIVE inner, inside, inward, interior. An *opposite word* is external.

interrupt VERB interfere, butt in, intrude, disturb, suspend. *Opposite words* are resume, continue.

interval NOUN interlude, break, gap, pause, intermission, recess, delay.

intervene VERB **1** interrupt, intrude, break in, interfere. **2** mediate, arbitrate.

interview NOUN meeting, consultation, talk, conference, press conference.

intolerant ADJECTIVE bigoted, narrow-minded, unfair, impatient, prejudiced, arrogant. *Opposite words* are tolerant, broad-minded.

Here are some different **inventions**.

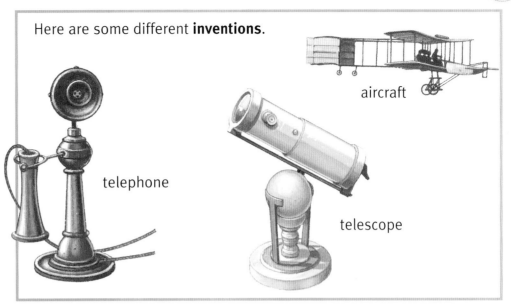

aircraft

telephone

telescope

intrepid ADJECTIVE brave, bold, fearless, valiant, courageous, daring. *Opposite words* are cowardly, timid.

intrigue VERB **1** fascinate, attract, charm. *An intriguing story.* **2** scheme, plot.

introduce VERB **1** start, inaugurate, launch, institute. **2** acquaint, make known, present. *Introduce me to her.*

intrude VERB interrupt, butt in, meddle, interfere, trespass.

inundate VERB flood, drown, submerge, swamp. *We were inundated with applications.*

invade VERB overrun, conquer, occupy, march into, raid, assault. *Opposite words* are evacuate, withdraw.

invalid NOUN patient, victim, sufferer.

invaluable ADJECTIVE precious, priceless, valuable. An *opposite word* is worthless.

invent VERB conceive, think up, create, devise, plan, concoct.

invention NOUN creation, discovery, development, design, gadget, device.

investigate VERB inquire into, examine, study, inspect, explore, research, probe.

invisible ADJECTIVE out of sight, unseen, hidden, concealed, undetectable. An *opposite word* is visible.

invite VERB ask, request, summon, call, tempt, encourage.

involve VERB **1** mean, result in, require, include, take in. *The job involves long hours.* **2** take part in, connect with, concern with. *Involved with smuggling.* **3** confuse, confound. *An involved account.*

irrigate VERB water, inundate, flood.

irritate VERB **1** annoy, upset, bother, enrage, vex. **2** chafe.

isolate VERB insulate, detach, set apart, keep apart, segregate.

item NOUN **1** object, article, thing, detail. **2** entry, report. *An item in the newspaper.*

wheel (invention)

jab VERB poke, prod, stab, thrust, elbow.

jacket NOUN coat, cover, case, wrapping. *A book jacket.*

jaded ADJECTIVE exhausted, tired, weary.

jagged ADJECTIVE uneven, ragged, notched, serrated, toothed. An *opposite word* is even.

jam NOUN preserve, conserve, jelly, marmalade.

jam VERB **1** stick, clog, block. *The door has jammed.* **2** cram, crush, squeeze, press, block, fill, squeeze. *He jammed everything into a suitcase.*

jangle VERB clatter, clank, clash, ring, rattle.

jar NOUN pot, beaker (UK). *See also* **container**.

javelin NOUN spear. *See also* **weapon**.

jealous ADJECTIVE envious, bitter, resentful, covetous, suspicious, possessive.

jeer VERB mock, sneer, laugh at, scoff, ridicule, deride.

jeopardy NOUN danger, risk, peril, hazard. An *opposite word* is security.

jest VERB joke, fool, banter, quip.

jet NOUN spray, fountain, spout, gush.

jewel NOUN gem, precious stone, ornament.

jingle VERB tinkle, chime, jangle.

job NOUN **1** work, occupation, profession, trade, employment, business, position, post. **2** chore, task, pursuit, function. Some jobs that people do to earn a living: actor, architect, artist, bus driver, builder/construction worker (US), butcher, carpenter, chef, cleaner, dentist, detective, doctor, electrician, engineer, farmer, firefighter, journalist, lawyer, musician, optician, pilot, plumber, police, postal worker, photographer, publisher, teacher, traindriver, vet.

jocular ADJECTIVE jolly, funny, jovial, witty, humorous. An *opposite word* is serious.

jog VERB **1** run, trot, sprint. **2** prod, jolt, nudge. *Jog your memory.*

join VERB **1** connect, link, unite, fasten, attach. *Opposite words* are divide, separate. **2** come together, meet, merge. *The roads join at the crossroads.* **3** enter, enrol, become a member of, enlist. *Join a club.*

joke NOUN jest, wisecrack, quip, gag, pun, prank, trick.

jostle VERB shove, push, crowd, elbow, jolt.

journal NOUN **1** newspaper, magazine, review, periodical, monthly, weekly. **2** diary, log.

journey NOUN trip, excursion, outing, tour, voyage, expedition, flight.

jovial ADJECTIVE cheery, cordial, jolly.

joy NOUN happiness, pleasure, delight, rapture, bliss, glee. *Opposite words* are gloom, sadness, grief.

judge VERB assess, decide, appraise, evaluate, consider, examine, convict, sentence, adjudicate, referee.

juggle VERB conjure, manipulate, rig, rearrange, fake.

jump VERB **1** bounce, leap, bound, hurdle, pounce, vault, hop. **2** start, flinch, wince. *You made me jump.*

jumpy ADJECTIVE nervous, fidgety, tense.

junk NOUN rubbish, trash, scrap, garbage, waste, odds and ends.

just ADJECTIVE fair, unbiased, objective, impartial, kind, good. *Opposite words* are biased, unfair.

just ADVERB exactly, precisely.

jut VERB protrude, stick out, project, extend. An *opposite word* is recede.

These pictures show some different kinds of **job.**

| surgeon | office worker | photographer | electrician | actress |

a snake
tied in a knot

keen ADJECTIVE **1** eager, enthusiasic, ardent. **2** clever, perceptive, sharp, penetrating. *A keen sense of smell. Opposite words* are **1** apathetic, **2** dull.

keep VERB **1** hold, guard, detain. *He was kept in prison.* **2** look after, save, mind, support. *She keeps three ponies.* **3** save, put away, store. *He keeps all his old clothes.* **4** obey, follow, observe. **5** continue. *She keeps asking questions.* **6** remain, stay. *Keep quiet. Opposite words* are discard, forsake.

keep off VERB stay away. *Keep off the grass.*

keep on VERB continue, persist.

keep out VERB not to enter. *Keep out!*

key ADJECTIVE important, principal, essential, crucial. A word that sounds similar is quay.

key NOUN guide, clue, lead.

kick NOUN excitement, stimulation, thrill.

kick VERB boot, strike with foot, punt.

kidnap VERB abduct, capture, carry off, seize, hijack.

kill VERB slay, put to death, murder, massacre, assassinate, slaughter, execute, bump off, destroy, put to sleep.

kind ADJECTIVE good-natured, friendly, considerate, thoughtful, generous, helpful, gentle, amiable. *Opposite words* are unkind, hard.

kind NOUN type, sort, species, breed, make, category, manner.

kindle VERB set light to, start burning, ignite, inflame, stir, thrill.

kindness NOUN tenderness, good nature, generosity, friendliness.

kiss VERB embrace, caress, greet, smooch.

kit NOUN equipment, gear.

knack NOUN skill, ability, facility, flair, gift.

knave NOUN rascal, scoundrel, rogue, scamp. A word that sounds similar is nave.

knock VERB hit, strike, beat, rap, tap, smite.

knock off VERB **1** stop, cease, finish. **2** steal, filch. **3** deduct. **4** kill, assassinate.

knot VERB tie, loop, entwine, secure. An *opposite word* is untie.

know VERB **1** recognize, identify, be acquainted with. *I know you.* **2** remember, recall, recollect. *Do you know where you left your keys?* **3** understand, perceive, comprehend, see, realize. *Do you know Italian?* A word that sounds similar is no.

know-how NOUN knowledge, talent, ability.

knowing ADJECTIVE astute, perceptive, shrewd, knowledgeable. An *opposite word* is ignorant.

knowledge NOUN experience, understanding, learning, education, wisdom, facts, information. *Opposite words* are ignorance, unawareness.

kudos NOUN honour/honor (US), praise, fame. *She received great kudos for her work in medicine.*

Here are some different kinds of **knot.**

thumb knot

lighterman's hitch

reef knot

label NOUN badge, tag, ticket.

labour/labor (US) NOUN work, job, chore, task, slog, toil, effort, exertion, drudgery.

lack NOUN shortage, need, scarcity, dearth, want. An *opposite word* is plenty.

lag VERB linger, dawdle, loiter.

lagoon NOUN *See* **lake**.

lair NOUN nest, den, burrow, earth, hole.

lake NOUN loch, lagoon, mere, reservoir. *See also* **water**.

lame ADJECTIVE **1** limping, disabled, crippled, hobbling. **2** weak, poor. *A lame excuse.*

lament VERB mourn, feel sorry for, grieve, sorrow, bewail. An *opposite word* is rejoice.

lamp NOUN lantern, torch, flare, light. *Light the lamp.*

lance NOUN spear, javelin, shaft, scalpel, lancet.

lance VERB cut, penetrate, pierce.

land NOUN **1** earth, ground, soil. **2** country, nation, district, region, province. *The plague spread throughout the land.*

land VERB come down to earth, alight, arrive, touch down, go ashore, disembark. *The plane landed early.*

landscape NOUN scenery, view, panorama, countryside. *A beautiful landscape.*

language NOUN speech, dialect, tongue, talk, jargon. Some languages of the world: (Germanic): Danish, Dutch, English, Flemish, German, Icelandic, Norwegian, Swedish. (Romance): Catalan, French, Italian, Portuguese, Romanian, Spanish. (Celtic): Breton, Gaelic, Irish, Scots, Welsh. (Slavic): Croatian, Czech, Polish, Russian, Slovenian, Slovak, Ukrainian. (Indian): Gujurati, Hindi, Punjabi. Sinhalese, Urdu, (Other languages): Bantu, Basque, Chinese, Finnish, Greek, Hebrew, Hottentot, Hungarian, Japanese, Lapp, Persian, Swahili, Turkish, Zulu.

lanky ADJECTIVE tall, gangly. *Opposite words* are stocky, squat.

lap NOUN orbit, circuit, loop, circle.

lapse NOUN error, fault, failing, slip.

lapse VERB slip, slide, sink, decline. deteriorate, die.

large ADJECTIVE big, sizeable, bulky, great, ample, broad, fat, huge, vast, massive. An *opposite word* is small.

last ADJECTIVE final, concluding, ultimate. An *opposite word* is first.

last VERB endure, stay, go on, remain, continue, survive. *Opposite words* are fade, vanish, cease.

late ADJECTIVE overdue, delayed, slow, behind-time, tardy. *Opposite words* are early, prompt, punctual.

lately ADVERB recently, latterly.

lather NOUN foam, bubbles, froth, suds.

laugh VERB chuckle, giggle, snigger, chortle, titter smile, guffaw. An *opposite word* is cry.

launch VERB **1** send off, propel, set in motion. **2** begin, start, inaugurate, embark on. *They launched a new magazine.*

lavish ADJECTIVE plentiful, luxuriant, abundant, profuse, liberal, generous, extravagant. An *opposite word* is frugal.

law NOUN rule, regulation, edict, decree, statute, legislation.

Here are two examples of different written **languages.**

Chinese

hieroglyphics

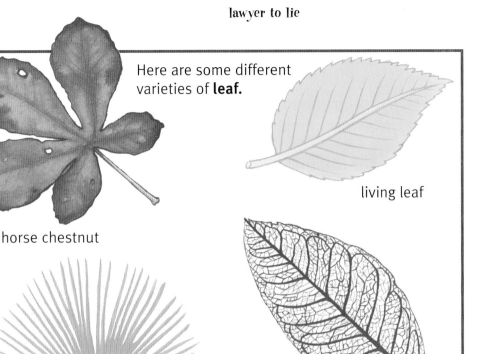

Here are some different varieties of **leaf.**

living leaf

horse chestnut

palm fronds

leaf skeleton

lawyer NOUN solicitor (UK), barrister (UK), advocate, counsel, attorney.

lax ADJECTIVE careless, negligent, slack, relaxed. *Opposite words* are strict, rigid.

lay VERB put, set down, place, leave. *Lay the basket on the ground.* **2** arrange, present. **3** produce an egg.

lay into VERB attack.

lay on VERB supply.

lay out VERB display, exhibit, arrange.

layer NOUN seam, stratum, thickness, coating.

lazy ADJECTIVE idle, indolent, work-shy, slothful. *Opposite words* are active, busy.

lead VERB **1** conduct, guide, steer, take. An *opposite word* is follow. **2** be in charge of, rule, command, manage, direct. **3** outstrip, surpass.

leader NOUN chief, ruler, commander, guide. An *opposite word* is follower.

leaf NOUN page, sheet.

league NOUN union, alliance, association, federation, group, category.

leak VERB drip, ooze, percolate, dribble, trickle, seep. *The shower leaks.* A word that sounds similar is leek.

lean ADJECTIVE thin, slim, scrawny.

lean VERB **1** bend, slant, tilt, slope, list, tend. *The Leaning Tower of Pisa.* **2** prop, rest, recline.

leap VERB **1** jump, spring, skip, vault, bound. **2** rise, increase.

learn VERB discover, find out, hear, memorize, understand, comprehend, grasp.

learned ADJECTIVE erudite, educated, scholarly. An *opposite word* is ignorant.

leave NOUN *See* **holiday.**

leave VERB **1** depart, quit, go. **2** abandon, forsake, desert. **3** put down, place. **4** bequeath, entrust, bestow.

lecture NOUN talk, discourse, address, sermon.

legal ADJECTIVE lawful, legitimate, permitted, allowed, above board. An *opposite word* is illegal.

legible ADJECTIVE readable, clear, decipherable. *Opposite words* are illegible, obscure.

legitimate ADJECTIVE *See* **legal.**

leisure NOUN time off, spare time, freedom, liberty, holiday.

lend VERB loan, grant, give, lease. An *opposite word* is borrow.

lengthen VERB extend, elongate, stretch, prolong. *Opposite words* are shorten, abbreviate.

lenient ADJECTIVE mild, gentle, tolerant, forgiving, merciful, clement. An *opposite word* is harsh.

lessen VERB cut, reduce, decrease, shrink, dwindle. *Opposite words* are increase, grow. A word that sounds similar is lesson.

let VERB **1** allow, permit, consent. An *opposite word* is forbid. **2** hire, lease, rent.

level ADJECTIVE **1** flat, smooth, even, horizontal. *A level teaspoon of sugar.* **2** equal. *The buildings are level with each other. Opposite words* are **1** uneven. **2** unequal.

liberate VERB free, set free, release. An *opposite word* is imprison.

liberty NOUN freedom, release, emancipation.

lie VERB **1** tell a lie, fib. **2** be located, be situated. **3** recline, sprawl. *He lay on the sofa.*

lift VERB hoist, raise, pick up.

light ADJECTIVE **1** lightweight, buoyant. **2** bright. **3** faint, pale. *Opposite words* **1** heavy. **2** dark. **3** strong.

light NOUN Some different kinds of light: candle light, daylight, electric light, firelight, gas light, lamp light, moonlight, street light, torch light, sunlight.

light VERB **1** kindle, set fire to, burn, ignite. **2** illuminate, lighten, brighten.

like ADJECTIVE similar, alike, identical. *An opposite word is unlike.*

like VERB **1** love, adore, have a soft spot for, be fond of, admire, respect, cherish. **2** prefer, choose, wish for, want, fancy.

likely ADJECTIVE probable, expected, liable.

likeness NOUN similarity, resemblance, image, portrait.

limit VERB restrict, curb, confine, hinder.

limp ADJECTIVE hobble, stumble, shuffle.

linger VERB dawdle, loiter, delay, hang about/hang around (US), tarry, lag. *An opposite word is hurry.*

link VERB connect, join, unite, bind, fasten, attach.

liquid ADJECTIVE fluid, flowing, runny.

lithe ADJECTIVE flexible, supple, pliable.

litter NOUN rubbish, debris, junk, waste, garbage.

little ADJECTIVE **1** small, compact, tiny, minute, wee. **2** brief, fleeting. *Opposite words* are **1** big. **2** lengthy.

live VERB **1** exist, survive. **2** dwell, reside, inhabit, occupy.

livelihood NOUN living, occupation. *See also* **job**.

lively 1 ADJECTIVE energetic, active, sprightly, animated, agile, frisky, busy, bustling. *An opposite word is lazy.* **2** bright, vivid. *Lively patterns.*

livid ADJECTIVE enraged. *See also* **angry**.

load VERB fill, pack, burden, pile up, encumber.

loathe VERB despise, abhor. *See also* **hate**.

local ADJECTIVE district, regional, provincial, parish, community.

locate VERB **1** discover, detect, unearth, find. **2** situate, establish, place. *Their house is located to the north of town.*

lock NOUN and VERB bolt, latch, padlock. *An opposite word is unlock.*

locked up

lodge VERB **1** stay, reside, dwell, inhabit, settle, shelter. **2** fix, get stuck in. *A fishbone lodged in his throat.*

loiter VERB *See* **linger**.

lonely ADJECTIVE **1** lonesome, unhappy. **2** remote, isolated, solitary, out of the way.

long ADJECTIVE lengthy, extensive, extended, prolonged, protracted, endless. *Opposite words* are short, quick.

long for VERB want, wish, yearn for, fancy, crave.

look VERB **1** gaze, see, regard, watch, stare, peer, observe, notice. **2** seem, appear. *The teacher looks angry.*

look after VERB protect.

look for VERB search, try to find.

look up to VERB admire, respect. *He's always looked up to his older brother.*

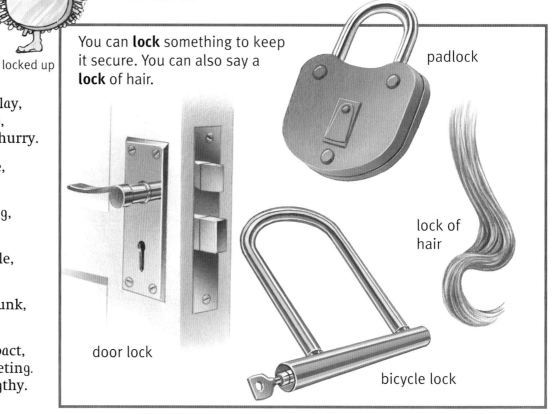

You can **lock** something to keep it secure. You can also say a **lock** of hair.

door lock

padlock

lock of hair

bicycle lock

Cupid, messenger of love

loom VERB appear, threaten, menace.

loop NOUN circle, noose, ring, hoop.

loose ADJECTIVE **1** flabby, baggy, slack, hanging, not tight, wobbly. *My little sister has another loose tooth.* **2** free, unattached. *The horse got loose and nearly ran out into the road.* **3** vague, indefinite, inaccurate.

lose VERB **1** misplace, mislay. **2** fail, to be beaten, be defeated. *Opposite words* are **1** find. **2** win.

lot NOUN **1** plenty, abundance. **2** fate, fortune.

loud ADJECTIVE **1** noisy, deafening, earpiercing, shrill, raucous. **2** strong, clear, powerful. *She has got such a loud voice.* **3** showy, brash, garish. *Opposite words* are **1**, **2** quiet, soft. **3** subdued, tasteful. Some different sounds: bang, boom, crash, howl, roar, shriek, uproar.

lovable ADJECTIVE dear, likeable, attractive, endearing, charming, sweet, amiable, winning. An *opposite word* is hateful.

love VERB adore, like, worship. *See also* **like**.

lovely ADJECTIVE *See* **beautiful**.

low ADJECTIVE squat, shallow, short, stunted. An *opposite word* is high.

lower ADJECTIVE inferior, lesser.

lower VERB **1** let down, fall, descend, sink. **2** reduce, lessen, decrease.

loyal ADJECTIVE faithful, staunch, true, trustworthy. *Opposite words* are disloyal, treacherous.

lubricate VERB grease, oil, smoothe, ease.

lucid ADJECTIVE clear, plain, easy to understand, intelligible.

luck NOUN fortune, chance, fate, accident, coincidence, success.

lucky ADJECTIVE fortunate, favoured/favored (US), happy, timely. *Opposite words* are unhappy, unfortunate.

ludicrous ADJECTIVE *See* **funny**.

lug VERB drag, heave, tow, tug, haul, pull.

luggage NOUN baggage, belongings, suitcase, holdall. *Put your luggage outside the door.*

lump NOUN **1** swelling, bump, tumour. **2** chunk, clump, block, mass, piece. *The teacher started with a lump of brown clay and made it into an amazing sculpture in minutes.*

lunatic ADJECTIVE *See* **mad**.

lunge VERB thrust, attack, charge at, pounce. *The tigers pounced on the gazelle in the high grass.*

lure VERB attract, tempt, ensnare, seduce. *We lured the kittens in front of the camera with a saucer of milk. Opposite words* are repel, repulse.

lurid ADJECTIVE shocking, startling, grisly, graphic, sensational, dismal. *There was a lurid description of the crime in all the papers.*

lurk VERB prowl, slink, snoop, skulk.

lush ADJECTIVE rich, abundant, luxuriant, prolific, green. *The lush landscape seemed to stretch for miles in every direction.*

lusty ADJECTIVE robust, tough, sturdy, vigorous, strong, rugged. An *opposite word* is weak.

There are many symbols and tokens of **love.**

heart (a symbol of love)

Romeo and Juliet fell in love

engagement ring (a token of love)

luxury NOUN comfort, ease, pleasure, opulence, splendour/splendor (US). *We pampered ourselves in luxury all weekend at the resort.*

macabre ADJECTIVE hideous, gruesome, grim, horrible, sinister.

macaroni NOUN pasta. Some different kinds of pasta: cannelloni, conchiglie, fettucini, lasagne/lasagna (US), ravioli, spaghetti, tagliatelle, vermicelli.

machine NOUN apparatus, instrument, tool, contrivance, engine, machinery.

mad ADJECTIVE **1** insane, deranged, lunatic, mentally ill, unbalanced. **2** angry. *She was mad at me.* **3** stupid, irrational, foolish, absurd. *It's a totally mad idea.*

magazine NOUN periodical, journal, review.

magic NOUN sorcery, wizardry, witchcraft, enchantment, spells.

magnificent NOUN grand, majestic, impressive, splendid, imposing. *Opposite words* are simple, plain.

magnify VERB enlarge, increase, amplify, boost, increase. An *opposite word* is reduce.

mail NOUN **1** post, correspondence, letters. **2** armour/armor (US). A word with a similar sound is male.

main ADJECTIVE principal, key, chief, basic, first, leading, most important. *Opposite words* are minor, secondary.

maintain VERB **1** look after, care for, support, provide for. **2** state, insist, assert, declare, affirm. *She maintained she was right.*

majestic ADJECTIVE splendid, imposing, grand, noble, dignified. *Opposite words* are unimportant, unimpressive.

major ADJECTIVE leading, important, bigger, larger, chief. An *opposite word* is minor.

majority NOUN most, bulk, mass, greater number, preponderance. An *opposite word* is minority.

make VERB **1** create, invent. **2** build, construct, put up. **3** manufacture, put together, form, mould/mold (US), shape. **4** add up, total, equal. **5** force, oblige, compel. *They made him clean his room.* **6** cause, produce, bring about. *The wind made the door slam.* **7** prepare. *If you make breakfast, I'll make lunch and dinner.* **8** compose, comprise. **9** get, earn. *He makes a lot of money.*

make for VERB go towards.

make believe NOUN fantasy.

makeshift ADJECTIVE rough and ready, temporary. *They arranged a makeshift shelter in the forest.*

malady NOUN *See* illness.

male NOUN masculine, manly. An *opposite word* is female.

malicious ADJECTIVE spiteful, bitter, hateful, bad, evil. *They've been spreading malicious stories.* An *opposite word* is kind.

maltreat VERB abuse, injure, ill-treat, harm, hurt, bully. An *opposite word* is help.

mammoth ADJECTIVE huge, enormous, massive, giant. An *opposite word* is small.

manage VERB **1** control, run, direct, be in charge of, look after, administer. **2** succeed, accomplish. *Do you really think you'll manage to finish on time?* **3** cope with, get along. *He is deaf but he manages very well.*

manager NOUN boss, director, controller, overseer, chief.

mangle VERB maim, disfigure, twist, maul.

mania NOUN craze, obsession, fad, enthusiasm. *Snowboarding at our school is an absolute mania now.*

Here are three very different kinds of **machine.**

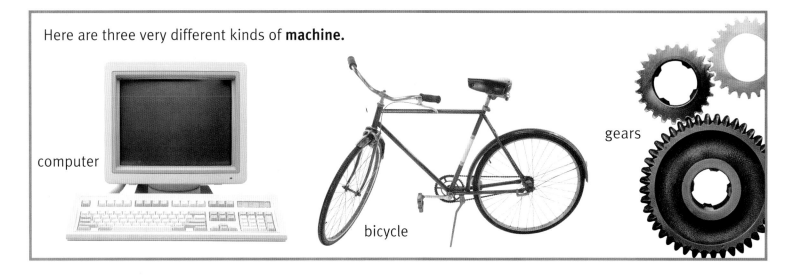

computer

bicycle

gears

manifest VERB show, reveal, declare, signify. An *opposite word* is hide.

manner NOUN style, way, fashion. *He has a rude manner.* A word that sounds similar is manor.

manners plural NOUN conduct, behaviour/behavior (US).

manor NOUN *See* **home.**

manslaughter NOUN homicide, *See also* **kill.**

manual ADJECTIVE automatic, by hand, hand-operated.

manual NOUN handbook, guide.

manufacture VERB make, produce, fabricate, build, turn out.

many ADJECTIVE numerous, various, a large number, sundry. An *opposite word* is few.

map NOUN chart, plan, diagram.

mar VERB damage, spoil, blemish, disfigure, scar.

march VERB **1** stride, walk, step out, trek. **2** parade, demonstration.

margin NOUN edge, limit, verge, border, rim, brink. An *opposite word* is centre/center (US).

marine ADJECTIVE maritime, naval, oceanic, nautical.

mariner NOUN sailor, seafarer, deckhand, seadog, tar.

mark VERB **1** notice, observe, note, see. **2** scratch, stain, blot. **3** grade, assess.

maroon VERB abandon, desert, leave. An *opposite word* is rescue.

marriage NOUN wedding, wedlock, matrimony, nuptials. An *opposite word* is divorce.

marry VERB get married, wed, join in matrimony.

A **mask** can be worn for protection or disguise.

surgeon's mask

ancient Greek tragedy mask

African carved ivory mask

marsh NOUN swamp, bog, morass, quagmire.

martial ADJECTIVE military, warlike, militant, belligerent. An *opposite word* is peaceful.

marvel NOUN wonder, spectacle, miracle.

marvellous/marvelous (US) ADJECTIVE wonderful, spectacular, splendid, fabulous, extraordinary.

masculine ADJECTIVE *See* **male.**

mask NOUN conceal, disguise, camouflage, cloak, veil, cover.

mass NOUN **1** load, lump, pile, quantity, mound. *A mass of paperwork.* **2** majority.

massacre VERB *See* **kill.**

massive ADJECTIVE huge, bulky, heavy, enormous, vast. *Opposite words* are small, little, light.

master VERB **1** control, tame, overcome, defeat. **2** learn, understand, grasp, get the hang of. *Japanese is difficult to master.*

match VERB **1** equal, copy, resemble, measure up to. **2** go with, suit, tone with.

match NOUN contest, competition, game.

mate NOUN companion, friend, pal, colleague, spouse, husband, wife.

mate VERB breed, pair, couple.

material NOUN **1** cloth, fabric, textile, stuff. **2** substance, matter, stuff. **3** information.

mathematics NOUN Words used in mathematics: **1** add up, divide, multiply, subtract, take away, times. **2** calculate, count, measure, work out. **3** digit, fraction, minus, plus. **4** circumference, diameter, radius. **5** angle, area, diagonal.

matrimony NOUN marriage, wedlock, nuptials.

matted ADJECTIVE tangled, twisted. *The dog's coat was matted.*

matter NOUN **1** substance, material. *Vegetable matter.* **2** problem, difficulty, worry, trouble. *What is the matter?* **3** topic, subject. *A matter for discussion.*

mature ADJECTIVE adult, grown-up, fully grown, developed, ripe. An *opposite word* is immature.

in disguise (mask)

maul VERB injure, hurt, beat, deform, abuse, rough up.

maxim NOUN saying, adage, proverb, rule.

meadow NOUN field, paddock, pasture, grassland.

meagre/meager (US) ADJECTIVE poor, scanty, sparse, insubstantial.

meal NOUN **1** repast, snack, banquet, feast. **2** breakfast, brunch lunch, tea (UK), dinner, supper, picnic, barbecue, take-away.

mean ADJECTIVE **1** stingy, selfish. **2** cruel, unkind. *Opposite words* are **1** generous, **2** kind.

mean VERB **1** stand for, convey, indicate. *What does this Italian word mean?* **2** intend, plan. *I meant to give you this.*

measurement NOUN size, dimension, height, depth, width, volume. Some ways of measuring: **1** inch, foot, yard, mile. **2** millimetre/ millimeter (US), centimetre/ centimeter (US), metre/meter (US), kilometre/kilometer (US). **3** square foot, square yard, square mile, acre. **4** pint, gallon, litre/liter (US).

mechanism NOUN **1** motor, machinery, workings, contrivance. **2** method, means, procedure, functioning.

meddle VERB interfere, tamper, butt in. A word that sounds similar is medal.

media NOUN press, newspapers, radio, television, internet.

medicine NOUN drug, medication, remedy, potion, tablet, pill, suppository, injection.

mediocre ADJECTIVE average, ordinary, middling, medium, inferior, commonplace. An *opposite word* is excellent.

medium ADJECTIVE average, normal, mediocre.

medley NOUN mixture, assortment, variety, collection, miscellany, jumble.

meek ADJECTIVE humble, modest, lowly, unassuming, docile. An *opposite word* is arrogant.

meet VERB **1** join, come together, converge. **2** encounter, run into, bump into. **3** gather, assemble. *Opposite words* are **1** diverge, **2** miss, **3** scatter.

meeting NOUN assembly, gathering, congregation, conference.

melancholy NOUN sad, unhappy, dejected, gloomy, miserable, downcast. An *opposite word* is joyful.

mellow ADJECTIVE mature, sweet, mild, melodious, smooth, soft.

melt VERB thaw, dissolve, liquefy. *Opposite words* are harden, freeze.

memorable ADJECTIVE unforgettable, famous, celebrated, outstanding.

memory NOUN remembrance, recall, recollection. An *opposite word* is forgetfulness.

menace VERB threaten, frighten, intimidate, alarm.

mend VERB repair, fix, restore, rectify, darn, patch, recover, heal. *His bone is mending. Opposite words* are damage, break.

mental ADJECTIVE **1** Intellectual, theoretical, abstract. *Mental powers.* **2** insane, loony. *See also* **mad**.

merchandise NOUN goods, produce, wares, commodities, cargo, freight.

merchant NOUN trader, dealer, retailer, shopkeeper, wholesaler, vendor.

merciless ADJECTIVE pitiless, callous, cruel, ruthless, unforgiving. *Opposite words* are merciful, compassionate.

mercy NOUN pity, forgiveness, compassion, clemency, kindness. An *opposite word* is cruelty.

merge VERB meld, combine, blend, amalgamate, join together.

merry ADJECTIVE jolly, cheerful, happy, jovial, lively. *Opposite words* are sad, gloomy.

mess NOUN **1** clutter, disorder, confusion, jumble, muddle, chaos.

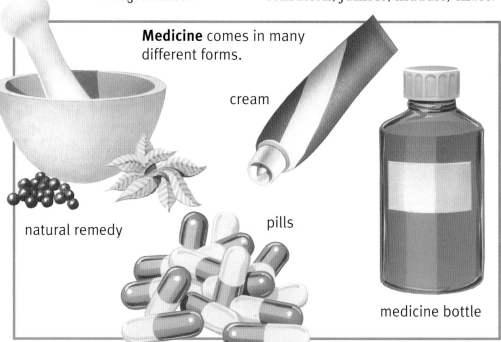

Medicine comes in many different forms.

cream

natural remedy

pills

medicine bottle

message NOUN letter, note, missive.

metal NOUN Some different metals: aluminium/aluminum (US), brass, bronze, copper, chromium, gold, iron, lead, mercury, nickel, platinum, silver, tin, zinc.

method NOUN system, way, manner, technique, mode.

middle NOUN centre/center (US), heart, midpoint, core.

mighty ADJECTIVE strong, powerful, dynamic, potent. *Opposite words* are weak, frail.

mild ADJECTIVE gentle, pleasant, warm, slight, calm. An *opposite word* is harsh.

militant ADJECTIVE aggressive, fighting, belligerent, contending. An *opposite word* is peaceful.

mimic VERB ape, copy, imitate, impersonate, take off.

mince VERB dice, grind, chop, cut up, hash. A word that sounds similar is mints.

mind NOUN **1** brain, understanding, wits, intelligence. **2** opinion. *She changed her mind.*

mind VERB **1** worry, care. *Do you mind if I open the window?* **2** care for, look after. *She is minding the children.* **3** Pay attention, obey, listen to, heed. *Mind your mother!*

mindless ADJECTIVE thoughtless, stupid.

mineral NOUN Some common minerals: alabaster, asbestos, blacklead, borax, calamine, calcite, chalcedony, chalk, chlorite, cinnabar, corundum, dolomite, feldspar, fluorite, galena, graphite, gypsum, jet, lapis lazuli, magnetite, malachite, mica, plumbago, quartz, rock salt, rutile, saltpetre, silica, talc, uranite, zircon.

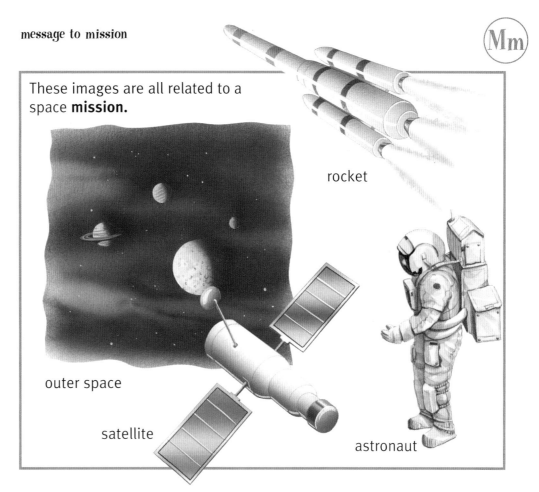

These images are all related to a space **mission.**

outer space

satellite

rocket

astronaut

mingle VERB mix, combine, blend, merge, join in.

minimize VERB **1** diminish, reduce. **2** belittle, discount, play down. An *opposite word* is maximize.

minimum NOUN least, smallest, slightest. An *opposite word* is maximum.

minor ADJECTIVE smaller, inferior, lesser, unimportant, trivial. *Opposite words* are major, important. A word that sounds similar is miner.

minute ADJECTIVE little, small, tiny, miniscule, wee, microscopic. *Opposite words* are large, gigantic. **2** precise, exacting. *Minute detail.*

mire NOUN mud, slime, filth, ooze, clay.

mirth NOUN laughter, fun, jollity, merriment, glee. *Opposite words* are gloom, seriousness.

misbehave VERB disobey, be naughty, offend, behave badly.

mischief NOUN naughtiness, pranks, devilment, harm, injury.

miserable ADJECTIVE **1** sad, unhappy, wretched. **2** awful, bad, poor.

misery NOUN grief, suffering, distress, sorrow, sadness.

misfortune NOUN bad luck, adversity, hardship, disaster, blow, trouble. An *opposite word* is success.

mislay VERB lose, misplace. An *opposite word* is find.

mislead VERB trick, delude, deceive, lead astray, fool.

miss VERB **1** avoid, dodge, steer clear of. **2** pine for. **3** omit, skip, leave out.

mission NOUN undertaking, assignment, errand, duty, job, business, crusade.

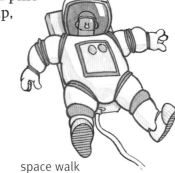

space walk

mist NOUN fog, vapour/vapor (US), cloud, haze. A word that sounds similar is missed.

mistake NOUN error, blunder, fault, gaffe, slip.

mistaken ADJECTIVE incorrect, inexact, wrong, erroneous. An *opposite word* is correct.

mistreat VERB abuse, harm, hurt, batter, maltreat.

misty ADJECTIVE hazy, dim, fuzzy, unclear. An *opposite word* is clear.

mix VERB blend, combine, mingle, shuffle, stir, jumble, scramble.

mixture NOUN blend, combination, variety, assortment, miscellany.

moan VERB groan, lament, wail, whimper, grumble, whine.

mob NOUN crowd, throng, rabble, flock, group, collection.

mock VERB tease, ridicule, taunt, make fun of.

model NOUN **1** pattern, prototype, copy, replica. **2** style, version, design, type. *They've bought a new model of car.*

moderate ADJECTIVE normal, ordinary, medium.

modern ADJECTIVE up-to-date, fashionable, new, recent.

modest ADJECTIVE humble, shy, bashful.

modify VERB amend, change, alter, revise, adjust.

moist ADJECTIVE damp, humid, dank, wet, clammy. An *opposite word* is dry.

molest VERB torment, tease, pester, annoy, harry, vex, upset, badger, harm, hurt.

moment NOUN second, tick, instant, jiffy. *See you in a moment.*

momentous ADJECTIVE important, notable, outstanding, serious. *Opposite words* are unimportant, insignificant.

monarch NOUN king, queen, emperor, empress.

money NOUN **1** cash, coin, banknote (UK)/bill (US), currency, change. **2** wealth, fortune.

monotonous ADJECTIVE boring, tedious, dull, uninteresting, repetitive. *Opposite words* are lively, interesting.

monster NOUN ogre, beast, vampire, werewolf.

month NOUN January, February, March, April, May, June, July, August, September, October, November, December.

mood NOUN temper, humour/humor (US), feeling, state of mind, *He is in a really bad mood.*

moody ADJECTIVE temperamental, morose, peevish, perverse, sullen.

moor VERB fasten, fix, berth, tie up. *Moor the boat.*

mope VERB be sad, grieve, pine, sulk, brood.

moral ADJECTIVE honest, good, virtuous. An *opposite word* is immoral.

more ADJECTIVE additional, extra, greater, further. *They're making more noise than usual.*

more ADVERB **1** again. *I saw her once more.* **2** longer, better. *You must try to make more of an effort.* An *opposite word* is less.

moreover ADVERB also, in addition, besides, also.

morgue NOUN *See* **mortuary**.

morose ADJECTIVE sullen, sulky, brooding, moody, sour. An *opposite word* is cheerful.

morsel NOUN scrap, bit, piece, fragment, fraction, nibble.

mortal ADJECTIVE **1** human, perishable, temporal, feeble. *We are mere mortals.* **2** deadly, fatal, lethal. *It was a mortal wound.*

mortuary NOUN morgue, necropolis, cemetery.

Here are two forms of **money.**

banknotes/bills (US)

coins

mostly ADVERB mainly, principally, usually, chiefly. An *opposite word* is seldom.

motherly ADJECTIVE maternal, loving, caring, gentle, tender.

motion NOUN **1** movement, action, change. **2** proposal, suggestion. *A motion to change the speed limit.*

motive NOUN reason, cause, purpose, inspiration, spur.

motto NOUN axiom, saying, adage, maxim, slogan.

mould/mold (US) VERB form, model, shape, fashion.

mouldy/moldy (US) ADJECTIVE bad, putrid, musty, off, stale, decaying. An *opposite word* is fresh.

mound NOUN pile, hillock, rise, embankment. *Every Sunday she walks along the river embankment.*

mount VERB **1** get on, clamber on, ascend, go up, rise. **2** exhibit, display. *Stamps mounted in an album.*

mountain NOUN peak, summit, volcano, elevation, pile.

mourn VERB grieve, sorrow, lament, regret, bewail. An *opposite word* is rejoice.

mournful NOUN sad, unhappy, sombre, melancholy. *Opposite words* are cheerful, happy.

mouth NOUN opening, aperture, orifice, gap, estuary.

move VERB **1** leave, go away, depart, quit. **2** go forward, proceed, advance, travel, walk. **3** run, race, gallop, rush. **4** stir, budge, shift. **5** take away, remove, disturb, carry, transport.

movement NOUN **1** action, motion, move, change. **2** party, group, cause, crusade. *The peace movement.* **3** section of music.

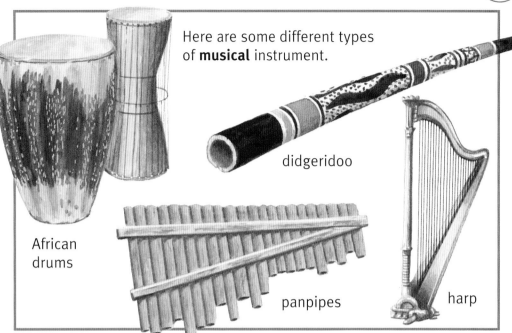

Here are some different types of **musical** instrument.

didgeridoo

African drums

panpipes

harp

moving ADJECTIVE stirring, emotional, thrilling, touching.

mow VERB cut, crop, scythe.

muck NOUN mud, filth, dirt, manure, dung.

muddle VERB **1** mix up, tangle, jumble. **2** bewilder, confuse.

mug VERB attack, rob, beat up.

multiply VERB increase, grow, spread, extend, reproduce, breed. An *opposite word* is decrease.

mumble VERB mutter, murmur.

munch VERB *See* **eat.**

murder VERB *See* **kill.**

murky ADJECTIVE dark, gloomy, cloudy, overcast. *Opposite words* are clear, bright.

murmur VERB whisper, mutter, mumble, grumble, complain.

muse VERB ponder, think about, meditate, reflect, cogitate.

music NOUN tune, melody.

musical notes

musical ADJECTIVE melodic, harmonious, dulcet, sweet. Musical instruments include: accordian, banjo, castanets, cello, clarinet, cymbals, drums, flute, guitar, horn, kazoo, lute, oboe, organ, piano, recorder, saxophone, trombone, trumpet, violin, xylophone.

musician NOUN player, performer, busker, singer, vocalist. *The musician worked hard for little money.*

mute ADJECTIVE dumb, speechless, voiceless, silent, quiet. An *opposite word* is loud.

mutilate VERB damage, maim, injure, disfigure, wound.

mutiny NOUN rebellion, uprising, riot, revolt, insurrection. *There was a mutiny on board the boat.*

mutter VERB mumble, murmur, grouse, complain.

mutual ADJECTIVE common, reciprocal, joint, shared. *A mutual admiration.*

muzzle VERB stifle, gag, suppress.

mysterious ADJECTIVE **1** strange, puzzling. **2** weird, ghostly, eerie.

Nn

nag VERB pester, annoy, badger, go on about, henpeck.

nail VERB fix, peg, fasten, hammer in.

naive ADJECTIVE innocent, simple, unsophisticated, gullible.

naked ADJECTIVE nude, bare, unclothed.

name NOUN **1** title, label, designation. **2** reputation, character, fame. *He's making a name for himself.*

name VERB call, christen, term, entitle, dub. **2** indicate, specify. *He named the culprit.*

nap VERB sleep, doze, snooze, rest.

narrate VERB tell, describe, recount, relate.

narrow ADJECTIVE fine, thin, slender, limited, tight, cramped. An *opposite word* is wide.

narrow-minded ADJECTIVE biased, bigoted, intolerant. An *opposite word* is broad-minded.

nasty ADJECTIVE **1** bad, dreadful, horrible, offensive, unpleasant, offensive. **2** dirty, filthy, foul. **3** unfriendly, unkind rude, mean, vicious. An *opposite word* is nice.

natter VERB chatter, gossip.

natural ADJECTIVE **1** normal, usual, common. **2** inborn, instinctive, hereditary. **3** frank, open, genuine, unsophisticated, artless. *Opposite words* are **1** unnatural, **2** learned, **3** artificial.

naughty ADJECTIVE bad, unruly, disobedient, mischievous. *Opposite words* are well-behaved, good.

nausea NOUN sickness, queasiness, squeamishness.

nautical ADJECTIVE *See* **naval.**

naval ADJECTIVE maritime, nautical, marine, seafaring.

navigate VERB sail, pilot, steer, guide, direct.

nearly ADVERB almost, not quite, practically, roughly.

neat ADJECTIVE smart, tidy, orderly, spruce. *Opposite words* are untidy, sloppy.

need NOUN necessity, shortage.

need VERB **1** want, require, call for. **2** rely on, depend on, count on.

needy ADJECTIVE poor, needful, penniless, destitute. An *opposite word* is rich.

neglect VERB ignore, overlook, forget. An *opposite word* is look after.

negotiate VERB bargain, haggle, mediate, deal, talk about, discuss.

neighbourhood/neighborhood (US) NOUN district, area, locality, surroundings.

nervous ADJECTIVE anxious, fidgety, edgy. An *opposite word* is calm.

nest NOUN burrow, den, lair.

net NOUN mesh, net, trap, snare.

neutral ADJECTIVE **1** impartial, unbiased, fair, even-minded. **2** dull, mediocre.

never ADVERB not ever, at no time, under no circumstances. An *opposite word* is always.

new ADJECTIVE **1** unused, fresh. **2** novel, original, unfamiliar. **3** modern, recent, just out, up-to-date, latest. *Opposite words* are second-hand, old-fashioned, out of date, stale, old.

news NOUN information, report, bulletin, account.

Travellers used to look at the stars to **navigate.** Today, sophisticated equipment is used. No one knows how migrating birds **navigate.**

bird migration

stars

radar

orienteering equipment

nibble VERB bite, peck, gnaw. *See also* **eat.**

nice ADJECTIVE **1** beautiful, fine, lovely, attractive, pretty, pleasant, good. **2** delicious, tasty, scrumptious **3** friendly, warm, kind, likeable, considerate, good-natured. **4** comfortable, cosy. *A nice, warm bed.* **5** smart (UK), stylish. *A nice new dress.*

nimble ADJECTIVE spry, agile, nippy, lively, swift. *Opposite words are* slow, clumsy.

nip VERB cut, bite, pinch.

nobility NOUN **1** aristocracy, gentry, nobles. **2** dignity, majesty, eminence, worthiness. *Opposite words are* **1** hoi polloi, common people. **2** meanness.

nod VERB **1** beckon, signal, indicate, gesture, agree. **2** doze, sleep.

noisy ADJECTIVE loud, rowdy, deafening, boisterous. *Opposite words are* quiet, silent.

nomadic ADJECTIVE wandering, roving, migratory, itinerant. *The travellers led a nomadic lifestyle.*

none PRONOUN not one, not any, nobody. A word that sounds similar is nun.

nonsense NOUN rubbish, drivel, rot, trash, gobbledegook.

nook NOUN corner, alcove, niche, recess.

normal ADJECTIVE common, ordinary, usual, natural, average. An *opposite word* is abnormal.

nostalgic ADJECTIVE longing, yearning, homesick, wistful, sentimental.

notable ADJECTIVE remarkable, outstanding, famous, notable, momentous. An *opposite word* is commonplace.

note NOUN **1** letter, message. **2** signal, symbol. *A musical note.*

note VERB **1** remark, notice, observe. **2** record, write down.

notice VERB see, note, perceive, detect, observe. An *opposite word* is overlook.

notify VERB inform, tell, announce, declare, advise.

notion NOUN idea, thought, whim. *I had a notion you might think that.*

nought NOUN zero, nil, nothing, naught.

nourish VERB feed, support, sustain. An *opposite word* is starve.

novel ADJECTIVE new, fresh, original, innovative, uncommon, unusual. *Opposite words are* trite, familiar, hackneyed.

novice NOUN beginner, learner, pupil, tyro, apprentice.

now ADVERB **1** instantly, at this moment, immediately. **2** at this time, at present.

nude ADJECTIVE naked, bare, undressed, unclothed, stripped.

nudge VERB elbow, prod, poke, push.

nuisance NOUN bother, pest, trouble, worry, plague.

numb ADJECTIVE insensible, dead, frozen, unfeeling.

number NOUN figure, amount, quantity, total.

numerous ADJECTIVE many, several, abundant. *Opposite words are* few, scant.

nurse VERB care for, mind, tend, look after, nourish.

nut NOUN Some different kinds of nut: almond, brazil, cashew, chestnut, cobnut, coconut, hazelnut, peanut, pecan, pistachio, walnut.

nutty ADJECTIVE foolish. *See also* **mad.**

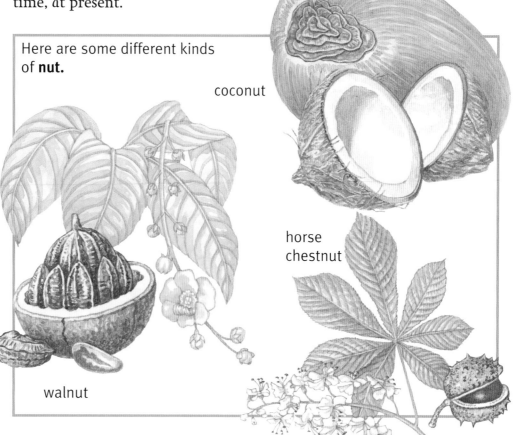

Here are some different kinds of **nut.**

coconut

horse chestnut

walnut

dolphin (ocean)

Oo

oath NOUN **1** promise, pledge, vow. **2** swear-word.

obedient ADJECTIVE well-behaved, law-abiding, deferential. *Opposite words* are rebellious, disobedient.

object NOUN **1** article, thing, item. *A useful object.* **2** target, purpose, mission, reason.

object VERB complain about, disapprove, oppose, mind.

objectionable ADJECTIVE offensive, disagreeable, unpleasant.

obliterate VERB wipe out, raze, erase, destroy, annihilate.

obnoxious ADJECTIVE disagreeable, disgusting, repulsive, unpleasant, horrid. An *opposite word* is pleasant.

obscene ADJECTIVE foul, dirty, unclean, indecent, smutty, coarse. An *opposite word* is decent.

obscure ADJECTIVE **1** dim, vague, hazy, indistinct. **2** puzzling, confusing. **3** little known.

observe VERB **1** watch, notice, perceive. **2** remark, mention. **3** keep, adhere to, comply. *Observing the speed limit.*

observer NOUN viewer, watcher, spectator, onlooker, bystander.

obsolete ADJECTIVE antiquated, old, out-of-date, disused.

obstacle NOUN hindrance, barrier, obstruction. An *opposite word* is help.

obstinate ADJECTIVE stubborn, pig-headed, dogged, mulish, headstrong.

obstruction NOUN *See* **obstacle**.

obtain VERB get, acquire, gain, achieve, earn.

obvious ADJECTIVE plain, clear, apparent, evident, unmistakable.

occasion NOUN **1** occurrence, event, incident. **2** opportunity, suitable time, chance.

occasional ADJECTIVE infrequent, rare, periodic. An *opposite word* is often.

occupation NOUN **1** job, work, business, employment. *See also* **job**. **2** activity, hobby. **3** possession, tenancy, occupancy.

occupied ADJECTIVE **1** settled, populated. **2** busy, employed.

occupy VERB **1** inhabit, live in, dwell, own, possess, keep. **2** engage, busy. **3** invade, capture. **4** use, fill. *Is this seat occupied?*

occur VERB happen, take place.

occurrence NOUN happening, event, incident.

ocean NOUN sea. Some famous seas and oceans: **1** Bering Sea, Black Sea, Caspian Sea, Irish Sea, Sea of Japan, South China Sea, Mediterranean Sea, North Sea. **2** Antarctic Ocean, Atlantic Ocean, Arctic Ocean, Indian Ocean, Pacific Ocean.

odd ADJECTIVE **1** curious, funny, peculiar, quaint, unusual, strange, weird. An *opposite word* is ordinary. **2** extra, spare, unmatched.

odious ADJECTIVE unpleasant, objectionable, loathsome, disgusting, hateful.

odour/odor (US) NOUN smell, aroma, fragrance, stench.

offend VERB **1** displease, insult, annoy, hurt. **2** sin, err. An *opposite word* is please.

offensive ADJECTIVE unpleasant, rude, hurtful, insulting.

The **ocean** is full of wildlife.

Atlantic Ocean

Pacific Ocean

Indian Ocean

Arctic Ocean

Antarctic Ocean

offence/offense (US) NOUN
1 crime, sin, misdeed.
2 insult, attack, injury.

offer VERB propose, put forward, present, submit. 2 volunteer.

office NOUN 1 bureau, work place.
2 responsibility, duty, job, position.

official ADJECTIVE authorized, formal, authoritative, proper, approved. An *opposite word* is unofficial.

officious ADJECTIVE meddlesome, self-important, pushy.

offspring NOUN child, children, heir, successor, descendant.

often ADVERB frequently, again and again, repeatedly. *Opposite words* are rarely, seldom.

ogre NOUN monster, fiend, devil, demon.

oil NOUN grease, fat, lubricant.

old ADJECTIVE 1 aged, elderly
2 out-of-date, old-fashioned.
3 stale. 4 worn out, shabby. 5 last, previous, former. *Opposite words* are 1 young, 2 fashionable, 3 fresh, 4 new, 5 present.

omen NOUN sign, warning, potent, premonition, augury.

ominous ADJECTIVE menacing, foreboding. An *opposite word* is auspicious.

omit VERB leave out, exclude, drop, overlook. An *opposite word* is include.

once ADVERB 1 one time. 2 in the past, previously, formerly.

onlooker NOUN *See* **observer.**

ooze VERB leak, exude, seep.

opaque ADJECTIVE clouded, murky, filmy, unclear, obscure. An *opposite word* is transparent.

Here are some things that are **old.**

old letters

old typewriter

ancient ruins

old telephone

open ADJECTIVE 1 frank, candid, sincere. 2 unfastened, unlocked, uncovered. 3 exposed, unsheltered.

open VERB 1 unlock, unfasten,undo. 2 begin, start.

opening NOUN 1 gap, crack, hole, space, aperture. 2 beginning, start, launch. *The opening of the new store.*
3 opportunity.

operate VERB use, work, handle, drive, manipulate. *Do you know how to operate a VCR?*

opinion NOUN view, thought, idea, belief, feeling. *In my opinion, we should cancel the meeting.*

opponent NOUN rival, competitor, adversary, challenger, enemy, foe. An *opposite word* is ally.

opportunity NOUN chance, occasion, break, scope.

oppose VERB resist, combat, stand against, confront, withstand, defy, fight. *We oppose all types of cruelty to animals.* An *opposite word* is support.

opposite ADJECTIVE 1 facing, fronting. 2 opposed, adverse, conflicting, different contrary. *They have completely opposite points of view.* An *opposite word* is similar.

opposition NOUN 1 hostility, resistance, antagonism, obstacle.
2 rival, opponent. *Opposition parties.*

oppress VERB overpower, overwhelm, crush, harass, persecute.

oppressive ADJECTIVE 1 stifling, airless, muggy, close. 2 tyrannical, overwhelming, cruel, savage. *Opposite words* 1 fresh, 2 mild.

opt VERB choose, select, prefer.

optimistic ADJECTIVE hopeful, cheerful, confident, bright. An *opposite word* is pessimistic.

option NOUN choice, selection, possibility, alternative.

opulent ADJECTIVE rich, wealthy, prosperous, affluent. An *opposite word* is poor.

oral ADJECTIVE spoken, said, verbal, unwritten. *There was an oral exam after the written test.*

oration NOUN speech, address, lecture, declamation.

orbit VERB circle, revolve. *Earth orbits the Sun.*

ordeal NOUN trial, torment, test, trouble, hardship. *They went through the whole ordeal of a trial.*

Oo

order NOUN **1** command, regulation, law, rule. **2** plan, pattern, arrangement. *In the right order.* **3** society, association, community. *An order of monks.*

order VERB **1** tell, command, instruct, direct. **2** arrange, control, classify. **3** ask for, send for.

ordinary ADJECTIVE usual, common, normal, customary, everyday, average, plain, simple. *Opposite word*s are unusual, extraordinary.

organize VERB arrange, order, establish, set up. *An opposite word is disorganize.*

organization NOUN **1** group, establishment, institute, society. **2** order, plan, pattern, system.

origin NOUN start, beginning, source, rise, root, cause. *An opposite word is end.*

original ADJECTIVE **1** first, aboriginal. **2** new, fresh, imaginative, novel. *Opposite word*s are **1** latest, **2** unoriginal.

ornament NOUN decoration, adornment, trinket, knick-knack, bauble.

ornate ADJECTIVE decorated, elaborate, adorned, showy, bedecked. *An opposite word is plain.*

orthodox ADJECTIVE conventional, accepted, traditional, recognized.

oscillate VERB swing, sway, vary.

oust VERB expel, eject, throw out, overthrow, dismiss.

outbreak NOUN **1** outburst, eruption, explosion. **2** rebellion, uprising, upsurge.

outcome NOUN result, consequence, conclusion, effect.

outing NOUN trip, day out, excursion, jaunt.

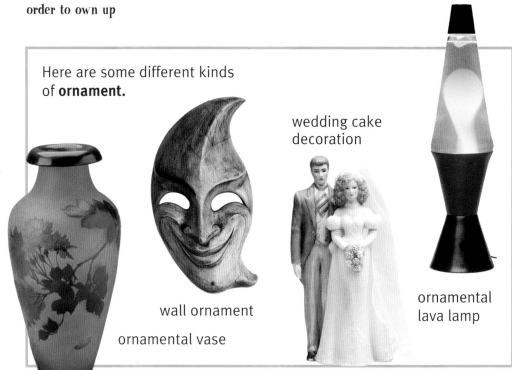

Here are some different kinds of **ornament**.

wedding cake decoration

wall ornament

ornamental vase

ornamental lava lamp

outlaw NOUN criminal, fugitive, bandit, desperado, highwayman.

outlet NOUN way out, exit, opening, vent.

outlook NOUN **1** view, scene, viewpoint, attitude. **2** chance, prospect, forecast. *The employment outlook is good.*

outrage NOUN fury, shock, anger, offence/offense (US). *The decision caused outrage.*

outskirts NOUN suburbs, borders, boundaries, edges.

outspoken ADJECTIVE frank, open, blunt, direct, straightforward. *Opposite word*s are reserved, diplomatic, secretive.

outstanding ADJECTIVE **1** notable, exceptional, noticeable, striking. **2** owing, unpaid. *An outstanding bill.* *Opposite word*s are **1** insignificant, ordinary.

overcome VERB conquer, overwhelm, defeat, overpower, subdue.

overflow VERB spill, run over, flood, inundate.

overhead ADVERB above.

overlook VERB **1** neglect, pass over, miss, ignore. **2** pardon, excuse, turn a blind eye. **3** look over, look onto. *They live in a beautiful house overlooking a lake.*

overseas ADJECTIVE abroad, foreign. *We have penpals overseas.*

oversight NOUN mistake, error, omission, blunder.

overtake VERB pass, catch up with, outdo.

overthrow VERB destroy, demolish, overwhelm, defeat, topple, beat, crush.

overturn VERB capsize, overbalance, keel over, abolish, set aside. *The raft overturned in the rapids.*

overwhelm VERB **1** *See* **overcome**. **2** confuse, overpower, inundate.

own VERB possess, have, keep. *My uncle doesn't own a television set and he refuses to buy one.*

own up VERB confess, admit, acknowledge.

pace NOUN step, rate, speed, tempo.

pacify VERB calm, placate, soothe, appease, soften. *Opposite words are anger, aggravate.*

pack NOUN *See* **package**.

pack VERB put, load, fill, cram.

package NOUN parcel, packet, bundle.

packed ADJECTIVE filled, full, crowded. A word that sounds similar is pact.

packet NOUN package, pack, parcel, box, carton, container.

pact NOUN agreement, treaty, contract, alliance. A word that sounds similar is pact.

pad NOUN cushion, pillow, bolster.

pad VERB fill, stuff, protect.

pad out VERB lengthen fill out.

paddock NOUN *See* field.

pageant NOUN parade, display, show, fair, spectacle, procession.

pain NOUN ache, sting, hurt, twinge, torment, torture, agony. A word that sounds similar is pane.

painful ADJECTIVE aching, hurting, sore, throbbing, stinging, distressing, unpleasant.

painstaking ADJECTIVE careful, diligent, thorough, scrupulous. *Opposite words are negligent, slipshod.*

paint NOUN colour/color (US), pigment, dye. Some different kinds of paint: eggshell, emulsion, enamel, gloss, matt, oil, poster.

paint VERB dye, tint, colour/color (US), embellish, decorate.

painting NOUN picture, mural, illustration, portrait, still-life, landscape.

pair NOUN two, couple, brace, twins, twain, duo. Words that sound similar are pare, pear.

pal NOUN *See* **friend**.

paperboy (paper)

palace NOUN mansion, castle, chateau.

pale ADJECTIVE **1** white, pasty, ashen, pallid, wan. **2** light, colourless/colorless (US), insipid. *Opposite words are* **1** ruddy, flushed. **2** dark.

pallid ADJECTIVE *See* **pale**.

pamper VERB spoil, pander to, indulge, cosset. An *opposite word* is neglect.

pamphlet NOUN leaflet, booklet, brochure.

pan NOUN pot, saucepan, frying pan, container.

panel NOUN board, group, committee, forum.

panic NOUN fear, terror, alarm, consternation, flap. *The real danger in a crisis is panic.* An *opposite word* is calmness.

panorama NOUN view, landscape, scenery, prospect.

pant VERB puff, gasp, blow, wheeze. *The runners were panting as they neared the end of the marathon.*

paper NOUN **1** newspaper, journal, periodical, tabloid, broadsheet. **2** document, report.

parade NOUN march, display, procession, pageant.

parcel NOUN bundle. *See* **package**.

parched ADJECTIVE dry, arid, thirsty, dehydrated.

pardon VERB forgive, let off, excuse, spare, reprieve.

Here are some different things used to make **packages.**

string

labels

brown paper

tape

pare VERB peel, skin, strip, trim, prune. Words that sound similar are pear, pair.

parent NOUN father, mother.

park NOUN enclosure, garden, grounds, green. Some different kinds of park: recreation ground, safari park, wildlife park.

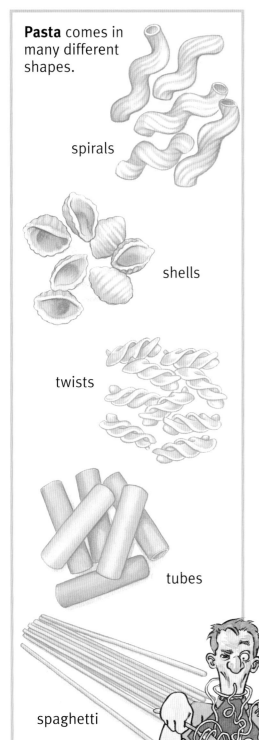

Pasta comes in many different shapes.

spirals

shells

twists

tubes

spaghetti

parliament NOUN assembly, congress, council. Some different names for parliament: Althing (Iceland), Congress (USA), Cortes (Spain), Dail (Ireland), Eduskunta (Finland), Folketing (Denmark), Knesset (Israel), Riksdag (Sweden), States General (Netherlands), Storting (Norway).

parody NOUN caricature, imitation, satire, spoof, burlesque.

part NOUN 1 piece, bit, component, fraction, portion, section, element, constituent. 2 area, district, region. 3 role, character. *A part in a play.*

part VERB 1 divide, separate, break. 2 leave, depart.

partial ADJECTIVE 1 incomplete, restricted, limited. 2 biased, favouring/favoring (US), unjust.

participate VERB take part, co-operate, contribute, share, help, partake.

particle NOUN speck, bit, morsel, fragment.

particular ADJECTIVE 1 individual, personal, private. 2 special, distinct, specific. *A particular time of day.* 3 fussy, choosy.

parting NOUN 1 leave-taking, departure, farewell. 2 separating, split. *A parting of the ways.*

partner NOUN companion, friend, colleague, helper.

party NOUN 1 festivity, celebration, get-together, dance, disco, ball, barbecue, wedding, birthday, anniversary. 2 group, faction, company. *The Green party.*

pass VERB 1 exceed, overtake. 2 experience, suffer. 3 cease, pass away, elapse. *Time passes quickly.* 4 enact, approve, authorize. 5 hand, transmit, give. *Please pass the salt.* 6 succeed. *Pass a test.*

pass away VERB die, expire.

pass out VERB faint, collapse.

pass over VERB ignore, disregard.

passage NOUN 1 corridor, hallway. 2 extract, section, quotation

passenger NOUN traveller/traveler (US), voyager, tripper, commuter.

passion NOUN enthusiasm, emotion, feeling, mania, craze.

past ADJECTIVE 1 done, finished, over. 2 previous, former. *Past president.*

pasta NOUN spaghetti, tagliatelli, tortellini, macaroni, lasagne/lasagna (US) cannelloni.

pat VERB tap, pet, fondle, touch, stroke.

path NOUN track, trail, footpath, lane, pavement, way, walkway bridleway.

pathetic ADJECTIVE 1 sad, pitiable, moving, lamentable. 2 worthless, useless, laughable. *A pathetic game.*

patient ADJECTIVE calm, long-suffering, uncomplaining, restrained. *Opposite words are impatient, intolerant.*

pattern NOUN 1 decoration, design, ornament, shape. 2 model, prototype, specimen.

pause VERB rest, stop, wait, hesitate, cease. *Opposite words are carry on, continue.*

pay VERB give, spend, settle, reward.

peaceful ADJECTIVE calm, quiet, restful, serene. *Opposite words are restless, turbulent, troubled, noisy.*

peculiar ADJECTIVE 1 odd, strange, unusual, funny, curious, bizarre. 2 special, characteristic.

peep VERB 1 look, glimpse, peer. 2 appear.

peer VERB look, examine, gaze, inspect. A word that sounds similar is pier.

penetrate VERB pierce, perforate, bore, pass through, cut, enter.

penetrating ADJECTIVE piercing, cutting, incisive, probing, perceptive, shrewd. *Opposite words* are blunt, stupid.

penniless ADJECTIVE poor, destitute, needy, broke. An *opposite word* is rich.

people NOUN human beings, populace, population, inhabitants, folk, tribe, nation.

perceive VERB 1 observe, see, notice. 2 understand, grasp discern, appreciate.

perception NOUN understanding, feeling, awareness.

perch VERB roost, rest, settle.

percussion ADJECTIVE crash, clash, collision. Some percussion instruments: bongo drums, cymbals, chimes, drum, kettledrum, snare drum, triangle, gong, xylophone.

perfect ADJECTIVE 1 ideal, excellent, faultless, flawless. 2 exact, precise. An *opposite word* is imperfect.

perform VERB act, 1 take part, play, appear in, sing. 2 do, achieve, carry out, accomplish, function.

performance NOUN 1 presentation, show, production. *There are two performances on Saturdays.* 2 behaviour/behavior (US), operation, work, action. *His performance at work has been disappointing.*

perfume NOUN scent. *See also* **smell**.

perhaps ADVERB possibly, maybe. An *opposite word* is certainly.

Here are some different kinds of animals that make good **pets.**

rabbit

hamster

dog

cat

peril NOUN danger, risk, hazard, risk, jeopardy, uncertainty.

period NOUN time, term, span, era, age, phase.

periodical NOUN *See* **paper**.

perish VERB rot, decay, wither, shrivel, die.

permanent ADJECTIVE lasting, stable, durable, perpetual, enduring. *Opposite words* are temporary, transient, fleeting.

permission NOUN approval, consent, leave, authorization. An *opposite word* is prohibition.

permit VERB let, allow, approve of, agree to. An *opposite word* is forbid.

perpetrate VERB do, carry out, commit, execute, perform, inflict.

perplex VERB bewilder, baffle, puzzle, confound.

persecute VERB harass, hunt, chase, torment, pester, hound.

persist VERB continue, carry on, persevere, remain.

person NOUN individual, human, being, character, man, woman, child.

perspective NOUN outlook, view, angle, standpoint, point of view.

perspire VERB sweat, drip.

persuade VERB tempt, urge, coax, entice, cajole, talk into. An *opposite word* is dissuade.

perturb VERB bother, trouble, disturb, upset, worry, alarm, distress. An *opposite word* is compose.

peruse VERB study, pore over, examine, inspect, scrutinize.

pervade VERB fill, permeate, spread, saturate.

perverse ADJECTIVE stubborn, obstinate, wilful, contrary. An *opposite word* is reasonable.

pessimistic ADJECTIVE gloomy, cynical, despondent, defeatist, downhearted. An *opposite word* is optimistic.

pester VERB annoy, worry, harass, nag, get at, trouble.

pet NOUN favourite/favorite (US), darling, idol. Some animals that people keep as pets: canary, cat, dog, gerbil, goldfish, hamster, parrot, rabbit, tortoise.

petty ADJECTIVE 1 small, unimportant, insignificant, trifling, paltry. An *opposite word* is important. 2 mean (UK), miserly. *She's petty about money.*

phase NOUN angle, view, aspect, period, stage.

philanthropic ADJECTIVE kind, charitable, benevolent, generous, unselfish. *Opposite words* are selfish, misanthropic.

philistine ADJECTIVE vulgar, uncouth, materialistic.

phobia NOUN dread, obsession, dislike, aversion. Some common phobias: acrophobia (heights), agoraphobia (open spaces), bibliophobia (books), claustrophobia (confined spaces), haemophobia (blood), homophobia (homosexuals), hydrophobia (water), necrophobia (corpses), ornithophobia (birds), xenophobia (foreigners), zoophobia (animals).

phone VERB telephone, call, ring.

photograph NOUN picture, snap, slide, transparency.

physician NOUN doctor, medic, healer, quack.

pick VERB 1 choose, select, elect. 2 pluck, collect, gather, harvest.

picture NOUN drawing, illustration, painting, photograph, snapshot, portrait, sketch, diagram, mural, collage.

picturesque ADJECTIVE pretty, attractive, scenic, pictorial, quaint.

piece NOUN bit, fragment, part, portion, sliver, chip, chunk.

pierce VERB penetrate, puncture, go through, prick, perforate.

pig NOUN 1 swine, hog, boar, sow. 2 glutton.

pigment NOUN *See* **colour/color (US)**.

pile NOUN heap, mound, mass, stack, collection.

pilgrim NOUN traveller, wanderer.

pillar NOUN column, post, support, mast.

pinch VERB 1 nip, squeeze, hurt. 2 *See* **steal**.

pioneer NOUN innovator, frontiersman/woman, explorer, trail-blazer.

pious ADJECTIVE holy, religious, saintly, godly. An *opposite word* is ungodly.

pipe NOUN hose, tube, conduit.

pit NOUN mine, well, hollow, hole, cavity.

pitch VERB 1 toss, hurl, throw, fling. 2 fall, plunge, drop. 3 erect, set up. *Let's pitch the tent here.*

pitiless ADJECTIVE ruthless, merciless, cruel. *Opposite words* are kind, merciful.

pity NOUN mercy, sympathy, compassion.

place NOUN 1 site, position, location, spot. 2 area, region, district, city, town. 3 home, dwelling, residence.

placid ADJECTIVE calm, composed, serene, mild.

plague NOUN 1 disease, pestilence, epidemic. 2 nuisance, bother, affliction, thorn in the side.

plain ADJECTIVE 1 simple, ordinary, everyday. 2 clear, obvious, definite. A word that sounds similar is plane. *Opposite words* are 1 ornate, 2 complicated.

plan NOUN 1 project, idea, scheme, proposal. 2 map, diagram, drawing, chart.

plane NOUN *See* **aircraft**. A word that sounds similar is plain.

planet NOUN The Sun's planets are: Earth, Mars, Jupiter, Saturn, Uranus, Venus, Mercury, Pluto, Neptune.

plant NOUN Some different kinds of plant: algae, aquatic plants, cacti, ferns, flowering plants, fungi, grasses, lichen, moss, shrubs, trees, vegetables.

play VERB 1 perform. *She's playing the violin.* 2 amuse yourself, have fun, sport, frolic.

plead VERB beg, implore, ask for, request.

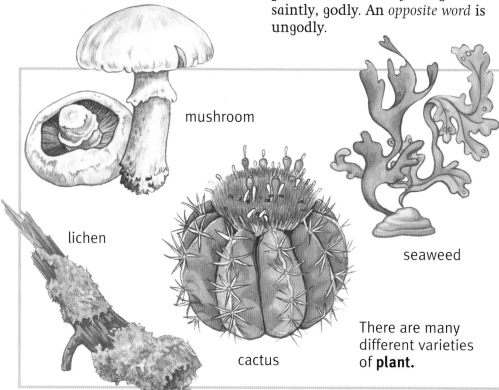

mushroom

lichen

cactus

seaweed

There are many different varieties of **plant.**

polluted atmosphere

pleasant ADJECTIVE
1 agreeable, cheerful, enjoyable, pleasing, nice. **2** friendly, kind, likeable. *They're pleasant people.* **3** fine, mild, warm. *Pleasant weather.* **4** attractive, peaceful, pretty. *A pleasant house.*

pleasure NOUN enjoyment, happiness, joy, delight, amusement, entertainment.

pledge NOUN promise, guarantee, vow, undertaking.

plenty ADJECTIVE abundance, lots of, loads of, enough. *Opposite words* are scarcity, need.

pliable ADJECTIVE flexible, pliant, bendable, supple.

plight NOUN difficulty, trouble, predicament, dilemma.

plod VERB trudge, lumber, labour/labor (US), slog.

plot NOUN story, theme, outline.

plot VERB conspire, plan, scheme, devise, scheme.

pluck VERB pick, gather, collect, snatch.

plump ADJECTIVE fleshy, portly, fat, round, corpulent, chubby. *Opposite words* are skinny, thin.

plunge VERB dive, jump, leap, drop, submerge, dip.

ply VERB use, employ, practise/practice (US).

poach VERB steal, pilfer, trespass, filch.

poetry VERB verse, rhyme. Some different kinds of poetry: ballad, limerick, lyric, haiku, sonnet, ode.

poignant ADJECTIVE bitter, sharp, distressing, piercing, moving.

---

point NOUN **1** spike, tip, end. **2** purpose, object, intent. *The point of studying hard.*

point VERB aim, direct, level, indicate, show.

pointless ADJECTIVE aimless, futile, meaningless.

poison NOUN pollute, contaminate, infect, taint, corrupt.

poke VERB prod, jab, dig, thrust, shove, nudge.

poky ADJECTIVE cramped, uncomfortable, small. *A poky little room.*

policy NOUN plan, tactics, stratagem, programme/program (US), strategy, procedure.

polished ADJECTIVE shiny, sparkling, bright, glossy, burnished. An *opposite word* is dull.

polite ADJECTIVE well-mannered, well-behaved, considerate, civil. *Opposite words* are rude, impolite.

polluted ADJECTIVE poisoned, contaminated, infected, defiled, adulterated.

pompous ADJECTIVE proud, pretentious, bombastic, self-important, flaunting. *Opposite words* are unassuming, modest.

pond NOUN *See* **pool**.

ponder VERB consider, study, contemplate, reflect.

pool NOUN pond, lake, swimming pool, puddle, loch, lough, lagoon.

poor ADJECTIVE **1** hard-up, broke, poverty-stricken, impoverished, penniless, needy, destitute. An *opposite word* is rich. **2** bad, inferior, faulty, third-rate. **3** barren, unproductive, infertile. *Poor soil.*

poorly ADJECTIVE ill, unwell, sick, under the weather, seedy. An *opposite word* is healthy.

Here are some things that make our environment **polluted.**

factory smoke

car fumes

deforestation

rubbish/litter

popular ADJECTIVE liked, well-known, admired, accepted, sought after, famous. An *opposite word* is unpopular, disliked.

port NOUN harbour/ harbor (US), haven, dock, anchorage.

portion NOUN helping, part, piece, share, slice. An *opposite word* is whole.

portly ADJECTIVE large, stout, plump, burly. *Opposite words* are slim, slender.

portrait NOUN picture, likeness, drawing, sketch.

pose VERB stand, affect, feign, pretend, model.

position NOUN **1** place, situation, spot, site. **2** posture, pose. **3** job, post, occupation. **4** rank, status, standing.

possess VERB have, own, hold, enjoy, occupy.

possession NOUN belongings, property.

post NOUN **1** column, pillar, pole, prop, support. **2** mail.

postpone VERB put off, defer, hold over, shelve, adjourn, delay, put on ice.

poultry NOUN Some different kinds of poultry: chicken, duck, goose, turkey.

pounce VERB strike, swoop, fall on, jump on, attack.

pour VERB **1** empty, tip, spill. *He poured water down the drain.* **2** flow, run, gush, stream.

poverty NOUN penury, hardship, impoverishment, need, distress, lack. An *opposite word* is wealth.

powerful ADJECTIVE mighty, strong, robust, potent, high-powered, leading. *Opposite words* are weak, powerless, impotent.

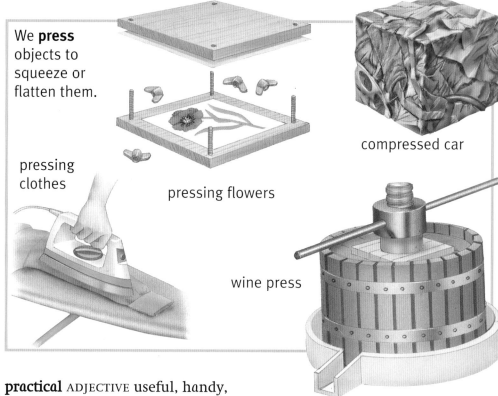

We **press** objects to squeeze or flatten them.

pressing clothes

pressing flowers

compressed car

wine press

practical ADJECTIVE useful, handy, efficient, workable. An *opposite word* is useless.

practise/practice (US) VERB **1** train, rehearse, exercise. **2** carry out, perform, do, pursue. *She practises medicine.*

pragmatic ADJECTIVE realistic, sensible, business-like. *Opposite words* are romantic, unrealistic.

praise VERB congratulate, praise, admire, compliment, applaud, flatter. An *opposite word* is criticize.

prattle VERB chatter, chunter, gossip, gabble, witter.

pray VERB beg, call on, ask, entreat, worship, beseech.

precaution NOUN care, wariness, safeguard, prudence.

precede VERB lead, come before, herald, head, go first. An *opposite word* is succeed.

precious ADJECTIVE costly, expensive, valuable, priceless. An *opposite word* is worthless.

precise ADJECTIVE exact, scrupulous, accurate, formal, strict.

predict VERB foretell, forecast, prophesy, project.

prefer VERB fancy, favour/favor (US), like better, select, support.

prejudice NOUN bias, partiality, unfairness, bigotry, discrimination. An *opposite word* is fairness.

premises NOUN grounds, buildings, property, site.

preoccupied ADJECTIVE distracted, involved in, engrossed, wrapped up, day-dreaming.

prepare VERB get ready, organize, plan, arrange, study. *She's busy preparing for an exam.*

preposterous ADJECTIVE absurd, ridiculous, unbelievable, unreasonable. An *opposite word* is reasonable.

prescribe VERB recommend, order, decree, rule, command, specify.

present NOUN gift, offering.

present VERB **1** award, hand over, give, bestow. **2** introduce. **3** exhibit, show.

presently ADVERB **1** soon, shortly, directly. **2** at present, now.

press VERB **1** push. **2** flatten, iron, smooth. **3** squeeze, compress, crush.

presume VERB suppose, take for granted, believe.

pretend VERB **1** act, impersonate, trick, imitate, bluff. **2** claim, aspire.

pretty ADJECTIVE beautiful, lovely, pleasing, dainty, attractive. *Opposite words* are plain, ugly.

prevent VERB stop, hinder, impede, slow down, ward off. *Opposite words* are cause, help.

previous ADJECTIVE former, preceding, earlier. *Opposite words* are later, subsequent.

previously ADVERB before, formerly, earlier.

price NOUN fee, cost, charge, payment, value, expense.

priceless ADJECTIVE invaluable, precious, prized.

prick VERB pierce, puncture, bore, perforate.

pride NOUN **1** self-respect, dignity. An *opposite word* is humility. **2** conceit, vanity, arrogance.

prim ADJECTIVE formal, stiff, prudish, priggish.

primary ADJECTIVE **1** earliest, first, original, beginning, basic, fundamental. **2** main, principal, leading, chief. An *opposite word* is secondary.

prime ADJECTIVE **1** best, excellent, first-class, choice. **2** principal, chief.

primitive ADJECTIVE early, rudimentary, simple, old, crude, prehistoric. *Opposite words* are cultivated, cultured, sophisticated.

principal ADJECTIVE chief, important, main, key, foremost. An *opposite word* is minor.

principle NOUN **1** law, rule, doctrine, code. **2** honour/honor (US), virtue, integrity.

print VERB imprint, mark, stamp, reproduce, copy.

prisoner NOUN captive, inmate, convict.

private ADJECTIVE personal, secret, confidential, hidden. An *opposite word* is public.

prize NOUN award, bounty, reward, recompense, trophy.

prize VERB cherish, esteem, value.

probe VERB **1** investigate, explore, examine, look into. **2** poke, prod.

problem NOUN **1** difficulty, dilemma, question, worry. **2** puzzle, question, enigma. An *opposite word* is solution.

proceed VERB **1** go forward, advance, progress. **2** arise, derive.

process NOUN method, procedure, way, technique.

procession NOUN march, parade, cavalcade, motorcade.

proclaim VERB announce, declare, make known.

procure VERB obtain, buy, get, purchase, secure, gain.

prod VERB poke, jab, dig, nudge, shove, stimulate.

prodigal ADJECTIVE wasteful, spendthrift, reckless, extravagant. An *opposite word* is thrifty.

produce VERB **1** make, create, manufacture, originate, invent. **2** publish, bring out, present.

production NOUN **1** manufacture, creation, construction, assembly. **2** presentation, staging. *The first production of the play.*

productive ADJECTIVE fruitful, creative, worthwhile, constructive. *Opposite words* are wasteful, useless.

profession NOUN occupation, career, calling, employment.

profound ADJECTIVE deep, penetrating, weighty, serious, shrewd. *It was a profound concept.*

progress VERB move forward, proceed, advance, make headway, improve. *Progress was slow but steady throughout the meeting.*

progressive ADJECTIVE advanced, forward-looking, increasing, growing.

Here are some different types of **print.**

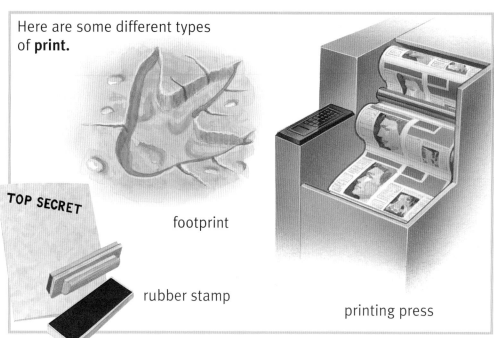

footprint

rubber stamp

printing press

prohibit VERB forbid, bar, deny, ban, hinder, veto, prevent. An *opposite word* is allow.

project NOUN plan, scheme, task, job, idea, proposal.

project VERB **1** forecast, predict, estimate. **2** protrude, jut out. **3** fling, throw.

prolong VERB lengthen, protract, draw out, extend. *Opposite words* are shorten, curtail.

prominent ADJECTIVE **1** noticeable, outstanding. *Prominent features.* **2** famous, distinguished, celebrated. *Opposite words* are insignificant, unknown.

promise VERB give your word, swear, vow, agree, pledge, undertake.

promote VERB publicize, advertise, sell, market, support, sponsor.

prompt ADJECTIVE punctual, on time, ready, alert. *Opposite words* are slow, late.

prone ADJECTIVE **1** face down, horizontal. **2** inclined, disposed to, liable, likely.

pronounce VERB **1** say, speak, utter, express. **2** declare, proclaim, decree. *I pronounce you man and wife.*

prop VERB lean, rest, stand, support, uphold.

propel VERB thrust, push, drive, shove, launch, shoot.

proper ADJECTIVE **1** correct, fit, appropriate, suitable. **2** decent, respectable.

prophesy VERB foretell, augur. *See also* **predict**.

proposal NOUN scheme, suggestion, project, offer, proposition.

propose VERB **1** recommend, suggest, offer, put forward. **2** mean to, intend. *He proposes to go on a trip around the world.*

prosaic ADJECTIVE ordinary, commonplace, everyday, uninspiring, unimaginative.

prosecute VERB sue, accuse, summon, put on trial, try. An *opposite word* is defend.

prospect NOUN hope, expectation, chance, likelihood, future, outlook.

prosperous ADJECTIVE, thriving, booming, successful, rich, wealthy. An *opposite word* is unsuccessful.

protect VERB **1** defend, guard, look after, preserve. **2** screen, shield, shelter. *Opposite words* are attack, endanger.

protective ADJECTIVE shielding, sheltering, defensive.

protest VERB object, complain, oppose, dispute, disagree.

prototype NOUN model, original, pattern.

proud ADJECTIVE **1** happy, pleased, honoured/honored (US). **2** boastful, arrogant, conceited, vain.

prove VERB show, demonstrate, verify, justify, confirm. An *opposite word* is disprove.

provide VERB supply, give, procure, furnish, equip.

provoke VERB **1** anger, upset, worry, irritate, annoy. **2** cause, give rise to, incite. *The announcement provoked an uprising.*

prowl VERB lurk, roam, rove, stalk.

prune VERB *see* **cut**.

pry VERB interfere, meddle, peep, snoop.

public ADJECTIVE general, national, common, communal, open, unrestricted, well-known, popular. An *opposite word* is private.

puddle NOUN *See* **pool**.

pull VERB **1** drag, tug, haul, tow, draw, heave. **2** stretch. *Pull the heavy table across the room.* **3** hitch. *Pull up your socks.* An *opposite word* is push.

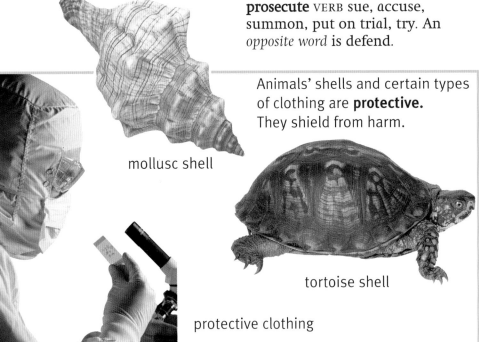

Animals' shells and certain types of clothing are **protective.** They shield from harm.

mollusc shell

tortoise shell

protective clothing

pull down VERB destroy, demolish.

pull through VERB recover, survive.

pull up VERB stop, halt.

punch VERB **1** hit, strike, bash, beat, rap, thump. **2** perforate, bore, puncture. *The machine punched the ticket.*

punctual ADJECTIVE prompt, on time, exact.

punish VERB scold, penalize, discipline, correct, flog, fine. An *opposite word* is reward.

puny ADJECTIVE weak, feeble, frail, stunted, insignificant. *Opposite words* are strong, sturdy.

pupil NOUN student, scholar, learner, beginner, schoolboy, schoolgirl.

purchase VERB buy, obtain, get, earn, procure. An *opposite word* is sell.

pure ADJECTIVE **1** clean, clear, natural, unpolluted. An *opposite word* is dirty. **2** real, undiluted, unmixed, neat. **3** chaste, blameless, innocent.

purge VERB **1** purify, cleanse. **2** eliminate, exterminate, kill, get rid of.

purpose NOUN **1** plan, reason, intent, object. **2** use, application, function. **3** determination, will.

purify VERB clear, clean, wash, cleanse, refine, purge. An *opposite word* is pollute.

pursue VERB **1** follow, chase after, hunt, harry. **2** carry on, continue, conduct. *Pursue an occupation.*

pursuit NOUN **1** hunt, chase, search, race. **2** occupation, vocation.

push VERB **1** shove, press, force, crush, propel. **2** poke, prod, nudge.

push off VERB go away.

push on VERB go on, continue.

push over VERB cause to fall, topple.

put VERB place, deposit, store, position, set out, lay, rest. An *opposite word* is remove.

put aside VERB save, preserve. *Let's put some of these aside for later.*

put away VERB replace, return.

put down VERB **1** note, record. *Start by putting down everything you know about the subject, then try to put each point in order of importance.* **2** defeat, crush, humiliate.

put on VERB **1** dress. **2** present, display. *We put on an exhibition of our science projects at school this year.*

put off VERB postpone, delay.

put on VERB **1** dress. **2** present, display.

put out VERB **1** stretch. **2** extinguish. **3** dislocate.

put through VERB connect by telephone.

put together VERB assemble, construct.

put up VERB erect.

put up with VERB endure, bear, tolerate, stomach.

putrid ADJECTIVE rotten, stinking, decayed, rancid, bad.

puzzle NOUN problem, riddle, question, enigma, crossword, brain-teaser, conundrum.

puzzle VERB confuse, mystify, perplex.

Here are some different kinds of **puzzle.**

crossword puzzle

mathematical puzzle

jigsaw puzzle

Qq

quagmire NOUN bog, marsh, swamp, mire.

quail VERB tremble, quake, back away, cower, tremble.

quaint ADJECTIVE unusual, curious, strange, picturesque, old-fashioned.

quake VERB shake, shudder, quail, tremble, quiver.

qualification NOUN 1 competence, suitability, ability, fitness. 2 condition, limitation, stipulation. *We agree with the plan with certain qualifications.*

quality NOUN 1 peculiarity, characteristic, attribute. 2 grade, standard, value, worth, goodness. *High quality goods.*

quandary NOUN dilemma, plight, difficulty, predicament.

quantity NOUN amount, volume, portion, sum, share.

quarrel VERB argue, disagree, fall out, fight, squabble, bicker. An *opposite word* is agree.

quaver VERB shake, tremble, oscillate, vibrate, shudder, sway.

quay NOUN jetty, pier, landing-stage, harbour/harbor (US).

queasy ADJECTIVE sick, nauseous, squeamish, groggy.

queer ADJECTIVE 1 strange, unusual, odd, funny, weird, peculiar. 2 suspicious, dubious.

quell VERB quash, crush, suppress, overcome, extinguish.

quench VERB 1 satisfy, slake, cool. *Quench your thirst.* 2 put out, extinguish, douse. *Quench the flames.*

query VERB question, ask, enquire, dispute, doubt, challenge. An *opposite word* is accept.

quest NOUN search, hunt, chase, adventure.

question VERB inquire, ask, demand, query, interrogate, quiz. An *opposite word* is answer.

quibble VERB argue, carp, bicker.

quick ADJECTIVE 1 fast, rapid, speedy, swift, express. 2 instant, prompt, immediate. *A quick answer.* 3 nimble, sprightly, brisk, lively, agile. 4 sharp, shrewd, quick-witted. *Opposite words are* 1 slow, 2 dull, unintelligent.

quiet ADJECTIVE 1 noiseless, still, peaceful, calm, tranquil, restful, hushed. 2 shy, meek, mild. *Opposite words are* noisy, loud.

quilt NOUN eiderdown, duvet, blanket, bedspread.

quip NOUN joke, wisecrack, witticism.

quirk NOUN whim, fancy, oddity, idiosyncrasy, notion.

quit VERB leave, go, abandon, stop, cease, give up, surrender, renounce.

quite ADVERB 1 totally, wholly, absolutely, utterly. *Quite certain.* 2 rather, fairly, moderately.

quiver VERB tremble, shake, quake, shudder, wobble.

quiz NOUN test, puzzle, riddle, enigma, questionnaire.

quota NOUN share, portion, allowance, ration.

quote VERB 1 cite, mention, recite, name, repeat. *He quoted from Shakespeare.* 2 suggest, estimate. *He quoted a price for the car.*

The cyclist and the cheetah are both going fast. The stopwatch can tell you how **quick** they are.

cheetah

stopwatch

cyclist

Rr

rainbow

rabble NOUN
crowd, mob, riff-raff.

race NOUN **1** nation, clan, tribe, people, ancestry. **2** chase, match, contest, sprint, steeplechase.

race VERB dash, run, sprint, speed, scamper.

racket NOUN noise, row, tumult, din, uproar.

radiant ADJECTIVE bright, beaming, brilliant, shining, splendid. An *opposite word* is dull.

radiate VERB emit, shine, beam, glow, spread, diffuse.

rage NOUN **1** anger, fury, wrath. **2** fad, fashion, vogue.

rail NOUN bar, railing, fence.

railway/railroad (US) NOUN Some different kinds of train: diesel, electric, steam, goods or freight, underground.

rain NOUN shower, drizzle, downpour, squall, precipitation. Words that sound similar are reign, rein.

rainbow NOUN The colours/colors (US) of the rainbow are: red, orange, yellow, green, blue, indigo, violet.

raise VERB **1** lift, heave, hoist, pick up. **2** collect, obtain, make, get. **3** rear, bring up, grow. A word that sounds similar is raze.

rake VERB scrape, scour, collect, assemble.

rally VERB **1** meet, gather, convene, congregate. **2** recover, get better.

ramble VERB stroll, wander, hike, trek, amble. **2** ramble, digress. *His mind is rambling.*

ramshackle ADJECTIVE rickety, tumbledown, unstable, decrepit. An *opposite word* is stable.

rancid ADJECTIVE sour, bad, off, rank, fetid, rotten.

random ADJECTIVE haphazard, chance, accidental, aimless.

range NOUN **1** scale, gamut, scope, extent. **2** variety, class, sort. *There is a wide range to choose from.*

ransack VERB plunder, rife, sack, pillage.

rapid ADJECTIVE fast, quick, speedy, swift. An *opposite word* is slow.

rare ADJECTIVE **1** scarce, uncommon, sparse. **2** excellent, choice, incomparable. *It is an object of rare beauty.*

rash ADJECTIVE hasty, reckless, headstrong, impetuous, impulsive, hot-headed. *Opposite words* are cautious, wary.

rate NOUN **1** speed, velocity. **2** charge, cost, tariff, tax, duty. **3** proportion, ratio, degree.

rather ADVERB **1** fairly, quite, moderately. **2** preferably, more.

ration NOUN portion, allowance, share, helping.

raucous ADJECTIVE, hoarse, rasping, rough, grating.

rave VERB **1** rage, storm, fume, rant. **2** enthuse, favour/favor (US). *They absolutely raved about the book.*

ravenous ADJECTIVE starving, hungry, voracious, famished.

raw ADJECTIVE **1** uncooked, fresh. **2** green, immature. **3** cold, freezing, biting.

ray NOUN beam, flash, shaft, glimmer.

raze VERB obliterate, destroy, level, flatten. Words that sound similar are rays, raise.

reach VERB **1** stretch, extend. **2** arrive, get to, attain.

read VERB study, interpret, peruse, decipher, understand. A word with a similar sound is reed.

ready ADJECTIVE **1** prepared, waiting, willing, prompt. **2** available, convenient handy. *Opposite words* are **1** unprepared. **2** inaccessible.

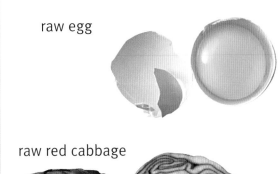

raw egg

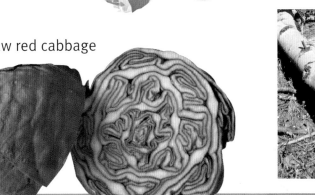

raw red cabbage

Here are some objects described as **raw.**

wood (a raw material)

Rr

realistic ADJECTIVE **1** life-like, natural. *A realistic portrait.* **2** practical, sensible, down-to-earth, pragmatic. *Realistic plans. Opposite words* are **1** unrealistic, **2** impractical.

realm NOUN kingdom, empire, state, territory, land, sphere, domain.

rear ADJECTIVE back, end, bottom, tail. *An opposite word* is front.

rear VERB raise, bring up, look after, cultivate.

reason NOUN **1** explanation, motive, cause, excuse. **2** intellect, sense, mind, brain, understanding.

reasonable ADJECTIVE **1** fair, moderate, average. **2** sensible, intelligent, wise, practical.

rebel VERB disobey, revolt, rise, mutiny. *Opposite words* are support, conform.

rebellion NOUN uprising, mutiny, insurrection, rising.

rebuke VERB scold, blame, reprimand, tell off. *An opposite word* is praise.

recall VERB remember, recollect. *An opposite word* is forget.

receive VERB **1** get, earn, obtain, acquire. **2** welcome, greet, let in.

rollerblading (recreation)

recent ADJECTIVE new, up-to-date, latest, modern. *Opposite words* are old, dated.

recite VERB relate, tell, narrate, describe, repeat, perform, declaim. *She was able to recite the poem exactly.*

reckless ADJECTIVE careless, thoughtless, rash. *An opposite word* is careful.

reckon VERB **1** add up, calculate, count, estimate. **2** think, consider, suppose, feel sure, believe, judge.

reclaim VERB recover, rescue, retrieve, regain, salvage.

recline VERB lean back, rest, repose.

recognize VERB know, remember, identify.

recollect VERB recall. *See also* **remember.**

recommend VERB **1** approve of, praise. **2** advise, suggest.

record NOUN diary, account, description, journal, log, minutes.

recover VERB **1** get better, improve. **2** get back, retrieve, find.

recreation NOUN enjoyment, fun, relaxation, amusement, pastime.

recuperate VERB get better, convalesce, rally, mend.

recur VERB reoccur, return, repeat.

reduce VERB lessen, cut, decrease, shrink, weaken.

redundant ADJECTIVE **1** out of work, unemployed. **2** surplus, unnecessary, excess.

reel VERB totter, sway, stagger, spin.

refer VERB **1** consult, look up. *Refer to a dictionary.* **2** comment on, mention. **3** concern, relate, pertain. **4** direct, transfer. *The child was referred to a specialist.*

reform VERB **1** improve, correct, better. **2** remodel, reconstruct, reorganize, revamp.

refuge NOUN asylum, shelter, protection, sanctuary.

refuse NOUN rubbish, junk, waste, dregs, litter, trash.

refuse VERB decline, reject, spurn, turn down, exclude. *Refuse entry. Opposite words* are agree, accept.

regal ADJECTIVE royal, majestic, noble, stately, kingly, queenly.

Here are some different kinds of **recreation.**

reading

playing football

sun bathing

walking

94

regard VERB think of, consider, notice, value, respect. An *opposite word* is disregard.

region NOUN district, area, territory, place, province, zone.

register VERB and NOUN record.

regret VERB repent, be sad about, grieve, mourn, apologize.

regular ADJECTIVE 1 even, steady, unchanging, uniform. *A regular drum beat.* 2 usual, normal, customary. *Opposite words are* 1 variable. 2 unusual.

regulate VERB adjust, correct, control, arrange, manage, govern.

rehearse VERB practise, prepare, repeat, run through, go over, train.

reinforce VERB strengthen, support, fortify, toughen.

reject VERB turn down, decline, refuse, scrap, throw out. An *opposite word* is accept.

rejoice VERB celebrate, exult, revel.

relapse VERB get worse, weaken, deteriorate, fall back, regress. An *opposite word* is improve.

relate VERB 1 describe, narrate, tell, report, mention. 2 connect, link, concern. *There was an unresolved matter relating to her death.*

relation NOUN 1 relative, kinsman, kinswoman, family. 2 link, connection, bearing.

relax VERB 1 rest, unwind. 2 weaken, slacken, loosen. An *opposite word* is 2 tighten.

release VERB 1 free, let loose, liberate, unfasten. 2 publish, circulate. *Opposite words are* 1 imprison, detain, arrest.

relentless ADJECTIVE remorseless, persistent, ruthless, cruel, unremitting. *Opposite words are* humane, merciful.

There are many sacred objects that are part of **religion.**

buddha

mosque

Hindu shrine

Star of David

reliable ADJECTIVE loyal, dependable, trustworthy, faithful, honest, staunch. *Opposite words are* unreliable, shaky, erratic.

relief NOUN help, ease, aid, support, assistance, comfort, release.

relieve VERB comfort, ease, smooth, alleviate, cure, lessen.

religion NOUN creed, belief, faith. Some of the main religions of the world: Branches of Christianity: Anglican, Baptist, Roman Catholic, Methodist, Orthodox, Presbyterian, Church of Scotland, Quaker, Unitarian. Other religions: Buddhism, Hinduism, Islam, Judaism, Sikhism, Taoism.

religious ADJECTIVE holy, devout, pious, godly, faithful, saintly, sacred.

reluctant ADJECTIVE unwilling, disinclined, hesitant, loath. *Opposite words are* willing, ready.

rely VERB depend on, count on, trust, swear by, believe in.

remain VERB 1 stay, stop, wait. 2 continue, last, persist, endure.

remainder NOUN balance, surplus, rest, remnant, residue.

remains NOUN remainders, relics, remnants, leftovers, dregs, ashes.

remark VERB 1 say, observe, mention, utter. 2 notice, regard, note.

remarkable ADJECTIVE unusual, amazing, extraordinary, outstanding, striking. *Opposite words are* ordinary, commonplace.

remember VERB recall, recollect, memorize. An *opposite word* is forget.

remind VERB jog the memory, prompt, nudge.

remnant NOUN *See* **remainder**.

remorse NOUN sorrow, regret, contrition, guilt, shame.

remove VERB 1 get rid of, take away. 2 extract, take out, wash off.

renew VERB restore, rebuild, renovate, mend, repair, rejuvenate.

renown ADJECTIVE fame, glory, celebrity, repute.

repair VERB mend, fix, put right, renovate, restore, make good, sew, darn, patch. *Opposite words are* break, shatter.

Rr

repay VERB **1** reimburse, refund. *Repay a debt.* **2** revenge, avenge, retaliate.

repel VERB **1** drive off, repulse, push back, oppose, withstand. *The two magnets repelled each other.* **2** revolt, disgust, nauseate.

replace VERB **1** substitute, supplant, succeed. **2** put back, restore, reinstate.

replica NOUN reproduction, facsimile, copy, likeness. An *opposite word* is original.

reply VERB answer, respond to, acknowledge.

report VERB announce, declare, state, tell, notify, publish.

repose VERB rest, sleep, recline.

represent VERB stand for, symbolize, depict, portray.

repress VERB control, curb, suppress, subdue, crush, overpower, hold back, bottle up.

reprieve VERB pardon, let off, acquit.

reprimand VERB rebuke, blame, scold, tell off, chide, admonish.*The teacher had to reprimand his pupils.*

reproduce VERB **1** imitate, mimic, copy, duplicate. **2** breed, multiply, generate.

reptile NOUN Some different kinds of reptile: alligator, crocodile, lizard, snake, tortoise, turtle.

repugnant ADJECTIVE repellent, revolting, repulsive, sickening, distasteful, horrible, hideous. *Opposite words* are pleasant, agreeable.

repulsive ADJECTIVE *See* **repugnant**.

reputation NOUN name, character, fame, renown, standing, good name, regard, repute.

request VERB ask for, beg for, appeal for, beseech, entreat.

require VERB need, desire, lack, want.

rescue VERB save, salvage, deliver, release, set free.

research VERB examine, study, explore, scrutinize, investigate.

resemble VERB look like, be similar to, take after. An *opposite word* is differ.

reserve VERB **1** keep, save, hold, hoard. **2** book, order, secure. *Let's reserve some tickets.*

reserved ADJECTIVE shy, withdrawn, secretive, aloof, distant. *Opposite words* are friendly, open.

reside VERB live, inhabit, dwell, occupy, lodge.

resign VERB leave, quit, abandon, give up, step down, surrender, renounce, abdicate.

resist VERB oppose, confront, defy, fight. An *opposite word* is submit.

resolve VERB **1** decide, determine, make up one's mind. **2** decipher, unravel, solve.

respect NOUN consideration, admiration.

respond VERB reply, answer, retort.

responsible ADJECTIVE answerable, guilty. *See also* **reliable**.

responsibility NOUN duty, obligation, burden, fault, blame.

rest NOUN **1** remainder, remnant. **2** break, pause, breather, repose, siesta, sleep.

rest VERB **1** relax, lie down, sleep, repose. **2** lean, prop.

restful ADJECTIVE relaxing, peaceful, quiet, calm. *Opposite words* are restless, disturbing.

restore VERB **1** mend, repair, renovate, renew, rebuild. **2** replace, reinstate. **3** refresh.

restrain VERB curb, repress, hold back, check, prevent, stop. *Opposite words* are encourage, impel.

Here are some different kinds of **reptile.**

snake

crocodile

lizard

restrict VERB limit, confine, control, restrain. *Opposite words* are amplify, free.

result NOUN effect, consequence, outcome, upshot, product. An *opposite word* is cause.

retain VERB keep, hold on to, withhold, save.

retire VERB *See* **retreat**.

retreat VERB run away, go back, depart, shrink. An *opposite word* is advance.

return VERB **1** come back. **2** repay, give back.

reveal VERB show, disclose, make known, divulge, tell, uncover.

revenge NOUN get one's own back, avenge, retaliate.

reverse VERB **1** go backwards, turn, retreat. **2** change, alter. *Reverse the usual order.*

review VERB examine, assess, criticize, survey, judge, reconsider.

revise VERB alter, amend, correct.

revolution NOUN **1** rotation, orbit, circle. **2** rebellion, uprising, revolt, riot, rising, reformation.

revolve VERB spin, rotate, circle, orbit, turn, swivel.

reward VERB prize, award, bonus, payment, honour/honor (US).

rich ADJECTIVE wealthy, prosperous. An *opposite word* is poor.

ride VERB travel, journey, move, trot, pedal.

ridiculous ADJECTIVE absurd, funny, laughable, comic, ludicrous, silly.

rigid ADJECTIVE **1** stiff, unbending, firm. **2** austere, stern.

right ADJECTIVE **1** correct, accurate, true, exact. **2** fair, honest, good, just. **3** appropriate, suitable. An *opposite word* is **1** wrong. A word that sounds similar is rite.

rim NOUN border, edge, lip, brim, flange.

ring VERB **1** chime, jingle, tinkle, peal. **2** call, telephone, phone. A word that sounds similar is wring.

rinse VERB wash, clean, swill, bathe.

riot NOUN disturbance. *See also* **revolution**.

rip VERB tear, split, slit, slash.

ripe ADJECTIVE mature, grown, mellow, developed, ready. An *opposite word* is immature.

rise VERB **1** climb, go up, ascend, lift, soar, take off, tower. **2** increase, escalate, jump. *Prices have risen since the last election.* **3** get up, stand up. *Opposite words* are **1** descend, **2** decrease, **3** sit down.

risk NOUN chance, danger, peril, jeopardy, possibility.

rival ADJECTIVE opposing, competing.

rival NOUN opponent, competitor. *Opposite words* are partner, associate.

river NOUN brook, stream, waterway, torrent, bourn.

road NOUN Some different kinds of roads and paths: alley, avenue, boulevard, bridleway, bypass, drive, lane, motorway/freeway (US), expressway (US), highway, pavement/sidewalk (US), ring road/beltline (US), street, thoroughfare, towpath, track.

roam VERB wander, stroll, meander, range, rove, drift.

roar VERB blare, bellow, cry, yell, boom.

roast VERB *See* **cook**.

rob VERB steal, loot, pilfer, plunder, pillage, rifle, strip, denude.

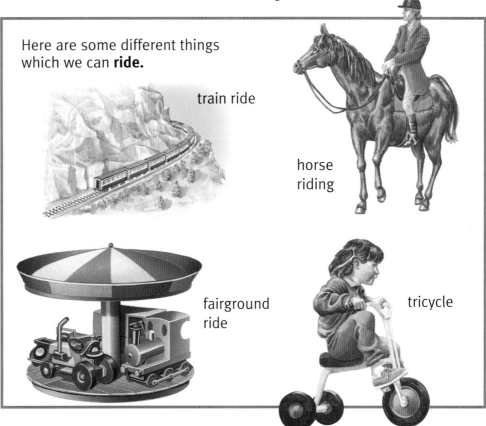

Here are some different things which we can **ride.**

train ride

horse riding

fairground ride

tricycle

robust ADJECTIVE strong, sturdy, stout, muscular, vigorous.

rock NOUN stone, boulder. Some different kinds of rock: aggregate, basalt, chalk, conglomerate, dolomite, gneiss, igneous, limestone, metamorphic, obsidian, oolite, pumice stone, schist, sedimentary, shale.

rock VERB 1 sway, swing, roll, soothe, lull. 2 stun, astonish.

rod NOUN pole, stick, staff, cane, baton, wand.

rodent NOUN gerbil, hamster, mouse, rat, squirrel.

rogue NOUN rascal, scoundrel, con, scamp, scallywag, good-for-nothing.

role NOUN 1 character, part. *He played the role of Hamlet.* 2 duty, function. *She had an important role in the company.*

roll VERB 1 rotate, revolve, turn, spin. 2 wrap, bind, enfold. 3 press, flatten, smooth. 4 roar, rumble, thunder. 5 swing, toss, pitch. A word that sounds similar is role.

room NOUN 1 chamber, bathroom, bedroom, kitchen, sitting room, lounge, dining room, study, toilet. 2 space.

roomy ADJECTIVE large, spacious.

rotten ADJECTIVE 1 bad, mouldy/moldy (US), putrid, decomposed, decayed. 2 useless, hopeless, nasty, inferior, crummy.

rough ADJECTIVE 1 coarse, harsh, scratchy. 2 bumpy, lumpy, uneven. 3 wild, violent, stormy. 4 severe, harsh, rude, impolite. *Opposite words are* 1 sleek. 2 smooth. 3 calm. 4 gentle, polite.

round ADJECTIVE circular, spherical, disc/disk (US), ball. *The skating rink was round.*

rout NOUN defeat, conquest, overthrow, thrashing.

routine NOUN method, system, procedure, pattern, custom.

rove VERB *See* **roam.**

row NOUN (rhymes with now) 1 quarrel, fight, squabble, disagreement. 2 uproar, din, noise, racket, commotion.

row NOUN (rhymes with go) file, line.

rowdy ADJECTIVE noisy, unruly, boisterous. An *opposite word* is peaceful.

rub VERB wipe, polish, stroke, caress, massage.

rubbish NOUN scrap, waste, refuse, junk, waste, garbage.

rude ADJECTIVE bad-mannered, impolite, coarse, curt, vulgar (UK). An *opposite word* is polite.

rugged ADJECTIVE 1 robust, sturdy, strong. 2 rough, uneven, craggy.

ruin VERB destroy, wreck, spoil, damage.

rule NOUN command, law, regulation, order.

rule VERB 1 govern, control, run, manage, command, reign. 2 judge.

ruler NOUN king, queen, monarch, emperor, empress, president, sovereign, sultan, tsar, rajah, dictator, tyrant, pharaoh.

rumble VERB *See* roar.

rumour/rumor (US) NOUN gossip, hearsay, scandal, report.

run VERB 1 race, jog, sprint, scamper, dash, trot, canter, gallop. 2 work, operate. *It runs on diesel.* 3 manage, control. *She runs a business.* 4 flow, pour. *Water running down the hill.*

rush VERB dash, hurry, run, speed, hasten. *Opposite words* are linger, saunter.

rusty ADJECTIVE 1 corroded, blighted, tarnished, rusted. 2 out of practice, unprepared.

ruthless ADJECTIVE pitiless, merciless, cruel, harsh, brutal, savage. *Opposite words* are merciful, kind.

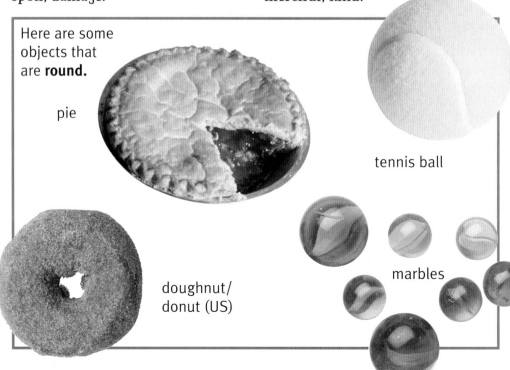

Here are some objects that are **round.**

pie

tennis ball

doughnut/donut (US)

marbles

weighing scales

Ss

sack NOUN bag, pouch, container.

sack VERB **1** dismiss, fire, make redundant, lay off (UK). **2** pillage, plunder, despoil.

sacred ADJECTIVE See **religious**.

sacrifice VERB give up, offer, surrender, renounce, forgo.

sad ADJECTIVE gloomy, miserable, depressed, melancholy, unhappy, upset, wretched.

safe ADJECTIVE **1** secure, unharmed, protected. **2** harmless, tame, trustworthy.

safeguard VERB defend, protect, shield, guard. *Opposite words* are endanger, imperil.

sag VERB droop, dangle, hang, bend.

sage ADJECTIVE See **wise**.

sail VERB cruise, float, put to sea, voyage, navigate, steer. A word that sounds similar is sale.

sailor NOUN mariner, seafarer, yachtsman, yachtswoman.

saintly ADJECTIVE See **religious**.

salad NOUN Some things we eat in a salad: carrot, celery, cucumber, lettuce, onion, pepper, radish, tomato.

salary NOUN pay, wages, earnings, income, remuneration.

sale NOUN trade, transaction, selling, marketing, auction. A word that sounds similar is sail.

salute VERB greet, hail, acknowledge, wave.

salvage VERB save, rescue, retrieve, reclaim, repair.

same ADJECTIVE similar, alike, equivalent, matching, changeless. *Opposite words* are different, changeable.

sample NOUN specimen, example, illustration.

sane ADJECTIVE normal, intelligent, sound, sober, rational, all-there. *Opposite words* are insane, mad.

sanitary ADJECTIVE clean, hygienic, pure, germ-free. An *opposite word* is insanitary.

sap NOUN weaken, undermine, tire out, exhaust.

sardonic ADJECTIVE bitter, jeering, mocking, biting, sarcastic.

satire NOUN ridicule, sarcasm, parody, burlesque, skit.

satisfy VERB **1** please, gratify, delight. *The teacher is never satisfied.* **2** meet, pay, fulfil, convince, assure.

saturate VERB soak, drench, steep, impregnate, souse.

saucy ADJECTIVE cheeky, impudent, rude, impertinent.

saunter VERB See **linger**.

savage ADJECTIVE cruel, brutal, ruthless, ferocious, heartless, violent, rough, uncivilized.

save VERB **1** keep, preserve, conserve, put aside, salvage, economize. **2** liberate, free, rescue, guard. *Opposite words* are **1** squander, waste.

savour/savor (US) VERB taste, smell, relish, enjoy, appreciate.

say VERB **1** talk, remark, speak, utter, declare, express, reply, retort. **2** tell, announce, order.

saying NOUN remark, proverb, axiom, adage, slogan, phrase, saw.

scale NOUN **1** measure, degree, range, gamut. **2** gradation, balance, calibration.

scale VERB ascend, clamber up. See also **climb**.

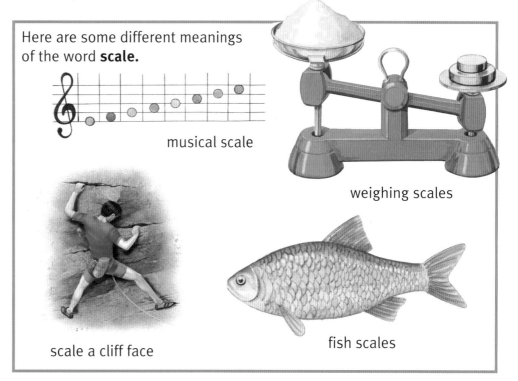

Here are some different meanings of the word **scale**.

musical scale

scale a cliff face

weighing scales

fish scales

scamper VERB scuttle, scoot, run, hasten, scurry, rush, scud.

scan VERB **1** inspect, scrutinize, examine, check. **2** glance at, dip into, skim. *She scanned the list of names.*

scandal NOUN disgrace, infamy, dishonour/dishonor (US), shame, ignominy, outcry, smear.

scanty ADJECTIVE scant, little. meagre/meager (US), small, insufficient, skimpy. *Opposite words* are plenty, adequate.

scar NOUN and VERB mark, wound, blemish.

scarce ADJECTIVE rare, uncommon, few, scanty, in short supply. *Opposite words* are common, plentiful.

scarcely ADVERB hardly, only, barely.

scare VERB frighten, terrify, alarm, upset, startle. *An opposite word is reassure.*

scared ADJECTIVE frightened, alarmed, nervous, terrified.

scatter VERB throw about, spread, sprinkle, sow, disperse.

scavenge VERB rummage, scrounge.

scene NOUN **1** view, landscape, location, setting, background, sight, spectacle, show, exhibition. **2** division, episode. *Act 2, Scene 3.*

scent NOUN smell, perfume, aroma, fragrance, odour/odor (US).

schedule NOUN agenda, plan, programme/program (US), timetable, catalogue/catalog (US).

scheme NOUN **1** plan, system, suggestion, arrangement. *A new scheme to make money.* **2** plot, intrigue, conspiracy, ruse, stratagem.

scholar NOUN student, pupil, academic, professor, highbrow, intellectual.

school NOUN college, academy, seminary, institute, kindergarten, comprehensive school (UK), boarding school.

science NOUN knowledge, technology. Some different branches of science: Biological sciences: anatomy, biochemistry, biology, botany, ecology, genetics, pharmacology, physiology, zoology. Physical sciences: astronomy, chemistry, electronics, engineering, geology, mechanics, metallurgy, meteorology, physics. Social sciences: anthropology, archaeology, geography, linguistics, philosophy, psychology, sociology.

scientific ADJECTIVE systematic, analytical, methodical, precise.

scoff VERB mock, make fun of, sneer, scorn, deride, ridicule, taunt.

scold VERB rebuke, tell off, reprimand, punish, blame. *An opposite word is praise.*

scope NOUN range, extent, field, room. *Scope for promotion.*

score VERB gain, earn, win, achieve, tally, notch up. *He scored 180 at darts.*

scorn NOUN despise, disdain, spurn, reject. *See also* **scoff.**

scrap NOUN bit, crumb, morsel. *See also* **fragment.**

scrap VERB abandon, discard, drop, throw away, dump.

scrape VERB scratch, grate, scour, graze.

scratch VERB scrape, mark, score, scuff, engrave, scrawl. *They scratched their names on the wall with a stone.*

scrawny ADJECTIVE *See* **lanky.**

scream NOUN AND VERB shout, yell, bawl, shriek.

screw NOUN fasten, twist, turn, tighten, force.

scribble VERB scrawl, scratch, write.

scrounge VERB cadge, beg.

scrub VERB clean, scour, wash, mop.

Here are some objects that are used in **science.**

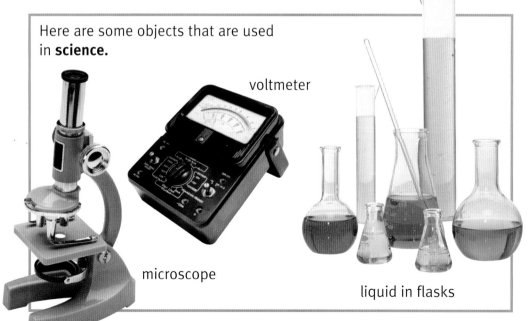

voltmeter

microscope

liquid in flasks

scruffy ADJECTIVE messy, unkempt, untidy, shabby.

sculpt VERB carve, chisel, cut.

sea NOUN **1** ocean, main. **2** lost, adrift, puzzled, bewildered. *I'm all at sea, I don't understand at all.*

seam NOUN **1** join, stitching, weld. **2** layer, stratum, vein. *A rich seam of ore.*

search VERB **1** hunt for, look for, seek. **2** examine, explore, frisk.

seaside NOUN beach, coast, shore.

season NOUN spring, summer, autumn, fall, winter, period, time.

season VERB flavour/flavor (US), spice, salt. *Season the vegetables.*

seat NOUN chair, stool, bench, armchair, sofa, rocking-chair, deckchair.

secondary ADJECTIVE minor, inferior, lesser, supporting. *Opposite words* are primary, main.

secret ADJECTIVE **1** personal, private, hush-hush, confidential. **2** concealed, hidden, unknown, mysterious, undercover, camouflaged. *Opposite words* are public, known.

sect NOUN faction, cult, group, party.

section NOUN portion, piece, part, segment, division, department. An *opposite word* is whole.

secular ADJECTIVE lay, worldly, non-religious.

secure ADJECTIVE safe, fixed, firm, stable, certain.

sedate ADJECTIVE serious, calm, thoughtful, grave. An *opposite word* is flippant.

sediment NOUN dregs, grounds, residue.

see VERB **1** look at, view, watch, behold. **2** notice, recognize, spot. *I see you've come by bus.* **3** understand, know, follow, comprehend. *I see what you mean.* A word that sounds similar is sea.

seedy ADJECTIVE shabby, worn, sleazy, tatty, grubby. *Opposite words* are smart, spruce.

seek VERB search, look for, hunt, ask, want.

seem VERB appear, look, feel, pretend. A word that sounds similar is seam.

seep VERB trickle, ooze, leak.

seethe VERB simmer, boil, froth, bubble.

segment NOUN bit, piece, portion. An *opposite word* is whole.

segregate VERB separate, isolate, keep apart.

seize VERB grab, snatch, arrest, capture.

seldom ADVERB, not often, rarely, occasionally.

select VERB pick, choose, opt for, prefer.

selfish ADJECTIVE greedy, mean, thoughtless. An *opposite word* is generous.

self-satisfied ADJECTIVE smug.

self-supporting ADJECTIVE independent, self-reliant.

sell VERB trade, vend, retail.

send VERB post, dispatch, forward, transmit.

senile ADJECTIVE old, aged, geriatric, decrepit.

senior ADJECTIVE elder, superior, high-ranking. An *opposite word* is junior.

sensation NOUN **1** excitement, surprise. **2** feeling, impression, sense, awareness.

sensational ADJECTIVE spectacular, staggering, astounding, shocking, scandalous.

sense NOUN **1** hearing, sight, smell, taste, touch, faculty. **2** intelligence, wisdom, understanding. **3** meaning, significance.

sensible ADJECTIVE wise, thoughtful, reasonable, intelligent. An *opposite word* is silly.

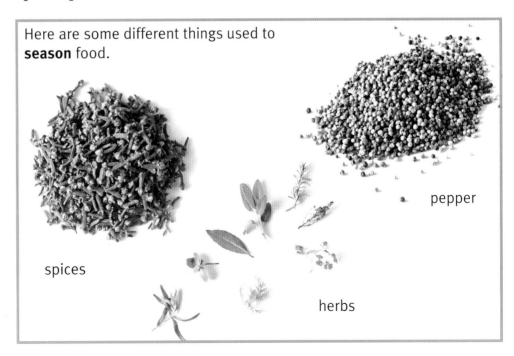

Here are some different things used to **season** food.

spices

pepper

herbs

separate ADJECTIVE apart, divided, isolated, segregated, detached, different. *Opposite words* are joined, connected.

serious ADJECTIVE careful, sincere, thoughtful, grave, sad, solemn, bad, terrible, severe.

servant NOUN domestic, employee, maid.

serve VERB help, assist, aid, wait on.

set VERB **1** harden, solidify, stiffen. *The concrete has set.* **2** arrange, place, lay out.

set off VERB depart, start.

settle VERB **1** colonize, populate, occupy. *They settled in New Zealand.* **2** fix, decide, agree, solve. *Settle an argument.* **3** pay. **4** fall, sink. *Settle a bill.*

severe ADJECTIVE **1** serious, bad. **2** strict, rigid, stern, harsh. *A severe discipline.* An *opposite word* is mild.

sew VERB stitch, darn, hem, tack, baste. Words that sound similar are so, sow.

shabby ADJECTIVE old, faded, shoddy, ragged, frayed, scruffy, threadbare. *Opposite words* are neat, smart.

shade NOUN **1** colour/color (US), hue, tinge. **2** shadow, darkness, gloom. **3** blind, screen, awning, umbrella, sunshade, parasol.

shadow NOUN shade, darkness, dimness.

shady ADJECTIVE **1** shaded, cool, shadowy. **2** crooked, suspicious, fishy. *A shady character.*

shaggy ADJECTIVE hairy, woolly, rough, rugged, tousled. *Opposite words* are smooth, shorn.

shake VERB *See* **quake.**

sham ADJECTIVE false, fake, imitation, bogus, mock, forged. An *opposite word* is genuine.

shame NOUN disgrace, disrepute, dishonour/dishonor (US), ignominy. An *opposite word* is pride.

shape NOUN form, outline, pattern, model, silhouette. Some different shapes: **1** circle, hexagon (six sides), oblong, octagon (eight sides), oval, pentagon (five sides), rectangle, semi-circle, square, triangle. **2** cone, cube, cylinder, pyramid, semisphere, sphere.

share NOUN *See* **ration.**

share VERB distribute, divide, allot, allocate, split, cooperate.

sharp ADJECTIVE **1** pointed, keen, cutting. **2** bright, quick, clever. **3** clear, distinct, bright. *Opposite words* are **1** blunt, **2** dull, **3** blurred.

shatter VERB smash, destroy, break, shock, wreck.

shelter NOUN cover, protection, safety, refuge, sanctuary.

shelter VERB guard, shield, protect, screen. An *opposite word* is expose.

shield NOUN guard, protection, screen, buckler.

shift VERB *See* **move 3.**

shifty ADJECTIVE sly, deceitful, foxy, untrustworthy. An *opposite word* is honest.

shimmer VERB glisten, gleam, sparkle.

shine VERB **1** glitter, gleam, sparkle, glisten, glow, twinkle. **2** polish.

shiny ADJECTIVE gleaming, glossy, polished, shining.

ship NOUN vessel, liner, craft. *See* **boat.**

shirk VERB avoid, shun, dodge.

shiver VERB tremble, shake, shudder, quiver.

shock VERB **1** startle, alarm, surprise, stun, scare, frighten. **2** disgust, upset, offend.

shocking ADJECTIVE horrible, scandalous, disgusting, repulsive, outrageous, disgraceful.

shoddy ADJECTIVE cheap, inferior, tawdry.

shoe NOUN Some of the things we wear on our feet: boots, clogs, pumps, slippers, sandals, sneakers (US), trainers (UK).

shoot VERB **1** aim, fire, discharge, explode. **2** bud, sprout.

Shoes can be made out of leather, cloth or even plastic and come in many different styles and colours.

brown leather lace-up shoe

cowboy boots

buckle shoes

shop NOUN store, departmental store, market stall, supermarket, hypermarket, emporium.

shore NOUN beach, seaside, sands, coast, waterfront, lakeside.

short ADJECTIVE **1** little, small, slight, dumpy. An *opposite word* is tall. **2** brief, concise, compact. An *opposite word* is long.

shortage NOUN lack, deficiency, need, scarcity, dearth.

shorten VERB reduce, abridge, abbreviate. *See also* **cut**. *Opposite words* are lengthen, prolong.

shortly ADVERB soon, presently, quickly, briefly.

shout VERB scream, yell, shriek, call, cry out.

shove VERB push, thrust, prod, jostle.

show NOUN exhibition, display, spectacle, performance.

show VERB **1** exhibit, display. **2** point out, indicate, explain, show, tell. **3** reveal, disclose. **4** illustrate, portray, represent.

showy ADJECTIVE flashy, garish, loud, ostentatious, flash.

shred NOUN scrap, fragment.

shred VERB mince, chop, dice, tear.

shrewd ADJECTIVE clever, smart, astute, sharp, artful, cunning, sly.

shriek NOUN and VERB *See* **shout**.

shrink VERB **1** shrivel, wither, diminish, shorten. *Clothes that have shrunk in the wash.* **2** draw back, recoil, flinch.

shrivel VERB shrink, wither, dry up, wilt.

shudder VERB quiver, tremble, shiver, quake, shake.

Here are some scenes of the **shore.**

beachball

shoreline

seabirds

rockpool

shuffle VERB **1** trudge, limp. *Shuffle through the snow.* **2** mix, jumble. *Shuffle the cards.*

shun VERB avoid, evade, steer clear of.

shut VERB close, lock, fasten, bar. An *opposite word* is open.

shy ADJECTIVE timid, bashful, nervous, diffident. *Opposite words* are bold, forward.

sick ADJECTIVE ill, unwell, unhealthy, poorly.

sickness NOUN **1** illness, malady, disease. **2** queasy, vomiting.

side NOUN **1** face, surface, margin, edge, bank. *The other side of the river.* **2** team, party, sect. A word that sounds similar is sighed.

sieve VERB strain, sift, riddle.

sift VERB strain, filter, separate, sort, examine. *Sift the evidence.*

sigh VERB grieve, moan, groan, lament.

sight NOUN **1** view, scene, appearance, spectacle. **2** vision, eyesight. Words that sound similar are cite, site.

sign NOUN **1** indication, symptom, signal, symbol. **2** notice, poster.

signal NOUN sign, mark, beacon, gesture.

significant ADJECTIVE meaningful, important, weighty, indicative, defining, historic.

silence NOUN calm, peace, quiet. *Opposite words* are noise, racket.

silent ADJECTIVE quiet, still, noiseless, hushed, dumb.

silhouette NOUN outline, shape, form.

silky ADJECTIVE smooth, fine, sleek. An *opposite word* is rough.

silly ADJECTIVE stupid, ridiculous, foolish, simple, weak, pointless. *What a silly idea!* **An** *opposite word* **is** sensible.

silt NOUN mud, ooze, sediment, alluvium.

simmer VERB seethe, bubble, stew, boil.

simple ADJECTIVE **1** easy, clear, straightforward. *It's really a simple question of economics.* **2** natural, unaffected, artless, naive, stupid, backward.

crab (shore)

simper VERB smirk, giggle.

simply ADVERB **1** merely, solely, only. **2** easily, openly.

sincere ADJECTIVE honest, genuine, real, truthful, straightforward. *Opposite words* are dishonest, false.

sing VERB chant, hum, croon.

singe VERB scorch, char, burn.

singer NOUN vocalist, chorister, prima donna, baritone, bass, tenor, countertenor, alto, treble, contralto, soprano, choir, chorus.

single ADJECTIVE **1** solitary, alone, sole. **2** unmarried, bachelor, spinster, celibate.

sinister ADJECTIVE evil, bad, unlucky, menacing, threatening.

sink VERB **1** immerse, submerge, drown. *A sinking ship.* **2** lower, drop, descend, disappear. *The sinking sun.* **3** lower, dwindle, decrease. An *opposite word* is rise.

sip VERB drink, taste.

sit VERB settle, rest, squat, perch.

site NOUN position, situation, spot, location. Words that sound similar are cite, sight.

situation NOUN **1** position, spot, locality. **2** plight, predicament.

size NOUN volume, extent, bulk, dimensions, width, breadth, length. *See also* **measurement**.

sizzle VERB sputter, fry.

sketch VERB outline, draw, design, trace, portray. *A rough sketch.*

skid VERB slide, slip, slither, glide, skate.

dream (sleep)

skilful/skillful (US) ADJECTIVE clever, talented, skilled, able, expert, adept. *Opposite words* are clumsy, inept.

skill NOUN talent, ability, knack.

skim VERB **1** float, glide, plane, touch. **2** glance, scan, look through. *Skim the newspapers.*

skinny ADJECTIVE thin, scrawny, lean, weedy.

skip VERB **1** hop, leap, jump. **2** pass over, omit, disregard.

slack ADJECTIVE **1** loose, limp, hanging, flabby, baggy. **2** lazy, idle, slow.

slam VERB close, bang. *She slammed the door shut.*

slander VERB abuse, malign, discredit, backbite.

slant VERB lean, slope, incline, tilt, list.

slap VERB smack, spank, hit.

slash VERB slit, cut, hack, rip.

slaughter NOUN murder, massacre, carnage, killing.

slave VERB toil, work, slog, drudge, labour/labor (US).

slay VERB *See* **kill**. A word with a similar sound is sleigh.

sledge NOUN sled, sleigh, toboggan.

sleek ADJECTIVE smooth, glossy, silky, slick. An *opposite word* is rough.

sleep VERB snooze, nap, nod off, slumber, doze.

sleet NOUN *See* weather.

slender ADJECTIVE slim, slight, thin, lean. An *opposite word* is fat.

slice NOUN piece, slab, wedge, section.

slice VERB cut, split, sever, shred. *Slice the bread.*

slick ADJECTIVE shiny, smooth, suave, polished.

People and animals need to **sleep.**

sleeping cat

sleeping man

sleeping child

slide VERB glide, skate, skid, skim, slip, slither.

slight ADJECTIVE small, minor, unimportant, trivial. An *opposite word* is serious. *There was a slight problem with the engine.*

slim ADJECTIVE slender, thin, slim, thin, narrow. *Opposite words* are fat, plump.

slime NOUN mud, mire, ooze.

sling VERB hurl, throw, chuck, fling, toss.

slip VERB **1** slide, skid, slither. **2** err, blunder.

slipper NOUN *See* **shoe.**

slippery ADJECTIVE smooth, icy, slimy, greasy, oily.

slipshod ADJECTIVE slapdash, slovenly, lax.

slit VERB cut, slash, rip, tear, gash.

slither VERB creep, slide, glide. *The snake slithered down the hill.*

slog VERB toil, work.

slogan NOUN motto, catchphrase, saying, jingle.

slope VERB slant, lean, tilt, incline.

sloppy ADJECTIVE **1** slovenly, unkempt, careless. *Sloppy work.* **2** wet, watery, runny slimy. *The stew was very sloppy.*

slot NOUN opening, slit, hole, aperture, place.

slouch VERB slump, stoop, lounge.

slovenly ADJECTIVE lazy, slipshod, untidy, dowdy. *Opposite words* are neat, tidy.

slow ADJECTIVE gradual, plodding, unhurried. *An opposite word is fast.*

slumber VERB *See* **sleep.**

sly ADJECTIVE cunning, crafty, wily, artful, sneaky.

smack VERB hit, slap, strike, tap.

small ADJECTIVE **1** little, compact, tiny, minute. **2** minor, slight, unimportant, trifling.

smart ADJECTIVE **1** neat, spruce, tidy. *A smart suit.* **2** clever, alert, intelligent.

smart VERB sting. *See also* **hurt.**

smash VERB break, shatter, destroy, crash, collide. *An opposite word is repair.*

smear VERB rub spread, daub, wipe, plaster.

smell NOUN odour/odor (US), scent, perfume, aroma, fragrance, stink, stench, whiff, smack, tang.

smelly ADJECTIVE stinking, fetid.

smile VERB grin, beam, smirk.

smirk VERB simper, smile.

smooth ADJECTIVE flat, even, level, sleek, shiny. *Opposite words* are rough, uneven, stormy.

smother VERB stifle, suffocate.

smoulder/smolder (US) VERB burn, smoke, seethe.

smudge VERB smear, streak, stain, blot.

smug ADJECTIVE conceited, self-satisfied, priggish, complacent.

snack NOUN titbit, morsel, nibble, bite to eat.

snag NOUN problem, handicap, catch, handicap, difficulty.

snap VERB **1** break, crack, split. **2** snarl, growl.

snare NOUN trap, net.

snarl VERB **1** growl. **2** entangle, knot.

snatch VERB seize, grab, clutch, grasp, take.

sneak VERB creep, prowl, lurk, snoop, slink.

sneer VERB ridicule, scoff, jeer, taunt.

snigger VERB titter, sneer.

snip VERB *See* **cut.**

snoop VERB sneak, pry, spy, eavesdrop.

snooze VERB *See* **sleep.**

snow NOUN *See* **weather.**

snug ADJECTIVE comfortable, cosy, warm, secure.

so ADVERB therefore, likewise. Words that sound similar are sew, sow.

soak VERB drench, wet, moisten, steep, saturate.

soar VERB rise, hover, fly, glide, tower. A word that sounds similar is sore.

sob VERB *See* **cry 1.**

social ADJECTIVE sociable, convivial, neighbourly/neighborly (US).

Here are some things that have a distinctive **smell.**

rose

pot pourri

coffee beans

society NOUN **1** people, human beings, community. **2** group, club, association.

soft ADJECTIVE **1** limp, spongy, squashy, flexible. An *opposite word* is hard. **2** smooth, silky, fluffy. An *opposite word* is rough. **3** low, quiet, gentle, restful. An *opposite word* is noisy.

soften VERB **1** lessen, ease, alleviate, calm. **2** melt, dissolve.

soggy ADJECTIVE wet, sodden, saturated, spongy.

soldier NOUN cavalry, infantry, army, troops.

sole ADJECTIVE single, only, unique. A word that sounds similar is soul.

solemn ADJECTIVE serious, grave, sedate, formal, ceremonial.

solid ADJECTIVE firm, hard, dense, compact. *Opposite words* are soft, hollow.

solitary ADJECTIVE sole, alone, only, lone, remote.

solution NOUN **1** explanation, answer. **2** mixture, blend, liquid.

solve VERB explain, answer, work out, decipher, unravel.

sombre/somber (US) ADJECTIVE serious, dull, dark, sad, dim, dismal. *Opposite words* are bright, cheerful.

song NOUN air, tune. Some different types of song: anthem, ballad, carol, folksong, hit, hymn, nursery rhyme, sea-shanty.

sonnet NOUN *See* **poetry**.

soon ADVERB shortly, before long, presently.

soothe VERB calm, relax, pacify, comfort, relieve, ease. *Opposite words* are upset, aggravate.

soppy ADJECTIVE sloppy, sentimental, slushy.

sordid ADJECTIVE slovenly, squalid, dirty, filthy, seedy, base, corrupt.

sore ADJECTIVE painful, tender, aching, inflamed. A word that sounds similar is soar.

sorrow NOUN sadness, unhappiness, misery, grief, remorse.

sorry ADJECTIVE apologetic, repentant, regretful, grieved.

sort NOUN type, kind, variety, breed, species, class, genre.

sort VERB classify, organize, arrange, catalogue, order.

sound ADJECTIVE **1** healthy, fit, well, strong, good. **2** valid, trustworthy, reliable.

sound NOUN noise, din, racket, tone. An *opposite word* is silence. Some of the sounds that animals make: bark, bleat, bray, buzz, chirp, cluck, croak, growl, grunt, hoot, hum, low, meow, neigh, purr, roar, squeak, yap.

sour ADJECTIVE sharp, acid, tart, bitter. An *opposite word* is sweet.

source NOUN origin, beginning, starting point, fount, spring, wellhead.

sow VERB scatter, strew, plant. Words that sound similar are so, sew.

space NOUN room, gap, area, expanse, hole, opening, blank.

span VERB stretch, reach, bridge, cross. *A bridge spans the river.*

spank VERB smack, slap, thrash.

spare ADJECTIVE extra, superfluous, additional, over, remaining.

sparkle VERB **1** flash, glitter, glisten, scintillate. **2** fizz, bubble.

sparse ADJECTIVE scanty, thin, meagre/meager (US). An *opposite word* is dense.

speak VERB talk, say, express, state, utter.

spear NOUN javelin, lance, harpoon, pike.

special ADJECTIVE important, distinct, unusual, particular, different, personal, individual.

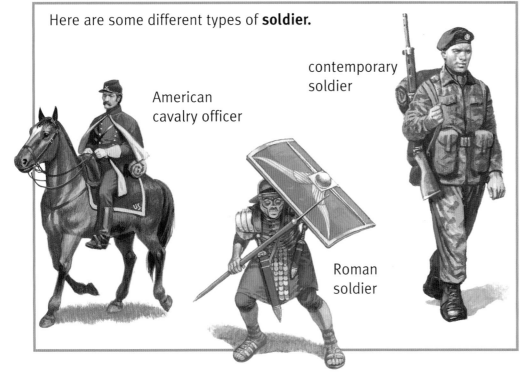

Here are some different types of **soldier.**

American cavalry officer

contemporary soldier

Roman soldier

species NOUN kind, type, group, sort, breed.

specimen NOUN example, sample, copy, illustration.

speck NOUN dot, bit, grain, spot, particle.

spectacle NOUN show, exhibition, display, scene, sight.

spectacular ADJECTIVE impressive, exciting, big, striking, stunning.

spectator NOUN onlooker, bystander, witness, observer, watcher.

speed NOUN pace, haste, swiftness, velocity, tempo, rate.

spell VERB 1 charm, enchantment, sorcery, magic power. 2 time, period, term.

spend VERB 1 pay, use up, fritter. 2 pass, use, employ.

sphere NOUN 1 globe, ball, orb. 2 field, area, domain.

spice NOUN seasoning, zest. *See also* **herb**. Some different kinds of spice: allspice, caraway, cardamon, cayenne, chili, cinnamon, clove, coriander, ginger, mace, nutmeg, paprika, pepper, turmeric.

spill VERB upset, overturn, tip, topple, shed, drop.

spin VERB turn, revolve, rotate, whirl, twirl, gyrate.

spite NOUN malice, ill-will, venom, hatred. An *opposite word* is goodwill.

splash VERB spatter, sprinkle, slop.

splendid ADJECTIVE impressive, superb, grand, brilliant, magnificent, gorgeous. *Opposite words* are drab, ordinary.

split VERB chop, crack, cleave, splinter, divide, cut.

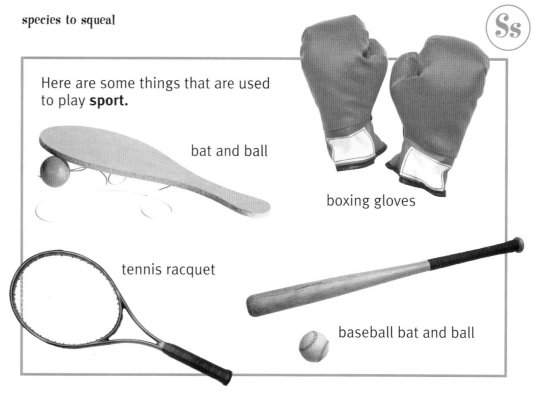

Here are some things that are used to play **sport.**

bat and ball

boxing gloves

tennis racquet

baseball bat and ball

spoil VERB 1 damage, ruin, injure, wreck, mar. 2 pamper, indulge. *A spoiled child.*

spooky ADJECTIVE frightening, eerie. *It's a very spooky house.*

sport NOUN recreation, play, fun, activity, pastime. *See also* **game.**

spot NOUN 1 mark, stain, blot, dot, speck, blemish. 2 pimple, boil. 3 place, position, situation. 4 plight, predicament. *In a bit of a spot.*

spot VERB recognize, identify, see, spy.

spotless ADJECTIVE unstained, immaculate, pure, chaste. *Opposite words* are dirty, impure.

sprawl VERB lounge, loll, stretch out, spread, straggle. *Sprawling plants.*

spray VERB splash, sprinkle, shower, scatter.

spread VERB unfold, open, lay out, expand. An *opposite word* is contract.

sprightly ADJECTIVE brisk, agile, lively, nimble. *My grandmother is sprightly for her age.*

spring VERB 1 jump, leap, bound, hop, pounce. 2 grow, shoot up.

sprinkle VERB scatter, rain, strew, pepper. *Sprinkle salt on the fries.*

sprint VERB race, run, dash.

spruce ADJECTIVE smart, tidy, neat. An *opposite word* is scruffy.

spurn VERB reject, turn down, despise, scorn.

spurt VERB gush, spew, stream, erupt.

spy VERB see, discover, detect, pry.

squabble VERB quarrel, fight, clash.

squalid ADJECTIVE filthy, foul, dirty, seedy, sordid. An *opposite word* is clean.

squander VERB spend, waste, fritter. *Opposite words* are save, hoard.

squash VERB crush, press, push, shove, squeeze, flatten.

squat ADJECTIVE stubby, stocky, crouching.

squeal VERB squeak, cry, squawk, screech.

sport

Ss

squeeze VERB pinch, nip. *See also* **squash**.

squirt VERB spurt, spray, spout, gush.

stab VERB pierce, jab, wound, spear.

stable ADJECTIVE firm, steady, staunch, fixed, secure, steadfast.

stack NOUN and VERB pile, heap, load, mount.

stage NOUN **1** period, phase, point, juncture. *The next stage in your career.* **2** platform, scaffold, podium.

stagger VERB **1** reel, totter, lurch. **2** shock, astonish. **3** alternate, vary. *Staggered working hours.*

stain NOUN mark, smudge, spot, blemish, soil, smear.

stale ADJECTIVE **1** dry, old, decayed. *Stale bread.* **2** flat, uninteresting, trite. *Stale ideas.* An *opposite word* is fresh.

stalk NOUN stem, twig, shank.

stalk VERB follow, pursue, track, trail, shadow.

stamina NOUN endurance, power, energy.

stamp NOUN mark, seal, label.

stamp VERB **1** mark, print, impress. **2** trample, pound, crush.

stand VERB **1** get up, rise. **2** arrange, place, put, position. **3** endure, tolerate, bear, put up with, abide. *She can't stand noise.*

stand down VERB resign, give up, quit, withdraw.

stand over VERB oversee.

stand up to VERB defy resist.

standard ADJECTIVE normal, consistent, regular. *Opposite words* are unusual, special.

standard NOUN **1** quality, level. **2** flag, banner, ensign, pennant.

staple ADJECTIVE basic, main, principal, chief. *Staple diet.*

stare VERB gape, gawk. *See also* **look**. A word that sounds similar is stair.

start VERB **1** begin, commence, open. **2** create, set up, found, establish. *Opposite words* are stop, finish, end.

startle VERB frighten, alarm, surprise, shock, scare.

starve VERB famish, be hungry, die, perish.

state NOUN **1** country, nation. **2** situation, condition.

state VERB say, declare, affirm, express, announce.

stately ADJECTIVE impressive, imposing, grand.

stationary ADJECTIVE motionless, unmoving, immobile, at rest, stable, fixed. A word that sounds similar is stationery.

stay VERB **1** remain, wait, abide, stop, dwell. **2** keep, carry on. *Opposite words* are go, stray.

steady ADJECTIVE **1** stable, solid, secure, firm. **2** constant, continuous, regular.

steal VERB pinch, take, thieve, burgle, pickpocket, rob, shoplift, pilfer.

steep ADJECTIVE sheer, precipitous, sharp.

steep VERB soak, submerge, souse.

steer VERB guide, pilot, direct.

stem VERB **1** arise, originate. *It stems from a Latin word.* **2** stop, oppose, check.

stench NOUN stink. *See also* **smell**.

step NOUN **1** pace, stride, tread. **2** stair, rung. **3** measure, action, deed. *The city is taking steps to reduce crime.*

stern ADJECTIVE strict, severe, hard, harsh, grim. *Opposite words* are lax, kind.

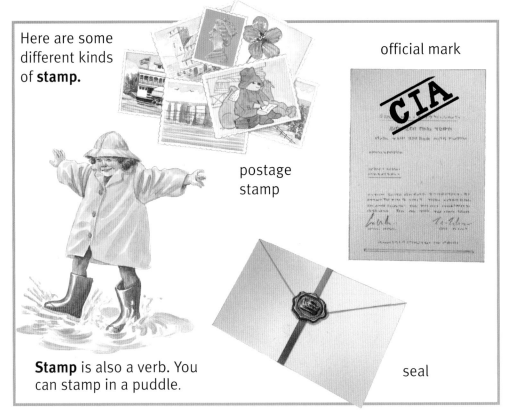

Here are some different kinds of **stamp.**

official mark

postage stamp

Stamp is also a verb. You can stamp in a puddle.

seal

stew VERB *See* **cook**.

stick NOUN pole, cane, walking stick, club, staff, wand, baton, stalk, twig.

stick VERB **1** glue, paste, attach, adhere. **2** pierce, thrust, stab.

stiff ADJECTIVE **1** rigid, hard, unbending. **2** hard, tough, difficult. *It's a stiff exam.*

still ADJECTIVE quiet, calm, tranquil, peaceful, hushed. An *opposite word* is noisy.

still ADVERB **1** always, even now, continually, ever. *Are you still living there?* **2** yet, even. *She wanted still more time.*

stimulate VERB excite, interest, encourage, arouse, inspire, motivate.

sting VERB wound, pain, prick.

stingy ADJECTIVE mean, miserly, niggardly, close. An *opposite word* is generous.

stink NOUN reek, whiff. *See also* **smell**.

stint NOUN job, task, work, shift, share.

stir VERB **1** mix, whisk, churn, shake. **2** arouse, stimulate, excite.

stool NOUN look at seat.

stoop VERB bend, crouch, squat, hunch, bow. **2** descend, sink. *Stoop to their level.*

stop VERB **1** end, cease, finish, pause, halt. **2** check, prevent, hinder. **3** stay.

store VERB save, put away, keep, reserve, accumulate. An *opposite word* is use.

storm NOUN **1** blizzard, hurricane, gale, tornado, rainstorm, squall, tempest, upheaval, thunderstorm. **2** uproar, commotion.

Here are some different kinds of **stick.**

magic wand

stick or twig, covered in blossom

stick with glue

walking stick

stormy ADJECTIVE wild, tempestuous, squally.

story NOUN tale, narrative, fairy-tale, fable, legend, myth, parable, yarn, anecdote, newspaper article.

stout ADJECTIVE plump, overweight, fat, tubby, big, chubby. An *opposite word* is thin.

straight ADJECTIVE **1** direct, undeviating, upright, vertical. **2** honest, fair, upright, frank. An *opposite word* is crooked.

straighten VERB disentangle, unbend, tidy, adjust.

strain VERB **1** struggle, try hard. **2** damage, injure, hurt, wrench. **3** exhaust, weaken, tire out. **4** filter, purify. *See also* **sieve**.

strange ADJECTIVE **1** unfamiliar, foreign, alien, unknown, novel. **2** extraordinary, unusual, queer, odd, peculiar, weird, bizarre, funny. *Something strange happened.*

stranger NOUN foreigner, newcomer, outsider, alien.

strangle VERB choke, asphyxiate. *See also* **smother**.

strap VERB **1** fasten, tie. **2** beat, belt.

strategy NOUN plan, scheme, tactics, design.

stray VERB wander, get lost, roam, digress.

stream NOUN brook, rivulet, beck, course, race, burn.

street NOUN lane, avenue. *See also* **road**.

strength NOUN **1** might, power, toughness, force, vigour/vigor (US), stamina. **2** soundness, sturdiness. An *opposite word* is weakness.

strengthen VERB reinforce, support, fortify. An *opposite word* is weaken.

strenuous ADJECTIVE energetic, vigorous, tough, demanding, exhausting.

stress NOUN strain, pressure, worry, tension.

stress VERB emphasize, underline, highlight, accentuate. *I must stress the importance of accuracy.*

stretch VERB lengthen, pull out, elongate, expand, reach.

strict ADJECTIVE **1** harsh, stern, austere, severe, rigorous. *It's a very strict diet.* **2** exact, precise, accurate. *Opposite words* are **1** lenient. **2** inaccurate.

sticky (stick)

stride NOUN walk, march, step.

strike VERB **1** hit, knock, beat, thump, smite, pound. **2** stop work, walk out, down tools.

string NOUN cord, rope, lace, twine, wire.

strip VERB remove, take off, peel, undress, expose, clear, plunder, loot.

strive VERB struggle, toil, try, endeavour/endeavor (US), attempt.

stroke VERB fondle, caress, rub, massage.

stroll VERB saunter, amble, promenade, ramble.

strong ADJECTIVE **1** tough, sturdy, muscular, powerful, robust, tough, unbreakable. *A strong personality.* **2** deep, eager, ardent.

stronghold NOUN castle, keep, citadel, fort, fastness, refuge.

structure NOUN **1** building, edifice. **2** form, design, framework, construction, composition.

struggle VERB wrestle, strive, try, grapple, contend, fight. An *opposite word* is give in.

stubborn ADJECTIVE obstinate, disobedient, pig-headed, dogged, wilful/willful (US).

student NOUN scholar, pupil, learner, apprentice.

study VERB **1** learn, revise, swot. **2** analyze, consider, investigate, think about, examine.

stuff NOUN **1** substance. **2** cloth, fabric, material, textile. **3** belongings.

stuff VERB **1** cram, pack, fill, compress. **2** guzzle, gorge.

stumble VERB trip, stagger, fall.

stun VERB daze, knock out, amaze, astonish, astound, surprise.

stunning ADJECTIVE amazing, gorgeous, beautiful, brilliant, spectacular.

stunt NOUN feat, exploit, performance.

stupid ADJECTIVE foolish, silly, idiotic, slow, thick, dim, senseless. *Opposite words* are sensible, clever, intelligent.

sturdy ADJECTIVE strong, robust, solid, well-built. *Opposite words* are weak, fragile.

style NOUN **1** fashion, chic, vogue. **2** way, method, manner, technique.

subject NOUN theme, topic, point. *What is the subject of the essay?*

submit VERB **1** present, put forward, tender, hand in. **2** give in, surrender, yield.

subject ADJECTIVE liable, prone, susceptible. *Subject to delays.*

subsequent ADJECTIVE following, succeeding, later, after. *Opposite words* are preceding, previous. *Subsequent meetings.*

subside VERB diminish, sink, decrease, lessen. *Opposite words* are rise, increase.

subtract VERB take away, deduct. *Opposite words* are add, remove.

succeed VERB **1** do well, prosper, work well, thrive, triumph. **2** follow, come after, replace, ensue. *George II succeeded George I.*

success NOUN luck, good fortune, triumph, achievement, victory. An *opposite word* is failure.

succulent ADJECTIVE juicy, moist.

sudden ADJECTIVE quick, hasty, abrupt, unexpected. An *opposite word* is gradual.

suffer VERB endure, bear, go through, undergo, stand, tolerate, allow.

sufficient ADJECTIVE enough, adequate, ample, plenty. An *opposite word* is insufficient. *Sufficient time.*

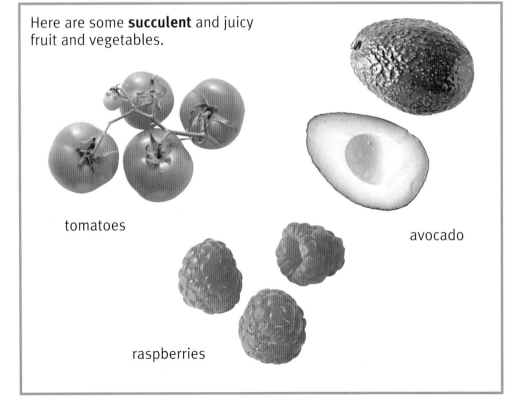

Here are some **succulent** and juicy fruit and vegetables.

tomatoes

avocado

raspberries

suffocate VERB smother, stifle, strangle, choke.

suggest VERB propose, advise, recommend, put forward, intimate.

suitable ADJECTIVE appropriate, apt, proper, fitting. *Opposite words are* unsuitable, inappropriate.

suitcase NOUN *See* **luggage**.

sulk VERB mope, glower, brood, grouch.

sullen ADJECTIVE morose, gloomy, glum, moody. *An opposite word is* cheerful.

sum NOUN total, whole, amount, aggregate. *A word that sounds similar is* some. *Can you work out the answer to the sum?*

summary NOUN resume, outline, digest, synopsis, precis, abridgment.

summit NOUN peak, top, apex, acme, pinnacle. *Opposite words are* base, bottom.

summon VERB send for, call invite, beckon, rally, mobilize. *An opposite word is* dismiss.

sunny ADJECTIVE bright, clear, fine, cloudless, cheerful, radiant. *A sunny smile.*

sunrise NOUN dawn, daybreak, daylight, morning. *Opposite words are* sunset, evening.

superb ADJECTIVE excellent, splendid, first-rate, magnificent, exquisite. *An opposite word is* poor.

superficial ADJECTIVE surface, exterior, skin-deep, shallow, trivial, slight. *An opposite word is* deep.

superintend VERB *See* **supervise**.

superior ADJECTIVE better, greater, higher, excellent, first-class. *Superior quality.*

superlative ADJECTIVE best, greatest, finest, outstanding.

supersede VERB replace, supplant, displace, replace.

superstitious ADJECTIVE illusory, false, credulous.

supervise VERB oversee, manage, control, direct, oversee, superintend, administer.

supple ADJECTIVE flexible, lithe, pliable, bending. *Opposite words are* stiff, rigid.

supply VERB give, provide, contribute, sell. *An opposite word is* withhold.

support VERB **1** aid, help, assist, encourage, back, defend. **2** hold up, bear, bolster, prop up. **3** feed, nourish, provide for, maintain. *She supports the family. Opposite words are* **1** oppose. **2** drop.

supporter NOUN fan, follower, defender, ally.

suppose VERB imagine, believe, pretend, guess, deduce, assume, conclude.

suppress VERB quell, put down, crush, subdue, stifle, stop. *The protests were suppressed. An opposite word is* free.

supreme ADJECTIVE highest, chief, best, greatest, foremost, leading, paramount. *An opposite word is* least.

sure ADJECTIVE certain, positive, confident, convinced. *Opposite words are* uncertain, doubtful. *A word that sounds similar is* shore.

surly ADJECTIVE morose, crusty, testy, bad-tempered.

surplus NOUN excess, remainder, residue. *Opposite words are* lack, deficit.

surprise VERB astonish, amaze, shock, startle, dumbfound, stagger.

Atlas supporting the Earth

a mother supports her child

stilts support this building

a person supported by crutches

Here are some different kinds of **support.**

surrender VERB give in, yield, concede, renounce, capitulate, forego.

surround VERB encircle, ring, enclose, besiege, invest.

surroundings NOUN environment, background, locality.

survey VERB investigate, study, inspect, scan, scrutinize.

survive VERB live, outlive, last, outlast, keep going, withstand, endure. *Opposite words* are die, perish.

suspect ADJECTIVE dubious, suspicious, unbelievable.

suspect VERB **1** think, fancy, guess. **2** mistrust, doubt.

suspense NOUN uncertainty, anxiety, anticipation, tension, excitement.

suspension NOUN break, stoppage, delay, postponement.

suspicion NOUN mistrust, doubt, misgiving.

swallow VERB **1** eat, drink, devour, gobble. **2** swallow up, absorb, accept, believe. *He swallowed the story.*

swamp NOUN bog, marsh, quagmire, fen.

swap VERB exchange, switch. *They swapped telephone numbers.*

swarm VERB crowd, collect, cluster, amass, teem.

swat VERB hit, clout, crush.

sway VERB **1** swing, wave, rock. **2** influence, convince, guide. *She was swayed by his promises.*

swear VERB **1** promise, declare, vow, pledge. **2** curse, damn.

sweep VERB brush, clean, clear.

sweet ADJECTIVE **1** sugary, honeyed, syrupy. **2** charming, agreeable, lovable. *The kittens are sweet.* **3** melodious, dulcet, mellow, tuneful. *Sweet music.*

swell VERB bulge, get bigger, grow, dilate, expand, puff up. *Opposite words* shrink, contract.

swelling NOUN bump, lump, bulge, boil, protuberance.

swerve VERB veer, turn, bend, dodge, deviate, lurch.

swift ADJECTIVE quick, fast, rapid, speedy, nimble. An *opposite word* is slow.

swill NOUN **1** rinse, wash. **2** swig, drink, tipple.

swindle VERB cheat, deceive, trick, defraud, diddle.

swing VERB sway, dangle, hang, vibrate, rock.

swipe VERB **1** hit, slap. **2** steal.

swirl VERB spin, whirl, churn, eddy.

switch VERB change, swap, replace, transpose, substitute.

swivel VERB spin, revolve, rotate, pivot, turn.

swoop VERB dive, pounce, plunge, pounce.

swop VERB See **swap.**

sword NOUN steel, brand, rapier, foil, cutlass, sabre, scimitar, claymore.

swot (UK) ADJECTIVE study, work hard, revise, cram.

symbol NOUN emblem, sign, token, mark, representation.

symbolize VERB signify, stand for, represent.

sympathy NOUN feeling, pity, compassion, understanding, condolence, harmony.

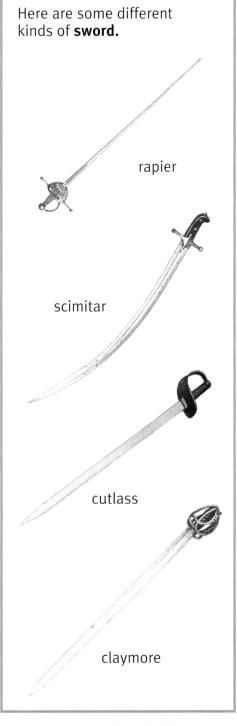

Here are some different kinds of **sword.**

rapier

scimitar

cutlass

claymore

symptom NOUN sign, indication, mark, evidence, warning.

synthetic ADJECTIVE artificial, manufactured, sham, mock.

system NOUN method, procedure, mode, process, scheme.

systematic ADJECTIVE logical, orderly, efficient, thorough.

Tt

tab NOUN label, sticker, tag.

tall

table NOUN **1** list, index. **2** board, slab, counter.

taboo ADJECTIVE banned, prohibited, unmentionable. *A taboo subject.*

tackle VERB try, attempt, take on, undertake, deal with.

tact NOUN discrimination, delicacy, skill, discretion.

tactics NOUN strategy, plan, policy, method.

tactless ADJECTIVE indiscreet, clumsy, blundering, inept.

tag NOUN label, ticket, docket.

tail NOUN rear, end, extremity.

tail VERB *See* **trail**.

take VERB **1** grasp, grab, snatch, clasp, hold, seize, pick, choose. **2** capture, catch. **3** carry, convey, deliver, transport. **4** steal, snatch, remove, pinch. **5** bear, tolerate, put up with.

take in VERB understand, realize, grasp.

take after VERB resemble, be like.

take away VERB subtract.

take place VERB occur, happen.

tale NOUN yarn. *See also* **story**. A word that sounds the same is tail.

talent NOUN skill, gift, ability, knack, flair, genius. *He has a real talent for making people laugh.*

talk VERB say, discuss, converse, speak, utter, chat, gossip, natter, prattle, shout, interview.

tall ADJECTIVE high, lofty, lanky, towering. *Opposite words* are short, low.

tame ADJECTIVE obedient, domesticated, trained, gentle. *Opposite words* are wild, savage, dangerous.

tamper VERB interfere, tinker, meddle.

tangle VERB knot, twist, coil, muddle. An *opposite word* is unravel.

tantrum NOUN outburst, temper, hysterics, scene, fury.

tap VERB knock, strike, hit, rap.

tardy ADJECTIVE *See* **late**.

target NOUN ambition, objective, aim, goal.

tarry VERB *See* **linger, loiter**.

task NOUN job, chore, undertaking, stint, errand, work.

taste NOUN **1** flavour/flavor (US), tang, salty, sweet, sour, bitter. **2** lick, nibble, mouthful, piece. *Have a taste of this ice cream.* **3** discernment, judgement.

tasty ADJECTIVE delicious, appetising, mouth-watering.

taunt VERB jeer, scoff, tease, sneer, make fun of, torment.

taut ADJECTIVE tight, stiff, tense, stretched. A word that sounds similar is taught.

tawdry ADJECTIVE gaudy, loud, flashy, vulgar, cheap.

teach VERB educate, instruct, train, drill, coach, lecture. An *opposite word* is learn.

teacher NOUN instructor, trainer, tutor, lecturer, professor, coach.

team NOUN side, group, company, crew.

tear VERB **1** rip, slit, slash, shred. **2** rush, dash.

tease VERB taunt, pester, badger, bait, make fun of, annoy, laugh at.

Here are some things that are **tall.**

a giraffe is very tall

a tall cactus

a tall skyscraper

tedious ADJECTIVE boring, dreary, humdrum. *Opposite words* are interesting, exciting.

teem VERB swarm, crawl with, abound. A word that sounds similar is team.

telephone VERB call, ring, phone.

tell VERB **1** inform, notify, reveal, admit, state. **2** narrate, relate, describe, recount. **3** order, command, instruct. **4** distinguish. *Can you tell butter from margarine?* **5** work out, figure out.

tell off VERB tick off, scold, rebuke.

temper NOUN mood, rage, anger.

temperamental ADJECTIVE sensitive, moody, touchy, emotional. An *opposite word* is calm.

tempest NOUN *See* **storm**.

temple NOUN sanctuary. *See also* **church**.

temporary ADJECTIVE transient, momentary, impermanent, makeshift. *Opposite words* are permanent, fixed.

tempt VERB lure, entice, persuade, coax, seduce.

tend VERB **1** be liable to, incline. **2** look after, protect, care for, mind, manage.

tender ADJECTIVE **1** kind, gentle, loving, caring. **2** delicate, soft. **3** sore, sensitive. *Opposite words* are **1** cruel, unkind. **2** tough.

tense ADJECTIVE tight, stretched, strained, edgy, nervous. An *opposite word* is relaxed. A word that sounds similar is tents.

tent NOUN wigwam, teepee, big top, marquee.

tepid ADJECTIVE cool, lukewarm, unenthusiastic.

term NOUN **1** time, period, semester. **2** expression, phrase.

terminate VERB end, stop, finish, conclude, close, compete. *Opposite words* are begin, start.

terrible ADJECTIVE awful, dreadful, horrible, vile, frightful, frightening, bad.

terrific ADJECTIVE **1** good, great, excellent. *We had a terrific time.* **2** huge, enormous.

terrify VERB frighten, scare, upset, alarm, horrify, petrify.

territory NOUN region, district, area, domain, country, land, estate.

terror NOUN fear, dread, alarm, panic, horror.

test VERB **1** examine, investigate, study, question. **2** try, check. *Test the light switch.*

tether VERB tie up, chain, fasten, secure, fetter.

texture NOUN grain, surface, pattern, feel.

thaw VERB melt, unfreeze, defrost, soften. An *opposite word* is freeze.

theatrical ADJECTIVE dramatic, affected, ostentatious, showy.

theme NOUN topic, subject, matter, thesis, keynote.

theory NOUN idea, conjecture, hypothesis, opinion.

therefore ADVERB **1** so, thus, consequently, hence. **2** for that reason.

thick ADJECTIVE broad, wide, chunky, dense, sticky, stodgy. *Thick porridge.* An *opposite word* is thin. **2** stupid, foolish.

thicken VERB congeal, clot.

thief NOUN robber, burglar, mugger, shoplifter, pickpocket, pilferer.

thin ADJECTIVE **1** slender, lean, skinny. *Thin, watery soup.* **2** fine, flimsy, delicate, sheer. *Thin wafers of chocolate.* **3** narrow. *Opposite words* are thick, fat, heavy.

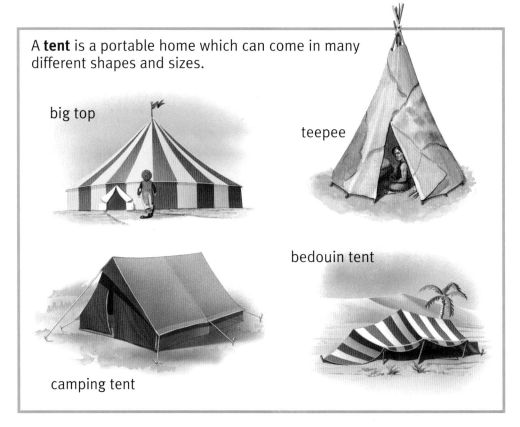

A **tent** is a portable home which can come in many different shapes and sizes.

big top

teepee

camping tent

bedouin tent

think VERB **1** believe, consider, fancy, reckon, feel, hold. **2** expect, guess, imagine, suppose. **3** concentrate, pay attention. **4** judge, conclude. **5** know, realize.

thirsty ADJECTIVE parched, dry, arid, desiccated.

though ADVERB however, all the same, even so, nevertheless. *The work is hard. I enjoy it though.*

though CONJUNCTION although, while, notwithstanding, and yet, in spite of. *I like the job though the hours are long.*

thought NOUN idea, concept, notion, opinion, fancy. *I had a thought.*

thoughtful ADJECTIVE **1** kind, friendly, attentive, considerate. **2** serious, solemn, pensive, reflective.

thoughtless ADJECTIVE unthinking, inconsiderate, careless.

threadbare ADJECTIVE frayed, ragged, shabby.

threat NOUN menace, danger.

threaten VERB menace, loom, bully, intimidate.

thrifty ADJECTIVE frugal, economical, careful, sparing. *Opposite words* are spendthrift, wasteful.

thrilling ADJECTIVE exciting, exhilarating, rousing, stirring. *A thrilling experience.*

thrive VERB flourish, boom, grow, thrive, bloom, succeed. *Opposite words* are fail, die.

throb VERB beat, pulsate, thump, pound.

throng NOUN crowd, mob.

throttle VERB choke, asphyxiate, gag, stifle, strangle, smother, suffocate.

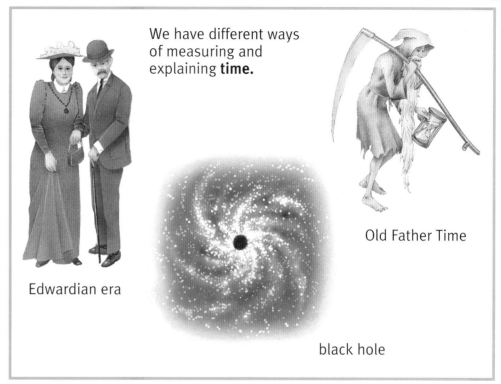

We have different ways of measuring and explaining **time.**

Edwardian era

Old Father Time

black hole

throw VERB hurl, lob, chuck, toss, bowl, fling, sling.

thrust VERB shove, ram, stab, push, poke, stick, jab.

thump VERB hit, punch, clout, batter.

tick VERB mark, indicate.

tide NOUN stream, flow, ebb, trend.

tidy ADJECTIVE neat, smart, orderly, shipshape. *Opposite words* are untidy, messy.

tie VERB fasten, fix, moor, tether, anchor, knot, secure.

tight ADJECTIVE small, close-fitting, fixed, secure.

tilt VERB lean, slope, incline, slant.

time NOUN age, era, period, interval, season.

timid ADJECTIVE nervous, shy, coy, timorous, diffident, fearful. An *opposite word* is confident.

tinge NOUN colour/color (US), shade, tint, tincture, hue, tone.

tingle VERB vibrate, thrill, throb, sting.

tint NOUN *See* **tinge**.

tiny ADJECTIVE little, minute, small, wee, microscopic. An *opposite word* is big.

tip NOUN **1** end, point, top, head. **2** advice, clue, tip-off. **3** reward, gratuity.

tipsy ADJECTIVE drunk, inebriated. An *opposite word* is sober.

tire VERB exhaust, fatigue, bore.

tiresome ADJECTIVE boring, annoying, irritating. *She's a tiresome woman.*

tired ADJECTIVE weary, sleepy, exhausted.

tiring ADJECTIVE exhausting, hard. *The journey was very tiring.*

title NOUN name, designation, rank, status.

titter VERB giggle, snigger, laugh.

toast VERB *See* **cook**.

115

There are many varieties of **transport.**

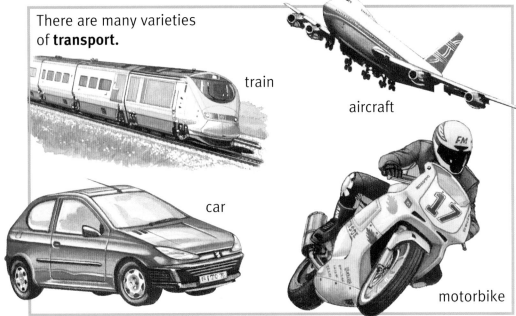

train

aircraft

car

motorbike

toil NOUN work, labour/labor (US), struggle, slave, grind.

token NOUN coupon, voucher, symbol, memento, souvenir.

tolerant ADJECTIVE easy-going, lenient, patient, open-minded. *Opposite words* are intolerant, bigoted.

tolerate VERB put up with, bear, endure, suffer, permit.

too ADVERB **1** as well, besides, in addition. *Can I come too?* **2** very, over, excessively. *Don't drive too fast.*

tool NOUN implement, gadget, instrument, utensil, device, contraption. Some different kinds of tool: adze, axe, bradawl, chisel, drill, fork, hammer, hoe, pick, pincers, plane, rake, screwdriver, scythe, shears, shovel, saw, spade, spanner, trowel, vice, wrench.

top NOUN **1** peak, summit. An *opposite word* is bottom. **2** cap, cover, lid, stopper.

topic NOUN theme, subject, matter.

torment VERB annoy, bully, tease, pester, provoke.

tornado NOUN *See* **storm.**

torture VERB hurt, be cruel to, torment, rack.

toss VERB throw, fling, hurl, chuck.

totter VERB stagger, reel.

touch VERB **1** handle, feel, finger, fiddle with, caress, fondle, hug, stroke, rub, contact, grope. **2** impress, stir.

tough ADJECTIVE **1** strong, firm, rugged, hard, leathery. *Tough meat.* **2** severe, harsh, rigid. **3** arduous, difficult. *A tough exam.*

tour NOUN visit, trip, excursion, ride.

tourist NOUN traveller/traveler (US), sightseer, tripper.

tow VERB haul, pull, drag, tug. A word with a similar sound is toe. *Tow the car away.*

toxic ADJECTIVE poisonous, dangerous, noxious.

trace VERB **1** track, hunt, follow, detect. **2** sketch, draw, copy.

track NOUN road, path, way, footprint.

track VERB follow, hunt, chase, trace, pursue.

tragedy NOUN disaster, calamity, catastrophe, blow.

tragic ADJECTIVE sad, dreadful, unfortunate, disastrous.

trail NOUN and VERB *See* **track, trail.**

train VERB teach, instruct, coach, exercise, practise/practice (US).

tranquil ADJECTIVE peaceful, quiet, placid, calm. *Opposite words* are upset, restless.

transfer VERB switch, change, move, transmit.

transform VERB turn, change, alter, adapt.

transmit VERB send, dispatch, relay, forward, communicate.

transparent ADJECTIVE clear, translucent, see-through, obvious, plain, lucid.

transport VERB carry, convey, move. Some different kinds of transport/transportation (US): **by road:** ambulance, bicycle, bus, car, coach, fire engine, motorcycle, taxi, tram, truck, van. **by rail:** diesel train, electric train, steam train, freight train, underground/subway (US), monorail. **by air:** airliner, glider, helicopter, plane. **by water:** barge, canoe, ferry, hovercraft, hydrofoil, jumbo jet, motorboat, rowing boat, sailing boat/sailboat (US) submarine, yacht.

trap VERB capture, catch, ensnare, ambush.

travel VERB journey, voyage, tour, trek, cycle, drive, fly, hitchhike, ride, sail, walk.

treachery NOUN disloyalty, unfaithfulness, betrayal. An *opposite word* is loyalty.

tread VERB walk, trample, plod, trudge.

treasure NOUN wealth, riches, booty, hoard.

treat VERB care for, look after, handle, nurse, doctor.

treaty NOUN agreement, pact.

tree NOUN evergreen, conifer, shrub. Some different kinds of tree: alder, ash, beech, birch, cedar, chestnut, elm, fir, holly, horse chestnut, larch, lime, maple, mulberry, oak, palm, pine, plane, poplar, spruce, sycamore, willow, yew.

tremble VERB quake, quiver, shake, shudder, shiver, vibrate.

tremor NOUN shaking, vibration, trembling, quake.

trend NOUN inclination, tendency, fashion, style, vogue.

tribe NOUN race, clan, family, dynasty, sect.

trick NOUN 1 fraud, deception, hoax. 2 prank, practical joke, jape.

trickle VERB drip, leak, dribble, seep.

tricky ADJECTIVE difficult, delicate, awkward. *A tricky situation.*

trim VERB 1 decorate, ornament. 2 *See* **cut**.

trip NOUN outing, excursion, visit, tour, jaunt, spin, drive. *Take a trip to the seaside.*

trip VERB stumble, slip, stagger.

triumph NOUN victory, achievement, success, conquest. An *opposite word* is defeat.

trivial ADJECTIVE unimportant, trifling, petty, paltry.

trouble NOUN 1 misfortune, distress, hardship, difficulty, worry. 2 unrest, row, bother, disturbance, disorder. 3 care, effort.

trouble VERB annoy, upset, bother, pester, worry.

truce NOUN peace, armistice.

trudge VERB plod, tramp, trek, march.

true ADJECTIVE 1 correct, right, factual, real, genuine, authentic. 2 loyal, reliable, honest, sincere, constant.

trust VERB count on, depend on, rely on, be sure of, believe in. *Opposite words* are distrust, doubt.

trusting ADJECTIVE trustful, innocent, unquestioning.

truth NOUN honesty, fact, reality. An *opposite word* is falsehood.

try VERB 1 attempt, strive, aim, endeavour/endeavor (US). 2 test, sample, try out, taste. *Try this coat for size.*

trying ADJECTIVE troublesome, annoying, irksome, aggravating. *She was being very trying.*

tuck VERB fold, insert, push. *Tuck your shirt into your jeans.*

tug VERB *See* **pull, tow.**

tumble VERB fall, topple, drop.

tune NOUN melody, song, air.

turmoil NOUN trouble, disorder, chaos, confusion.

turret

turn VERB 1 spin, rotate, revolve, twirl, twist. 2 become, change into. 3 curve, twist, bend. 4 convert, transform.

turret NOUN tower, spire, steeple, minaret.

tussle VERB struggle, fight, scuffle.

twaddle NOUN nonsense, prattle, drivel, bunkum, gossip.

twine NOUN *See* **string.**

twinkle VERB sparkle, shine, flash.

twirl VERB whirl, turn, spin.

twist VERB 1 writhe, distort. 2 interweave, intertwine, wind, wreathe.

type NOUN kind, sort, variety, species, breed, style.

typhoon NOUN *See* **storm.**

typical ADJECTIVE usual, normal, common, characteristic.

tyrant NOUN dictator, despot, autocrat. *He was a cruel tyrant.*

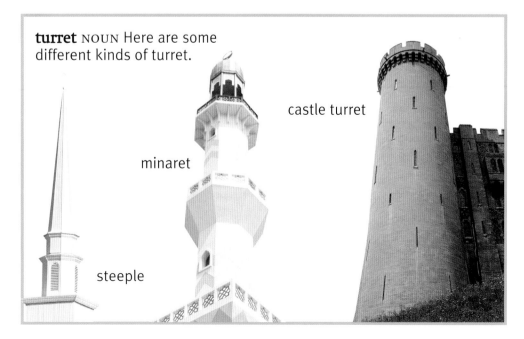

turret NOUN Here are some different kinds of turret.

minaret

castle turret

steeple

ugly ADJECTIVE unattractive, unsightly, hideous, repulsive. An *opposite word* is beautiful.

ultimate ADJECTIVE last, eventual, final. An *opposite word* is first.

umpire NOUN referee, judge, arbiter.

unable ADJECTIVE incapable, helpless, ineffective. An *opposite word* is effective.

unanimous ADJECTIVE agreeing, consenting, uniform, united. An *opposite word* is disunited.

unbiased ADJECTIVE fair, unbiased, impartial, disinterested. An *opposite word* is biased.

unbroken ADJECTIVE **1** whole, complete. **2** continuous, endless. **3** unbeaten.

uncanny ADJECTIVE strange, weird, unearthly, eerie, bizarre.

uncertain ADJECTIVE unsure, doubtful, unconvinced.

uncommon ADJECTIVE rare, infrequent, unusual, odd, scarce. An *opposite word* is common.

unconscious ADJECTIVE **1** insensible, stunned, knocked out. **2** unaware, ignorant, oblivious.

uncouth ADJECTIVE clumsy, loutish, boorish, crude, coarse.

uncover VERB reveal, expose, show, unmask, unveil. *Opposite words* are cover, conceal.

undecided ADJECTIVE unsure, hesitant, dubious, wavering, in two minds.

undergo VERB bear, suffer, tolerate, endure, go through, weather.

underhand ADJECTIVE sly, deceitful, stealthy, sneaky, dishonest. *Opposite words* are honest, open.

underline VERB emphasize, highlight, underscore.

undermine VERB **1** excavate, tunnel. **2** weaken, sap. *His confidence was undermined.*

understand VERB **1** comprehend, see, grasp, realize, twig, sympathize. **2** hear, learn, believe.

undertaking NOUN venture, attempt, enterprise. *The project was a huge undertaking.*

undo VERB untie, unfasten, open, loosen, free, unravel. An *opposite word* is fasten.

undue ADJECTIVE excessive, unnecessary, undeserved. *Undue praise and attention.*

unearth VERB uncover, dig up, find.

unearthly ADJECTIVE strange, weird, uncanny, eerie, supernatural.

uneasy ADJECTIVE worried, anxious, restless, edgy.

unemployed ADJECTIVE out of work, unoccupied, jobless, redundant. An *opposite word* is employed.

unequal ADJECTIVE uneven, disproportionate, varying. An *opposite word* is equal.

uneven ADJECTIVE **1** bumpy, rough. **2** irregular. *Opposite words* are **1** smooth. **2** regular.

unexpected ADJECTIVE sudden, surprising, unforeseen, chance. An *opposite word* is expected.

unfair ADJECTIVE unjust, wrong, prejudiced, biased, one-sided. *Opposite words* are fair, impartial.

unfasten VERB undo, detach, open, release, untie, unlock.

uncommon ADJECTIVE All these animals are uncommon and rarely seen.

leopard

tiger

white rhino

orang utan

unfit ADJECTIVE **1** incompetent, unable, unqualified, incapable. **2** unhealthy.

unfold VERB open, unroll, unwrap, spread, reveal, disclose.

unfortunate ADJECTIVE unlucky, unhappy, deplorable. An *opposite word* is fortunate.

unfriendly ADJECTIVE cold, unkind, hostile, aloof.

ungainly ADJECTIVE awkward, clumsy, lumbering. An *opposite word* is graceful.

unhappy ADJECTIVE sad, gloomy, miserable, depressed. An *opposite word* is happy.

uniform ADJECTIVE unchanging, constant, steady, regular.

unify VERB combine, unite, amalgamate. *Italy was unified in the 19th century.*

unimportant ADJECTIVE petty, trivial, trifling, irrelevant. *Opposite words* are important, significant.

uninteresting ADJECTIVE boring, dull, tedious, monotonous, prosaic.

union NOUN **1** alliance, association, combination, amalgamation, blend, mixture, fusion. **2** agreement, harmony. An *opposite word* is separation.

unique ADJECTIVE single, only, exceptional, sole.

unison NOUN harmony, agreement, unity.

unit NOUN one, individual, component, part, element.

unite VERB combine, join, connect, link, merge, marry. An *opposite word* is separate.

universal ADJECTIVE world-wide, general, whole, entire, total, unlimited.

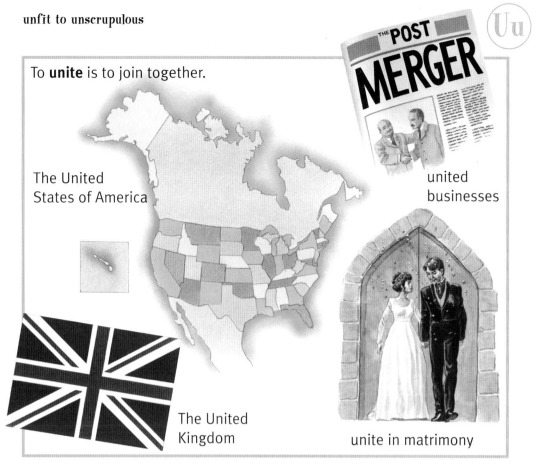

To **unite** is to join together.

The United States of America

The United Kingdom

united businesses

unite in matrimony

unkempt ADJECTIVE dishevelled/disheveled (US), scruffy, tousled. An *opposite word* is neat.

unkind ADJECTIVE cruel, callous, pitiless, heartless, unfriendly. An *opposite word* is kind.

unlikely ADJECTIVE improbable, incredible, dubious, far-fetched, remote. An *opposite word* is likely.

unlock VERB open, release, unbolt.

unlucky ADJECTIVE unfortunate, ill-fated, unsuccessful. An *opposite word* is lucky.

unnatural ADJECTIVE **1** unusual, uncommon, abnormal. **2** artificial, affected, forced, false, stilted.

unoccupied ADJECTIVE empty, vacant, open, uninhabited. An *opposite word* is occupied.

unpleasant ADJECTIVE **1** dreadful, frightening, terrible, upsetting. **2** rude, unfriendly. **3** nasty, disgusting, obnoxious, offensive. An *opposite word* is pleasant.

unpopular ADJECTIVE disliked, friendless, shunned, rejected. An *opposite word* is popular.

unravel VERB disentangle, unwind, sort out, decipher, solve.

unreasonable ADJECTIVE irrational, immoderate, unwise, excessive. *Unreasonable demands.* An *opposite word* is reasonable.

unreliable ADJECTIVE untrustworthy, unsound, undependable, fickle. *Opposite words* are reliable, trustworthy.

unrest NOUN disturbance, turmoil, upset, agitation, anxiety. An *opposite word* is calm.

unruly ADJECTIVE disobedient, uncontrollable, rebellious, riotous, rowdy, disorderly.

unscathed ADJECTIVE unharmed, undamaged.

unscrupulous ADJECTIVE dishonest, unprincipled.

Here are some different kinds of **utensil.**

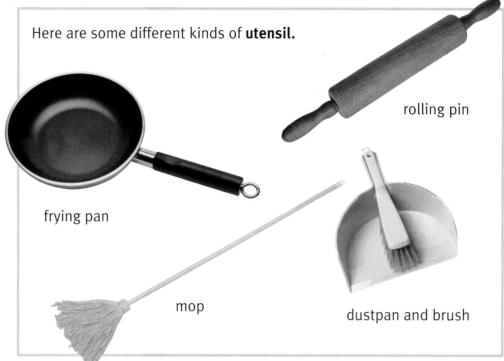

frying pan

rolling pin

mop

dustpan and brush

unseemly ADJECTIVE shocking, indecent, improper.

unsightly ADJECTIVE ugly, hideous, unattractive.

unskilled ADJECTIVE inexpert, inexperienced.

unsound ADJECTIVE **1** imperfect, impaired, unhealthy, feeble, sickly, poorly. **2** wrong, incorrect, false.

unstable ADJECTIVE shaky, unsteady, wobbly, fickle, changeable, variable.

unsuitable ADJECTIVE unacceptable, inappropriate, unfitting.

untidy ADJECTIVE disorderly, jumbled, muddled, scruffy, disorganized, cluttered. An *opposite word* is tidy.

untie VERB undo, unfasten, release, free.

untold ADJECTIVE countless, measureless, undreamed of.

unusual ADJECTIVE uncommon, odd, strange, curious, surprising.

unwell ADJECTIVE sick, ill, ailing, poorly.

unwelcome ADJECTIVE uninvited, rejected, not wanted, upsetting, disagreeable, distasteful, unpleasant.

unwieldy ADJECTIVE heavy, unmanageable, cumbersome. An *opposite word* is manageable.

unwilling ADJECTIVE averse, reluctant, opposed, loath. An *opposite word* is willing.

unwrap VERB open, unfold, undo. *Opposite words* are fold, wrap.

update VERB modernize, revise, revamp, improve.

upheaval NOUN disruption, turmoil, confusion, hubbub, uproar.

uphold VERB support, keep up, back, defend.

upkeep NOUN support, maintenance, care, conservation. An *opposite word* is neglect.

upright ADJECTIVE **1** perpendicular, vertical. **2** honest, good, just, honourable/honorable (US).

uproar NOUN disorder, turmoil, noise, tumult. *See also* **upheaval.**

uproot VERB pull up, eradicate, destroy, remove.

upset VERB **1** spill, knock over, topple. **2** frighten, trouble, worry, bother.

uptight ADJECTIVE angry, nervous.

urge NOUN wish, desire, compulsion, impulse, drive.

urge VERB entreat, encourage, beg, goad, plead, press, incite. An *opposite word* is deter.

urgent ADJECTIVE important, vital, pressing, immediate, crucial, priority. *It's urgent and can't wait.*

usage NOUN **1** tradition, custom, habit, routine, practice, fashion. **2** handling, use, treatment.

use VERB **1** employ, utilize, apply. **2** consume, finish.

useful ADJECTIVE helpful, valuable, handy, practical, convenient.

useless ADJECTIVE unusable, incompetent, worthless, futile.

usual ADJECTIVE ordinary, regular common, expected, habitual, customary. *Opposite words* are unusual, out of the ordinary.

utensil NOUN *See* **tool.**

utilize VERB employ, use, exploit.

utmost ADJECTIVE greatest, extreme, last, distant, farthest.

utter VERB speak, say, pronounce, express.

fork and spo (utensils)

utterly ADVERB completely, entirely, wholly.

U-turn NOUN about-face, reversal, turn about.

Vv

vacant ADJECTIVE unoccupied, free, not in use, void. *Opposite words* are occupied, full.

vacation NOUN holiday, rest, recreation.

vacuum NOUN emptiness, space, void.

vague ADJECTIVE **1** forgetful, absent-minded. **2** indefinite, imprecise, uncertain, undetermined, obscure.

vain ADJECTIVE proud, conceited, arrogant. Words that sound similar are vane, vein.

valiant ADJECTIVE brave, gallant, courageous, intrepid, heroic, stout, staunch. *Opposite words* are cowardly, fearful.

valley NOUN dale, vale, dell, glen.

valuable ADJECTIVE **1** precious, priceless, expensive. **2** helpful, worthwhile, constructive. *Opposite words* are **1** worthless, **2** useless.

value NOUN cost, price, worth, use.

value VERB prize, treasure.

vandal NOUN wrecker, barbarian.

vanish VERB disappear, go away, fade, depart, go. An *opposite word* is appear.

vanity NOUN pride, conceit, big-headed. An *opposite word* is modesty.

vanquish VERB beat, conquer, subdue, overcome.

vapour/vapor (US) NOUN steam, fog, haze, smoke.

varied ADJECTIVE mixed, diverse, assorted.

variety NOUN **1** difference, assortment, mixture. *A variety of ice cream*. **2** kind, type, sort, class.

various ADJECTIVE mixed, different, numerous, varied, several. *She has various names*.

vary VERB change, alter, differ, diverge.

vast ADJECTIVE enormous, immense, colossal, huge, wide. An *opposite word* is minute.

vault VERB *See* **jump**.

veer VERB shift, change, swerve.

vegetable NOUN. Some different kinds of vegetable: artichoke, asparagus, broad bean, broccoli, Brussels sprouts, cabbage, carrot, cauliflower, celery, French bean, kale, kohlrabi, lentil, okra, onion, parsnip, pea, potato, radish, shallot, soybean, spinach, squash, sweet potato, tomatoes, turnip, yam.

vehicle NOUN conveyance, transport carriage, car. *See also* **transport**.

veil VERB cover, hide, mask, conceal. A word with a similar sound is vale.

velocity NOUN speed, swiftness, rate.

vengeance NOUN revenge, retaliation.

ventilate VERB air, freshen.

venture NOUN chance, risk, undertaking.

verbal ADJECTIVE spoken, oral, said, unwritten.

verbose ADJECTIVE wordy, long-winded, loquacious.

verdict NOUN decision, judgement, conclusion, sentence. *The jury reached their verdict*.

verge NOUN edge, margin, rim, border.

verge VERB incline, lean, come close to.

verify VERB authenticate, confirm, bear out, testify.

versatile ADJECTIVE adaptable, flexible, capable, skilled.

Here are some different kinds of **vegetable**.

onions

carrots

cabbage

peas

verse NOUN rhyme, poem, jingle.

vertical ADJECTIVE perpendicular, upright, erect. An *opposite word* is horizontal.

vessel NOUN **1** craft. **2** bowl. *See also* **boat**, **container**.

veto VERB forbid, prohibit, reject, turn down.

vex VERB *See* annoy.

viable ADJECTIVE workable, practicable, feasible. An *opposite word* is unworkable.

vibrate VERB shake, quiver, shudder, oscillate, tremble.

vicinity NOUN surroundings, proximity.

vicious ADJECTIVE savage, cruel, ruthless, malicious, wicked, depraved.

victim NOUN prey, dupe, sufferer, casualty.

victory NOUN triumph, win, success, conquest, achievement. *Opposite words* are defeat, loss.

view NOUN **1** scene, spectacle, vista. **2** opinion, belief, impression.

view VERB watch. *See* **see**, **observe**, **survey**.

vigilant ADJECTIVE watchful, wary, alert, on the look out.

vigorous ADJECTIVE **1** active, energetic, dynamic. **2** healthy, strong, robust. An *opposite word* is weak.

vile ADJECTIVE wicked, mean, nasty, disgusting, foul, revolting.

vindictive ADJECTIVE spiteful, unforgiving.

violent ADJECTIVE **1** strong, severe, destructive, rough. **2** fierce, fiery, cruel, brutal, passionate, ferocious. *Opposite words* are mild, gentle.

virile ADJECTIVE manly, strong, vigorous, robust, lusty.

virtual ADJECTIVE essential, substantial.

virtue NOUN goodness, excellence, honesty. An *opposite word* is vice.

visible ADJECTIVE clear, plain, obvious, evident, noticeable, observable. An *opposite word* is invisible.

vision NOUN **1** seeing, sight. **2** perception, foresight. **3** ghost, spectre/specter (US), apparition.

visit VERB call, drop in, stay at, stop.

visitor NOUN caller, guest, tourist.

visualize VERB imagine, picture.

vital ADJECTIVE essential, necessary, indispensable, fundamental.

vivacious ADJECTIVE lively, sprightly, animated, high-spirited.

vivid ADJECTIVE colourful/colorful (US), bright, lucid, clear, striking. *A vivid sunset.*

vocation NOUN calling, career, profession, occupation, business, pursuit.

vogue NOUN style, fashion, mode, trend, fad.

void ADJECTIVE **1** empty, unoccupied. **2** null, invalid, annulled.

volume NOUN **1** amount, mass, size, capacity, quantity. **2** book, tome.

vomit VERB spew, throw up, be sick, retch, bring up.

vote VERB elect, choose, select, ballot, opt.

vow VERB promise, pledge, swear, give your word.

voyage NOUN journey, cruise, passage, crossing.

vulgar ADJECTIVE rude, coarse, common, bad-mannered, impolite, indecent. An *opposite word* is polite, refined.

vulnerable ADJECTIVE unprotected, exposed, sensitive, defenceless/defenseless (US).

A **vessel** is any kind of container.

vase of flowers

bucket

FIRE

boat

tumbler and carafe

Ww

wad NOUN pack, packet, bundle. *A wad of money.*

waddle VERB shuffle, wobble, toddle.

wag VERB flap, wave, shake, wiggle.

wage NOUN earnings, pay, salary, fee.

wage VERB undertake, conduct, carry on. *Wage war.*

wait VERB stay, remain, stop, halt, linger, pause, delay, hesitate. An *opposite word* is go. A word that sounds similar is weight.

waive VERB forego, renounce, yield. *He waived his right to a special car.* An *opposite word* is insist. A word that sounds similar is wave.

wake VERB rouse, awaken, call.

wakeful ADJECTIVE alert, vigilant, observant, wary.

walk VERB march, step, tread, stroll, amble, hike, trek, tramp, trudge, saunter, plod, creep, stride, shuffle, strut, tiptoe.

wall NOUN screen, partition, barrier.

wallow VERB **1** roll, flounder, loll, wade. *Wallowing in a bath.* **2** enjoy, revel, indulge. *Wallowing in wealth.*

waltz NOUN *See* **dance**.

wander VERB stray, roam, rove, meander, drift, digress. *They wandered from shop to shop.*

wane VERB decrease, decline, lessen, recede, ebb, sink, shrink. *Opposite words* are wax, increase. *The moon wanes.*

want VERB wish for, desire, crave, long for, need, require.

war NOUN battle, fighting, combat, hostilities, invasion, siege. An *opposite word* is peace. A word that sounds similar is wore.

warden NOUN custodian, guardian, keeper, protector, supervisor, caretaker.

warehouse NOUN depot, store, repository.

warm ADJECTIVE **1** tepid, luke-warm, sultry. **2** enthusiastic, kind, friendly. *A warm welcome.* *Opposite words* are chilly, cool.

warn VERB give notice, caution, alert, notify, admonish.

warrior NOUN hero, champion, soldier.

wary ADJECTIVE careful, cautious, watchful, prudent, vigilant.

wash VERB clean, cleanse, bath, scrub, rinse, shampoo, mop.

washing NOUN laundry, cleaning.

waste NOUN *See* **rubbish**.

wasteful ADJECTIVE extravagant, lavish, spendthrift, prodigal. An *opposite word* is thrifty.

watch VERB **1** *See* **gaze at**, **observe**, **view**. **2** look after, mind, guard, oversee.

watchful ADJECTIVE attentive, vigilant, wakeful, alert. An *opposite word* is inattentive.

water VERB dampen, moisten, wet, sprinkle, spray, irrigate, douse.

watery ADJECTIVE **1** damp, wet. **2** diluted, watered-down, weak.

A **warrior** is someone who fights.

Maori warrior

Greek footsoldier

Samurai warrior

David killed Goliath with a slingshot

wave VERB flutter, flap, flourish, shake, signal, gesticulate. *She waved goodbye.*

waver VERB hesitate, dither, swither, vacillate, falter.

wax VERB increase, grow, enlarge. An *opposite word* is wane.

way NOUN **1** method, system, technique. **2** style, manner. *The way she walks.* **3** route, direction, path, road. *Do you know the way to my house?*

way-out NOUN exit, outlet, exodus, departure, farewell. An *opposite word* is entrance.

weak ADJECTIVE delicate, faint, feeble, frail, fragile, puny, flimsy, watery, weak tea. *A weak excuse.* An *opposite word* is strong.

wealthy ADJECTIVE rich, prosperous, affluent, prosperous. An *opposite word* is poor.

weapon NOUN dagger, dirk, bomb, mine, bow and arrow, longbow, crossbow, catapult, boomerang, torpedo, tomahawk, truncheon. *See also* **gun, spear, sword.**

wear VERB **1** have on, dress in, carry, bear. **2** rub, use, scrape, corrode, consume, deteriorate. *Your soles have worn thin.*

weary ADJECTIVE tired, exhausted, worn out, dead beat, whacked. An *opposite word* is fresh.

weather NOUN climate, condition, temperature.

weather VERB **1** last, endure, survive, resist, withstand. **2** ill, depressed. *Under the weather.* Some different kinds of weather:
1 chilly, cold, cool, freezing, frosty, icy, snowy, wintry. **2** close, fair, fine, hot, mild, sunny, warm.
3 damp, drizzly, rainy, showery, wet. **4** cloudy, foggy, hazy, misty.
5 blustery, breezy, stormy, windy.

weave VERB plait, braid, knit, entwine, unite.

wedding NOUN marriage, wedlock, matrimony, nuptials. An *opposite word is* divorce.

wedge NOUN chock, block, chunk.

wedge VERB force, push, jam, thrust, ram.

weedy ADJECTIVE skinny, thin, weak, wimpish/wimpy (US).

week NOUN The seven days of the week are: Monday, Tuesday, Wednesday, Thursday, Friday, Saturday, Sunday. A word that sounds similar is weak.

weep VERB *See* **cry 1.**

weigh VERB balance, gauge, evaluate, consider, think. A word that sounds similar is way.

weird ADJECTIVE strange, odd, peculiar, scary, creepy, uncanny, unearthly.

well ADJECTIVE healthy, fit, hale, sound.

well ADVERB properly, adequately, properly, correctly, ably, greatly. *She swims well.*

wet ADJECTIVE **1** damp, dank, moist, soaking, drenched, wringing-wet, soggy. **2** rainy, showery, drizzly. *Opposite words* are dry, arid, parched. **3** feeble (UK). *See also* **weedy.**

wet VERB moisten, dampen, soak, water, sprinkle, spray, drench, drown.

whet VERB **1** sharpen, grind, strop. **2** stimulate, excite. *Whet the appetite.*

whiff NOUN a whiff of scandal. hint, breath, trace. **2** *See* **scent, smell.**

whim NOUN fancy, notion, impulse, humour/humor (US).

whimper VERB whine, moan, cry, wail, complain.

whine VERB *See* **whimper,**

whip VERB flog, thrash. *See also* **hit.**

whirl VERB *See* **spin.**

whisper VERB murmur, mutter, hint, disclose.

whistle VERB cheep, chirp, tweet.

whole ADJECTIVE complete, entire, undamaged, sound.

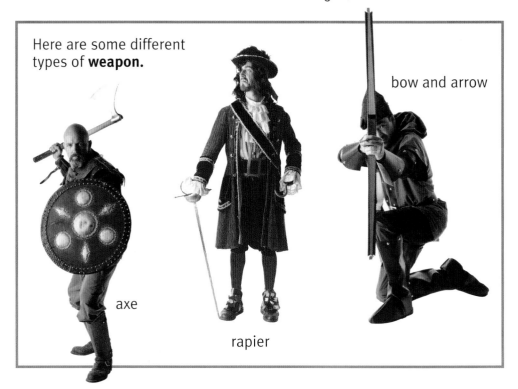

Here are some different types of **weapon.**

axe

rapier

bow and arrow

wicked ADJECTIVE evil, bad, wrong, depraved, immoral. An *opposite word* is good, virtuous.

wide ADJECTIVE broad, large, extensive, vast. An *opposite word* is narrow.

widespread ADJECTIVE far-flung, universal, general. An *opposite word* is narrow.

width NOUN breadth, wideness, thickness, range.

wield VERB use, handle, brandish, control. *Wield power.*

wild ADJECTIVE **1** untamed, savage, undomesticated. **2** stormy, violent, rough. **3** noisy, rowdy, turbulent, unruly. *A wild party.* **4** uncultivated. *A wild forest.*

wilderness NOUN wasteland, desert, outback.

will NOUN **1** choice, preference, wish, order, command. **2** determination, decision. **3** legacy, testament.

willing ADJECTIVE ready, eager, disposed, agreeable, helpful. *Opposite words* are unwilling, reluctant.

wilt VERB wither, shrivel, sag, droop, dry up. An *opposite word* is thrive.

wily ADJECTIVE sly, sneaky, cunning, scheming, designing, crafty. *The wily monkeys got into our tent and stole some food. Opposite words* are straightforward, sincere.

win VERB **1** earn, gain, acquire, receive. **2** succeed, triumph. An *opposite word* is lose.

wince VERB flinch, blench, shrink, start.

wind NOUN draught, air, gust, gale, breeze, hurricane, cyclone, typhoon, whirlwind. *There was a sudden gust of wind.*

Here are some different kinds of **wind instrument.**

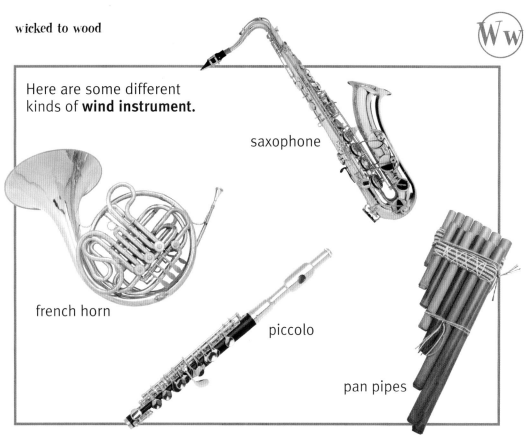

saxophone

french horn

piccolo

pan pipes

wind VERB curl, twist, coil, twine, curve, meander. *The road winds up the hill.*

wind instruments NOUN oboe, clarinet, flute, piccolo, bassoon, saxophone.

wink VERB blink, squint, flicker, flash.

winner NOUN victor, champion. An *opposite word* is loser.

wipe VERB clean, dust, polish, dry, mop, swab, take away.

wise ADJECTIVE sensible, intelligent, thoughtful, astute, sage. An *opposite word* is silly.

wish VERB **1** want, desire, long for. **2** require, order.

wit NOUN humour/humor (US), sparkle, intelligence, wisdom, cleverness, discernment. *He had a very sharp wit.*

withdraw VERB **1** retreat, retire, pull back, depart, flee. **2** recant, retract, revoke.

withdrawn ADJECTIVE aloof, shy, unsociable.

wither VERB pine, languish. *See also* **wilt.**

withhold VERB retain, keep back, reserve. *Opposite words* are give, grant.

witness VERB observe, notice, see, watch, bear out.

witty ADJECTIVE funny, humorous, droll, amusing, clever, facetious.

wobble VERB shake, tremble, sway.

woe NOUN sorrow, grief, anguish, misery, unhappiness. An *opposite word* is joy.

wonder VERB ask yourself, question, ponder, conjecture, marvel at.

wind instrument

wonderful ADJECTIVE amazing, fabulous, superb, astonishing. An *opposite word* is dreadful.

won't VERB the short form of 'will not'. *She won't go.*

wood NOUN **1** copse, grove, thicket, forest. **2** timber, boards, planks, logs.

word NOUN **1** term, expression, statement. **2** news, information. *We sent word of the president's arrival.* **3** command, order, instruction. *Stop, when I give the word.* **4** promise, pledge. *Always keep your word.* Some different kinds of word:
nouns names of people, things or ideas for example John, men, hope.
pronouns words used in place of a noun as in he (for John), they (for men), it (for hope).
adjectives words that describe a noun or adjective for example **white** houses, **dark green** shirt.
adverbs words that tell how or when something happens for example talk **loudly**.
prepositions words that show connections between a noun or pronoun and another word for example 'She walked **into** the room.'
verbs words that describe action, experience or state for example 'Jim **worked** hard.'
conjunctions words like 'but' and 'and' that link words and phrases.

work NOUN **1** labour/labor (US), effort, toil, chore, drudgery. **2** employment, job, career, profession, occupation, business, trade.

work VERB **1** toil, labour/labor (US), struggle. **2** go, function, operate, act, play. *The TV doesn't work.* **3** use, operate. *Can you work a computer?*

worn-out ADJECTIVE **1** exhausted, weary, whacked, dead beat. **2** used, ragged, shabby.

worry VERB be anxious, be concerned, fret. **2** upset, irritate. *See also* **annoy**.

worsen VERB deteriorate, get worse, decline, aggravate. An *opposite word* is improve.

worship VERB adore, venerate, idolize, exalt, love. *Opposite words* are detest, despise.

worth VERB value, merit, cost, usefulness. An *opposite word* is uselessness.

worthless ADJECTIVE useless, valueless, cheap. An *opposite word* is valuable.

worthy ADJECTIVE honest, admirable, fine, praiseworthy, deserving. An *opposite word* is unworthy.

wound VERB **1** hurt, injure, harm, cut, damage, bruise. **2** is upset, distress, insult. *Wounded pride.* An *opposite word* is **1** heal.

wrap VERB cover, enclose, pack, envelop, enfold. *Opposite words* are unwrap, unfold.

wrath NOUN anger, fury, rage, indignation.

wreck VERB destroy, break, smash, shatter, ruin, ravage. *Opposite words* are reconstruct, rebuild.

wreckage NOUN remains, rubble, flotsam and jetsam.

wrench VERB twist, strain, sprain, pull, yank, rick.

wrestle VERB fight, battle, contest, struggle.

wretched ADJECTIVE **1** unhappy, miserable, forlorn. **2** pitiable, pathetic.

wriggle VERB writhe, twist, squirm, worm.

wring VERB twist, squeeze, force, mangle. A word with a similar sound is ring.

write VERB **1** scribble, pen, scrawl, jot down, type. **2** compose. *She writes music.* Words with a similar sound are right, rite.

writer NOUN author, novelist, journalist, poet, playwright, hack, scribe.

writhe VERB *See* **wriggle**.

wrong ADJECTIVE **1** evil, wicked, criminal, sinful, immoral. **2** incorrect, false, untrue, mistaken. *A wrong answer.* **3** unfair, unjust. An *opposite word* is **2, 3** right.

wry ADJECTIVE twisted, distorted, crooked, ironic, sardonic. *She has a wry smile.*

There are many different types of **writer.**

novelist

journalist

playwright

yank VERB jerk, snatch, pull.

yap VERB bark, yelp, prattle.

yard NOUN court, enclosure, quadrangle, garden.

yardstick NOUN measure, criterion, standard.

yarn NOUN **1** tale, story, anecdote. **2** thread, fibre/fiber (US).

yawn VERB gape, open.

year NOUN The months of the year: January, February, March, April, May, June, July, August, September, October, November, December.

yearly ADJECTIVE and ADVERB annually, once a year, per annum.

yearn VERB long for, hanker after, desire, want, crave.

yell VERB shout, call out, cry, shriek, scream.

yield VERB **1** surrender, give in, succumb. **2** produce, provide, bring in.

yoke NOUN harness, link, chain, bond, burden, oppression. A word with a similar sound is yolk.

yonder ADJECTIVE and ADVERB over there, in the distance.

young ADJECTIVE youthful, juvenile, junior, little, immature. *Opposite words* are adult, old, mature.

youth NOUN **1** lad, youngster, young man, boy. **2** adolescence, childhood.

zany ADJECTIVE funny, clownish, comical, goofy, daft. An *opposite word* is serious.

zap VERB **1** attack, shoot, destroy. **2** switch suddenly. **3** delete data.

zeal NOUN enthusiasm, fervour/fervor (US), passion, devotion, dedication. An *opposite word* is indifference.

zenith NOUN peak, apex, summit, climax, high point, pinnacle. An *opposite word* is nadir.

zero NOUN nil, nought, nothing, duck, zilch.

zest NOUN relish, gusto, zeal, enthusiasm. An *opposite word* is apathy.

zigzag VERB twist and turn, wind, snake. An *opposite word* is straight.

zilch NOUN *See* **zero**.

zodiac NOUN The signs of the zodiac: Aries (The Ram), Taurus (The Bull), Gemini (The Twins), Cancer (The Crab), Leo (The Lion), Virgo (The Virgin), Libra (The Scales), Scorpio (The Scorpion), Sagittarius (The Archer), Capricorn (The Goat), Aquarius (The Water-carrier), Pisces (The Fishes).

zone NOUN area, district, region, sector, territory.

zoo NOUN zoological gardens, menagerie, aquarium, aviary.

zoom VERB flash, streak, whizz, shoot.

Here are the different signs of the **zodiac.**

Scorpio

Gemini

Cancer

Aries

Virgo

Libra

Taurus

Sagittarius

Leo

Capricorn

Pisces

Aquarius

Acknowledgements

The publishers would like to thank the following
artists who have contributed to this book:

David Ashby (Illustration Ltd.), Andrew Clark, Wayne Ford,
Mike Foster (Maltings Partnership), Jeremy Gower, Kuo Kang Chen,
Martin Sanders, Mike Saunders, Guy Smith, Mike White (Temple Rogers).

All photographs from Miles Kelly archives.